The Farmers' Market Book

QUARRY BOOKS

AN IMPRINT OF
INDIANA UNIVERSITY PRESS
Bloomington and Indianapolis

The Farmers' Market Book

Growing Food, Cultivating Community

Jennifer Meta Robinson
and J. A. Hartenfeld

Photographs and Illustrations by Dan Schlapbach
and Jennifer Roebuck

This book is a publication of

Quarry Books

AN IMPRINT OF

Indiana University Press
601 North Morton Street
Bloomington, IN 47404-3797 USA

http://iupress.indiana.edu

Telephone orders   800-842-6796
Fax orders   812-855-7931
Orders by e-mail   iuporder@indiana.edu

The paper used in this publication meets the minimum requirements of
American National Standard for Information Sciences—Permanence of Paper
for Printed Library Materials, ANSI Z39.48-1984.

Manufactured in China

Library of Congress Cataloging-in-Publication Data

Robinson, Jennifer Meta, date
  The farmers' market book : growing food, cultivating community / Jennifer
Meta Robinson and J. A. Hartenfeld ; photographs and illustrations by Dan
Schlapbach and Jennifer Roebuck.
        p.   cm.
  Includes bibliographical references and index.
  ISBN-13: 978-0-253-21916-9 (paper : alk. paper) 1. Farm produce—
Marketing—Indiana. 2. Farmers' markets—Indiana. I. Hartenfeld, J. A., date
II. Title.
  HD9007.I6R63 2007
  630.68'8—dc22
                                        2006032171

1 2 3 4 5   12 11 10 09 08 07

To Those Who Grow

Journeying through the world
To and fro, to and fro
Cultivating a small field
Basho, Japanese poet, seventeenth century

CONTENTS

Part 1. Settings

Part 3. Harvests

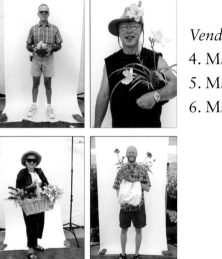

ACKNOWLEDGMENTS

.

When we first started working on the book, the only perspectives we knew were our own as vendors. Even when we walk around as customers to buy the produce that does not do well in our gardens, we wear market aprons with *Hart Farm* stenciled across the pockets and see through the eyes of growers. So it is with great thanks that we acknowledge all of the customers who shared their stories and their time with us. And thanks go, too, to all the vendors who took time out to talk, open their farms to us, and generally broaden our view of the collective enterprise. Special thanks go to the many people we talked with who are not named in the book but who contributed their wisdom to it. We are grateful to all of them for their patience and generosity. Without them, there would be no market and no book.

We are grateful to Indiana University Press for its faith in the project and especially to Linda Oblack for her valuable counsel in the development of the book and to Miki Bird for her careful reading and wise questions about the manuscript. Loyola College provided crucial support for the photography. Marcia Veldman generously fielded many inquiries by e-mail, telephone, and in person and also found time to make excellent suggestions for correcting and improving the chapter on the Bloomington market. She and the Bloomington Parks and Recreation Department have been tremendously supportive, including opening their archives to us and loaning us twelve-foot ladders and a canopy that made some of the photography possible. Thanks, too, to Marti Crouch for readings and years of rich conversations. And to Anne Brann for her help with transcription.

We are grateful to the many friends, old and new, who gave us newspaper clippings, books, references, watermelons, surplus tomatoes, dinners, and other most-welcome supports during the writing of the book. Thanks to generations of the farm crew for their hard work and stimulating conversations over the flowers and to our neighbors in the valley. In their own, unique ways, the following people have taught us much: Sam and Catherine Robinson, Mike and Sally Hartenfeld, Paul and Gloria Schlapbach, and Rhonda Roebuck. We extend heart-felt thanks for your help with cultivating our small field.

Customer, Vendor, Customer   *Bloomington*

Introduction

> The life and soul of a place, all of our experiences there, depend not simply on the physical environment, but on the patterns of events which we experience there. . . . It is the people around us, and the most common ways we have of meeting them, of being with them, it is, in short, the ways of being which exist in our world, that make it possible for us to be alive.
>
> —CHRISTOPHER ALEXANDER, *The Timeless Way*

It's clear that something is awry.

Corporations own the growing potential of seeds, and farmers are outlaws when they plant them without permission. Manufacturers strip the nutritional value from food and then rebuild on the blank palette. Apples are transformed into grape-flavored "grapples." Americans purchase produce in vast depopulated megastores with automatic misters and self-service check-out stands. Increasingly, the world comes to us through screens; televisions, computers, and automobiles spare us real contact.[1] Cell phones and music pods overlay a pervasive roar. Too often, food is not quite food; communication not quite communication; "myspace" remains an unreachable no place. We know more but understand less, as direct experience falls casualty to the fabulous but second-hand.

Yet in this time of virtual reality, screen-mediated experience, and air-conditioned isolation, people all over the United States gather weekly, out in the weather, with neighbors and strangers, to experience local community. At farmers' markets, customers and vendors, performers and pamphleteers meet neighbors, face to face and with the contrast, confirmation, and responsibility that contact implies.

Based on an ancient hallmark of society, farmers' markets today sate a hunger not calculated in the FDA's recommended daily allowances. They incorporate patterns of community and

Top: Greene County

Bottom: Bloomington

exchange that feed us deeply. The recent resurgence of farmers' markets nationwide signals a desire among many for a sense of authenticity and locality that is not found in the high-tech supermarket experience. Buying local potatoes with traces of soil from a grower who still has the same dirt on his boots apparently provides a kind of sustenance not accounted for in the latest nutritional pyramid.

Markets may seem at first nostalgic or idealistic, but the props and atmosphere of each come out of the present time and place, as fresh and diverse as those allow. Food assumes the role of the main character, but upon closer examination, we see something less tangible. At farmers' markets, an individually felt, but cooperatively generated experience plays out on a human scale. Different classes, races, neighborhoods, religions, and backgrounds meet to exchange food, yes, and also language, music, recipes, news, information, and ideas. In the marketplace, both our dependence on each other and our independence, our similarities and our differences come into focus. A market creates intersecting trading zones where histories, social groups, and cultures reinforce, share, and challenge. Some of the players arrive as vendors and some as customers, but the exchange goes both ways and through all the senses. Through the purposeful, life-sustaining, and often surprisingly engaging exchanges of the market, people come to know each other as more than assumptions and stereotypes. Eye to eye, out from behind the screens, we take on responsibility and accountability for the stories we tell.

Farmers' markets bring traditions together with current lifestyles. They help us to envision both rural and urban lives that can be satisfying and viable in the modern world. Growers have one foot in the agricultural methods and know-how of centuries past and the other in some of the most influential innovations of recent times. Some try to wrestle the juggernaut of progress toward sustainability. Some are eager to try the next great invention. Many lessen the vagaries of weather, markets, and health with jobs off the farm as newspaper reporters, medical doctors, janitors, university professors, graphic artists, store clerks, truck drivers, carpenters, language teachers, or any of countless other more reliable occupations. But inevitably, all try to make a place in contemporary society for the timeless concerns of growing produce and husbanding the land.

The customers, too, hail from as many professions and nations as the locality provides. Their interest in what they eat and where it comes from is keen. Their quest—for fresh food, favorite varieties, and assorted produce ever earlier or later in the season—drives the vendors to learn more, do more, and risk innovation. Customers may be interested in hunting for their grandmothers' bleeding heart plants or adding to their granddaughter's herb garden. At least a few are willing to try a potent new goat cheese or choose idiosyncratic heirloom tomatoes for their flavor instead of their looks. On the whole, customers are willing to weave the contrarian pace of the farmers' market into their busy lives.

Market sales are one to one. They put growers and consumers back in touch for real-time exchange at the scale of the individual. And the implications are significant. Over the course of the twentieth century, the United States transformed from a rural country to a vastly more urban one. In 1910, a third of the population of the United States was farmers living on farms. Ninety years later, less than 1 percent work in agriculture, fishing, forestry, and hunting combined.[2] Even among those few, most do not live on the land they work. The trend seemed unstoppable, what Wendell Berry calls a "catastrophe now virtually complete."[3] Along the way, retail farmers' markets languished, until they had mostly disappeared from the United States by the mid-1960s, like family farms, casualties of corporate farming and global food market experiments. Those that did survive presented a hybrid of anachronism and oasis. Since the 1970s, however, the number of people producing food for sale at farmers' markets has grown. By 2004, more than 3,700 farmers' markets were operating in the United States, growing in number by nearly 50 percent during the previous ten years. And some 19,000 growers sold their produce only at farmers' markets.[4] As people find contemporary culture increasingly homogenized, superficial, and rootless, many look to farmers' markets for good food and a sense of community.

Markets present the possibility of common ground for a diverse society. Their very regularity (usually weekly) makes them more intimate and socially complex than other public events. While farmers' markets obviously present opportunities for growers and customers to participate in a commercial exchange, something bigger often compels both sides against the national tide of convenience, uniformity, and brand appeal. Take, for example, the Waltham, Massachusetts, farmers' market at which customers line up in an empty lot where a dozen vendors display their wares. On one particular market day, no one seemed deterred by a rather loud band that had set up in front of the brick wall of an adjacent building. The customers, like the vendors, were apparently regulars. At one stand, a blind man stood while his raspberries and lettuce were bagged. His German shepherd guide dog alertly watched a little Pomeranian across the way. As the man began to pay for his produce, he told the vendor he felt he was forgetting something and asked what else she had. She rattled off, "arugula, lettuce, onions, tomatoes, soap, and patty-pan squash." Yes, he said, it was the squash he had forgotten and could he get a pound of that. She held out a sample so that he could be sure. He took it in his hands and declared it good. As she was making his change, he commented that he could always find her stand because of the cinnamon in her soap. He liked that smell, he said. He would see her next week, he said, then corrected himself. No, he would be away. And she wished him a safe trip.

Or consider the questions wildly out of touch with how things grow. One summer Saturday, a Bloomington, Indiana, customer soberly asked a vendor selling garlic braids how he got the garlic to grow that way; other customers routinely ask a flower farmer at the same market how long it takes cut flowers to grow roots or whether the flowers of perennial plants will come back the same color every year. Such exchanges are humorous, but they also require special care and respect. Opportunities to teach and to learn, they open conversations that cannot occur in the supermarket aisles over a box of genetically patented mashed potatoes grown and processed a thousand miles away. In a sense, such questions are crucial ones. How do plants grow? By what human effort? What of their character is attributable to nature and what to human nurture? What choices and trade-offs do they represent? What would it mean to make these choices sustainable?

A vendor at a farmers' market may grow eight kinds of potatoes of various hues and wear the most fantastically gnarled one on a string around his neck. He will likely invite questions—about these potatoes, the history of potatoes, their cultural resonances, the ways they can be grown and prepared. He invites questions, and he has answers for them. His answers may rest on the latest agricultural science, intuitive theories, eclectic reading, or family tradition. The answers will vary by vendor; the questions will vary by customer.

No one can ask these questions in a supermarket for, quite simply, there is no one to ask them of. Not the truck driver unloading a dolly of food from a warehouse across the country and filled with ingredients from countries across the world nor from the cashiers swiping bar codes at the register. Yet, the future depends on this kind of exchange.

The bigger, flawless produce of supermarket aisles we now know means de-natured, less nutritious crops that wreak havoc on water systems, soil, health, and communities.[5] The capital that we inherited—nutrients banked in the fertility of the soil, knowledge of growing in a particular place, and the health of a well-fed population—we fritter away at an alarming rate, only inadequately replacing the losses with a long-distance food chain. Farmers' markets are one way to make the necessary commitment to a local produce system, to return farming to a sustainable scale and keep the old, necessary skills of cultivating food and engaging our local communities. The growers at farmers' markets are learning or relearning weather, soil, labor, and mutual exchange. Consumers—and they are consumers in the most concrete sense—are recognizing, in the food itself and in their trade with growers, value that trumps the corporate competition. The stories that emerge from the farmers' market experience, from both sides of the exchange, suggest that these events are one way to foster a community physically, economically, and socially.

In the past few years, hardly a week goes by that farmers' markets do not get national notice: publications from *The New York Times* and *Time Magazine* to *Martha Stewart Living, Organic Living,* and *Organic Style* to *Sierra* and *Audubon* magazines take up the topic. Articles by community supported agriculture proponents, "slow foods" advocates, fitness buffs, and urban planners cite the benefits of farmers' markets. Books about markets offer start-up and public works recommendations, economics analyses, anthropological case studies, personal reflections, and culinary strategies.

In this book, we honor these ideas and hope to contribute a new perspective, one that derives from the intersection of our observations as long-time participants at one market with considerations of the broader social, ecological, and economic power of farmers' markets, generally. Focusing on a particular place, we look at (and listen to) how the people at farmers' markets engage each other and how they talk about their experiences. In these observations, we seek patterns of human action and interaction that can help to describe the phenomenal success of farmers' markets in ways that can extend to the experience of other people in other communities.

Like many markets, Indiana's Bloomington Community Farmers' Market is comprised of many small vending stands that are autonomous and specialized but that together create the market atmosphere. Not unique in its features, the Bloomington market is only a particularly well done example of what is possible. Seattle, San Francisco, Washington, D.C., Madison, Chattanooga, New York City, little gatherings in thousands of towns large and small around the country, all have similar elements and their own remarkable stories. Some markets offer only food, sometimes only local organic or sustainably produced food. Some allow lo-

Bloomington

cally made crafts; some open their vending spaces to crafts of the world. Some have locally prepared pies, roasted meats, beer, or wine. Some provide a view of a bay or mountains or fields or a town green or the brick back of an old building. Many have musicians, some living statues, dancers, circus stunts, and other kinds of performers as well. Free samples, scents, and tastes are ubiquitous.

All are open for the walking around, no purchase necessary. All offer free editorials on local and national news. They include colorful variegations of dress and language. At farmers' markets people mingle with those like and unlike themselves. They are places where a Baptist might exchange pleasantries with a Buddhist or a Rastafarian with a Methodist, a carpenter with a banker, a teacher with a janitor, an Asian-born grower of apples with a Hoosier selling native Korean flowers. There are few places left where the many differences of our social worlds mingle so genuinely; yet here, at least temporarily, obvious differences are set aside in order to get to the important though ordinary business at hand.

That ordinary business—the acquisition of foodstuffs—is, in some ways, merely an opening: to stories, histories, recipes, politics, and worldviews. While making a purchase, it is not unusual for someone to pull a visiting relative into a vendor's stand to shake hands. Nor is it unusual to hear about grandmothers who grew pussywillows or about last week's successes with the lemon basil, someone's health, someone else's home remedy. One customer uses photos of her favorite vendors as her computer screensaver at work. Vendors and customers alike see children grow up and hair grow gray. They see generations come of age, marry, divorce, and regroup in countless ways. Political buttons appear in November; pink ribbons at another time; and yellow ones, it seems, every few years.

In writing this book, we, as farmers' market vendors, have tried not to fool ourselves in thinking we know the real market. We come as stakeholders to our subject, both participants and observers of the market and its place in the current cultural climate. We recognize that we see ourselves as the stationary points against which we measure change. And we know best only one of the market's stories. Ours marks time by the varieties that we

Bloomington

have grown—basil back when it was newly popular, sunflowers before the deer attacks, the wholesale years—and in our growing partners and committed apprentices. We remember when we were the only flower vendors in a sea of vegetable stands. We remember the days before box stores had discovered bedding plants.

J. A. Hartenfeld has been "outstanding in the field" since 1977. A defector from a more institutional lifestyle, he struck out into the life of an organic grower of ornamental plants in south central Indiana. Joining the Bloomington farmers' market in its second full season, he sold his flowers from the back of a pickup at the edge of a city park. He persists now as one among the six most senior vendors at the market. Having lived out of sight of neighbors for nearly thirty years and making no more than weekly trips to town during that time, Hartenfeld can rightly be called an outside observer of many of the surges of popular culture. His winter activities, which include stacking firewood in ornate configurations and painting, hold some clue to a past life as a college teacher of photography and graphic design. He was joined in the business by his wife, Jennifer Meta Robinson, in 1991. After pursuing less traveled paths, she found Hart Farm and took up transplanting, hoeing, flower cutting, and bouquet making in her spare time, while she finished her doctorate in English. She nowadays directs the instructional consulting center at Indiana University in Bloomington. Our farm consists of fifty mostly wooded acres, six in production, with some in ornamental trees, shrubs, and grasses. The business has shifted over the years from back-of-a-truck retail to exclusively dried wholesale flowers. In the early 1990s, our primary outlet for dried flowers changed the business, pushing us back into marketing locally, both fresh and dried, directly to florists and to retail customers through the farmers' market. The pressure of competition—from wildlife, foreign markets, and other local market vendors—has kept our business innovative and changing.

Dan Schlapbach and Jennifer Roebuck moved to Bloomington, Indiana, in the summer of 1992 for Schlapbach to pursue his Master of Fine Arts degree in photography from Indiana University. In response to an ad placed on a bulletin board in the Fine Arts building ("Flower farm needs crew. Hard work, low pay, beautiful place"), Schlapbach and Roebuck both found themselves working on Hart Farm. In subsequent years, Schlapbach transplanted, weeded, watered, made bouquets, and sold flowers at two Bloomington farmers' markets and one Indianapolis farmers' market. In the summer of 1995, in the peak of August heat and surrounded by cockscomb, sunflowers, and tithonia, Schlapbach and Roebuck were married on Hart Farm. After Schlapbach received his degree in 1996, they moved to Baltimore, Maryland, where he is now Associate Professor of Fine Arts and the director of the photography program at Loyola University. His photographic work has been exhibited and published nationally. Roebuck received a Bachelor of Fine Arts degree at Maryland Institute College of Art in 1992. Her mixed-media artwork has been exhibited nationally.

All the contemporary photographs in this book were taken by Schlapbach and Roebuck in Indiana in 2005 and 2006. Their market photographs, including the customer and vendor portraits, come exclusively from the Bloomington Community Farmers' Market, a Saturday market held at Showers Common in downtown Bloomington. These portraits, taken mere steps from the activity of the market, allow a focus on individuals and relationships without background noise. The farm photographs were taken in five rural counties of south central Indiana.

The historical photographs, shot between 1935 and 1944, are from the Farm Security Administration (FSA) archive and are used courtesy of the Library of Congress. The Michael Hampshire painting "A Cahokia Market" is used courtesy of Cahokia Mounds State Historic Site in Collinsville, Illinois.

We have endeavored to get beyond our personal perspectives by interviewing many farmers' market participants and visiting with some on their farms.[6] Just short of fifty people agreed to one or more extended interviews. Without exception, all of those we spoke with were exceedingly generous with their wisdom, time, and forbearance.

Part 1 of the book provides a quick look at the rich history of market places and farmers' markets, primarily in Europe and America. Not meant to be exhaustive, this section sets the stage for some of the persistent structures, themes, and patterns that participants in today's farmers' markets will recognize. The first chapter describes the centrality of markets to human community and provides a quick look at some of the more distant history. It also introduces some of the substantial challenges to farmers' markets today. The second chapter traces the social strands that positioned farmers' markets for their remarkable resurgence at the end of the twentieth century. The third chapter proposes the Bloomington, Indiana, farmers' market as a case study through which to discuss the phenomenon of farmers' markets.

Part 2 begins to tease out who participates in farmers' markets and what their experiences are, as often as possible through their own voices and stories. Chapters 4 and 5 explore the perspectives of customers and vendors separately. Chapter 6 looks more closely at how farmers' markets and the activities surrounding them can act as sites of transformation for both vendors and customers, confirming their membership in a community that bridges the past and the future.

Part 3 looks ahead at harvests and futures. Chapter 7 visits with people who have, with ambitious vision and varying degrees of success, taken a shot at market vending. Their lives, like all those described here, are journeys in progress, full of midstream course corrections but still based on glimpses of a guiding light. Chapter 8 comes from a discussion among eight stakeholders in farmers' markets. Market administrators, customers, and vendors gathered to discuss the future promise and dilemmas of markets and local food. The final chapter proposes a few conclusions and directions meant to open a dialogue with the reader. We hope this ignites further conversation.

This is a book of fieldwork. It comes from seasons of damp mornings and hot days, plowing by the tractor headlights at night, cutting field bunches of snapdragons, dianthus, sunflowers, liatris, basil, and cockscomb, making mixed bouquets late on a Friday night, sometimes to the drumming of rain on the barn's tin roof with hope of clear skies for the market the following morning. The fieldwork begins early in the spring with the turning in of the green manure crops and ends late in the fall with garlic planting and the sowing of winter rye. It is an infinite cycle of beginnings that are endings and endings that renew.

This is a book of work in the field told by the people of the Bloomington Community Farmers' Market. This particular farmers' market, its people, and its practices do not represent all markets nor does it tell all the compelling stories of the marketplace. But it does serve as a point of entry into a community and a site of

Greene County

community making. The people attending the Bloomington market gather to grow and share the fruits of life in southern Indiana. As with all markets, they draw on the idealistic and utopian while also responding practically to social, political, and economic currents. This book is full of people's stories. Their voices together sketch the borders of a field—one in which we are all much alike for all our differences, much different for all our common ground.

Bloomington

Part 1. Settings

Even a quick perusal of farmers' markets shows that they emerge from both innovation and tradition. While each market arises uniquely from its local context and time, it also shares a common character with other markets around the world and through history. For this reason, a field study of one market can ground a discussion of the common and differing experiences of growing food and cultivating community.

Vendor Notes _____

On the opening morning of the farmers' market season, the alarm goes off at 3:30. Coffee, fried eggs, toast and jam before 4:00. We showered the night before, and clothes are all laid out. The coffee gets more than its fair share of attention, and the dogs look bleary-eyed at our early awakening. We, on the other hand, are bright, expectant. With the sky still thoroughly dark, any moon hidden behind clouds, we drive off the quiet farm by 4:30.

The trip to the market is lively. We come upon deer in unexpected places: standing in the road at one bend, climbing a rugged hill at another. Is this their last loop toward bed or are they just up, like us, looking toward the dawn? We pass a few cars going out to the country from town. Some places must just have closed up at 4 a.m. Someone walks along the verge with a gas can toward a car with blinking lights.

By the time we get to town, a few other cars are going our way. We pass one at the first traffic light at the edge of town. In the rear view mirror we watch it sit and sit as we move on. We pass empty fast food places and you-wash car bays standing ready. We pass vast parking lots and pizza joints lit as though they were open. All the stoplights flash.

At the market site, a roofed parking lot beside the city hall, a couple of vendors have beat us in. They are all old-timers, not in age but in experience: old enough to know what they are doing but young enough to be ambitious in doing it. Still flush with strength, they draw on the physical capital banked over a slow winter. No one can afford to hire much help, or not the experienced kind, so they rely on themselves. Only later in the morning will the aged vendors arrive with family, or friends, or an apprentice to do the heavy lifting. Farmers learn to move less and with more precision over time. More of the motion goes on in the mind, so the body works less, with fewer wasted moves, fewer mistakes, fewer injuries. We all know someone who in one mo-

ment was stung by a nest of yellow jackets, or tore a ligament, or flipped a tractor—usually by moving against the grain or against the proper pace. So these men and women move deliberately as they situate the compact station wagon, the lightweight card table, the greens and roots and buds that will bring in just what they seem to need to continue the market journey.

We set up quietly, with a nod or a wave to others and curious sideways glances around to see what there is to see of what the winter months have wrought. Then, there goes a kind of testing: Will this old umbrella really last through one more season? Does the leg on that table still stick? If I give this box just a bit of a kick, I won't have to bend down this one time to line it up with the front of my space.

The air is warm and dry, but as the sun rises, we see that the sky is overcast, and later arrivals bring the TV weather news. Everyone knows the weather has been too dry for early spring, but no one wants opening market morning to be the time we get the big rain.

More people set up, and the noise rises. Little conversations sputter between neighbors. Trucks and their clouds of exhaust fill the air. All manner of umbrellas go up in the uncovered spaces, in anticipation of rain now, of sun later. They are single-poled or four-legged. They have banners, stripes, things that hang. The foresighted people bring chairs, maybe a newspaper to read for the slow times, and raincoats. The rest pace around, watching the sky, checking their stand. A few who set up early take the grand tour. They eye their competitors, the prices, the packaging, the displays. Only one has tomatoes on the first of May. Asparagus is up. People have eggs. No one has morels. The milk people don't come at all. Nor does the CSA farm that lost two of its three growers when they moved on suddenly this winter. The alpaca woman brought vegetable plants this time and a few greens. The elk meat people are back. The dark-haired woman has her plants as always and a new truck and no husband. He, now ex-, is working with another vendor, unwilling to give up the market. The bread people come, and so do the organic farmers who fight the new highway. Their teenage son is apparently sleeping in. One of the kids who grew up at the market is now tall, a teen himself, and carrying the clipboard of the assistant market mas-

ter, a position created for him. The Bob Dylan fanatic races in, CD player blaring.

At 6:00 the first customers arrive, an hour before the official opening. Some vendors will sell to them, a few refuse to break the rules. The first to make the rounds are women, always elders, singly or in pairs, some very old in clear rain bonnets. The first men come as a pair, hatless, spending their social security money on vegetables and cleaned hickory nuts at stands manned by vendors older than they.

At 6:45 vendors without permanent spaces are let in to fill the gaps. They are regulars gambling on a second stand, those who missed picking their space at the winter meeting, or newcomers willing to give the market a try. Like the rest, they defy the forecast.

It's a damp morning that moves into rain with the dawn. By 7:30, a deluge starts. But it is the first market of the season, and the customers come. They know that the vendors, enough of them to be worth it, will be there. People don't know each other's names, have not seen each other for six months, and would only vaguely recognize these faces on the street. Still, warm hellos are exchanged. People note that it was a long winter, but a good one, and we all survived, which makes it a good one. Those who didn't survive and other sadnesses of the dark months are mostly left unsaid. Perhaps if it were a bright morning, warm and balmy, we might talk about those who do not return. But beyond a quick tally of the vendor spots, there is little mention of those things. It is spring after all. The lilacs, violas, kettle corn all perfume the air.

What is it that draws the vendors on a day they clearly will make little money? What is it that draws the customers on a day that will leave them rushing from stand to stand, buying quickly, with little contact, huddling under umbrellas, water dripping down their backs, shorts and flip-flops seeming hideous errors in this wind? Yes, there are greenhouse tomatoes and eggs, fresh and real, but by 8:00 they are gone. What is it that draws us all here? Why do we smile?

How long have you been coming here? Oh, forever, as long as I have been in town—twenty-two years. What brings them here year after year? A visitor from Maine buys daylilies for his *grandson's house, on a day that seems like summer back home. That couple there has moved back to Bloomington from Florida. Don't they know much of a generation moved to Florida from this very state? This is home; this is a community, they say. There are bigger farmers' markets, but none better. This one is home.*

That first wave of customers comes early—some just early risers, some with events later in the day: a christening, a derby party. By 9:00 another wave arrives, not crossing paths with the first. It's early in their day, and they never know about the tomatoes, never hoped to see any before June. They find the goat cheese, organic beef, jalapeno-pepper scones, and hot coffee they were looking for. Plenty left for them. The vendors are cold by 10:00 and thoroughly soaked. Some have slipped over to the bathrooms to put on long johns or change their shirts. Flannels and jackets appear from the cabs of trucks. Wool hats replace straw ones.

At 11:00 the rain quits. And as though masses of people waited in their cars for the first break in the weather, the market is hopping with customers. Just hopping. They all want to buy, and buy quick. They do little perusing, little mulling, even little comparison shopping. With just an hour until close and the rain still threatening, they rush around waving money. Juggling loaded sacks, they speculate about soccer games, the weather next week, and when the first beans will be in.

The vendors are happy then. Tee shirts and straw hats appear. They are still wet, and their feet hurt, but the smiles are brighter; the chatter is cordial and snappy. A fiddler strikes a lively tune.

Can the last hour salvage our day's earnings? Can this first market actually herald a lucrative season? It matters when we count the money, but in the flush of that first market, when all the rows lie out before us with promise, with dogwoods still blooming, mushrooms waiting in the woods, asparagus peeking through, and everything in the field now thoroughly watered, it's a sure thing we'll be back next week.

Vendor   *Bloomington*

1. Markets Past

In a colorful, bustling marketplace, a customer approaches a watermelon vendor. Any place. Any time. She wants, of course, a ripe one:

> *Customer: Are they good ones?*
> *Vendor: These are the only ones I'll grow.*
> *Customer: But they have seeds?*
> *Vendor: They have seeds.*
> *Customer: They're not mushy? They're all right? All right, I'll trust you.*
> *Vendor: As long as you can wait until it's ripe. Don't get impatient.*
> *Customer: Right. Do you have any more back there that might be ripe? I'd like a five-dollar one.*
> *Vendor: These are five and all those back there are all four. Feel free to look through them and thump them and smell them or whatever test you like to do.*
> *Customer: This one looks good.*
> *Vendor: I try and go by the sound test. There's cues when to pick them. When the tendril dies back where the stem is attached—where the main stem is, there is a little tendril that will die. And then the spot on the bottom will get darker. And then the final test is the ping-pang-punk thump test.*
> *Customer: Punk is good?*
> *Vendor: Ping is good. Punk is a little overripe.*
> *Customer: [She thumps the melon.] This one's good, right?*
> *Vendor: I'll tell you how many hours you have to wait.* [He thumps the melon.] *This one's pretty close. Tonight or tomorrow for breakfast.*
> *Customer: It's got to be for today!*
> *Vendor: My final test is I put a knife in it. Not all the way. And you slightly twist the knife and if it doesn't split open, it isn't ready. It bursts open when it's ripe. That's our final test.*
> *Customer: I'm buying this because I want it for today to*

take to my family. I guess I don't know what it's supposed to sound like—I'm expecting you to know.
Vendor: If you're not satisfied, come back next week, and I'll give you another one.

The fruits on offer and the markers of their ripeness may differ, but the essential market experience is the same—buyer and seller meet one-to-one to make a trade. They do so at a marketplace that is instantly recognizable—many traders gathered together in small stalls designated by front doors, kiosks, awnings, umbrellas, or simple mats on the ground. Negotiations about price and quality play out as explicit or implicit, vocalized or interior haggling. Most typically the meetings take place out of doors, in the morning before the offerings show the effects of heat or cold or rain. They happen on a regular basis, every day or every week or during the harvest season. People in the marketplace linger to observe, editorialize, and gossip, passing on news, wisdom, and wit.

This exchange could occur at any market, though it happened to take place over watermelons at a Midwestern American market. An ancient institution, in many ways markets seem the same around the world and through history. But they also differ from place to place. At the floating markets in Vietnam and Thailand, sellers row small boats full of oranges, grapes, papayas, cabbages, beans, and onions that they have grown in their own orchards and fields along canals to waterborne marketplaces. Some customers rent boats in order to go among the vendors to haggle. Bangkok's Chatuchak Weekend Market offers acres of live animals, handicrafts, books, produce, and more. In Marrakech's Bab Doukkala market, wine from local vineyards is the order of the day, and sheep's heads, lamb, recently butchered cows and chickens can be found along with eggplants, artichokes, lemons, mint, and marjoram. The giant Kumasi market in Ghana is organized by type of product, with all the cloth, plantains, yams, onions, and so on, each in its designated section. If a vendor finds that her area is drifting into a different line of produce, then she may change her own offerings rather than move her stall.[1] At the renovated Vero-peso market in Belém do Pará, Brazil, customers often travel by boat from their homes on islands in the Amazon River. In La Paz, vendors in bowler hats at the Weekend Women's Market sit on the ground beside neat bundles and heaped baskets. In Zanzibar's

Old Town Market, men do most of the shopping along narrow winding streets, often several times a day for lack of refrigeration at home. Shoppers in Ecuadorian markets may insult vendors as a calculated way to pressure them into lowering prices.[2] And in markets around the world, sellers cut better deals, longer measures, and cheaper prices to people they consider their own.

Lively, energetic, bustling, traditional, exotic, classic, trendy, historic, idyllic, groovy, ancient, distinctive, gorgeous, and imaginative are a few of the words that the people who love markets use to describe them.[3] The distinctive character and success of each market comes from its roots in the landscape, seasons, social orders, and foodways of its locale. Thus, farmers' markets provide particularly rich insights into how those elements intersect for a particular community. Marketplaces bring together the best of staying put—temporally and spatially—with the bounty of moving around.

Thousands of years ago, long before the Common Era, in areas as diverse as China, Burma, India, and Mesopotamia, markets were set in motion. The reasons they developed are not clear. Some indications exist that societies that have stratification (such that groups of people have different access to food), that tend to stay put, and that grow crops with purpose were the ones to develop markets. In that case, hunter-gatherer societies and shifting-cultivator societies, which moved their fields and homes when land fertility dropped, would not have had markets.[4] Possibly, markets started when those with too much of one thing—through luck or specialization—traded with those who were, through crop failure or alternative specialization, in need.[5] This scenario describes a horizontal rationale, trade among peers. Or perhaps markets started when political rulers who levied taxes on crops and possessions forced the conditions for markets that could move unmanageable surpluses into positions where they would have value. This version relies on a vertical impetus. Some hold that traditional societies gathered in marketplaces to redistribute and reciprocate goods, while others indicate that marketplaces address our tendency to compete and to maximize choice and profit. Whatever the cause, markets took hold around the world as places to sell and buy items such as clothing, equipment, live animals, and "keeper" foods that could withstand a trek to and fro.[6]

Top: Monroe County

Bottom: Greene County

Markets around the world developed ways of regulating their trade, resolving disputes among vendors, and ensuring customers get fair measures and prices for what they buy. Governments became involved in overseeing markets as early as fifth century B.C.E. in Greece, where the markets were known as *agorae*. For the protection of the consumer and to be able to levy taxes on the trade, Greek market officials (*agoranomoi*) regulated weights and measures and the frequency, location, and organization of markets.[7] Bailiffs or mayors policed medieval English markets in the name of the king, who licensed those markets to individuals, towns, and church officials. These market enforcers exacted rental fees for stalls and tolls on the transactions made there,[8] and they ensured that vendors employed the weights and measures that had been standardized across the kingdom. For example, the accounts records from the Framlingham market in England note that, in 1274–1275, the rent of the stalls totaled sixteen pennies. Those fees provided the market's landholder not only a "modest income" but also enough extra to improve the market with the purchase of several standard measuring devices to ensure fair trades—two gallons, one bushel, one ell (a 45" length), and a seal for making the measurements official.[9]

At that time, most Europeans lived as subsistence farmers, producing most of what they ate and eating most of what they produced. Most of the arable land then was in wheat, barley, oats, and beans. Highly fertile areas could support several plow teams of eight oxen on a square mile of cultivated ground, while poorer farmland might support only one team every two miles or more. In 1085, William the Conqueror ordered a general survey of the resources of all of England so that he could levy taxes on ownership and production to greatest effect. Issued as the *Domesday Book,* it shows that more than six thousand watermills ground grain in England, and sheep, pigs, goats, cows, oxen, horses, and bees were the most important farm animals. The survey also considered fisheries in rivers and ponds to be valuable enough to tally: "A millpond at Stratford in Warwickshire is said to have produced 1000 eels per year; Petersham in Surrey rendered 1000 eels and 1000 lampreys."[10] Such comprehensive taxation moved not only eels and lampreys but also staple goods like grains and sheep's wool into trade, which in turn stimulated more trade and strengthened the marketing system in England and Europe. Weekly markets commonly featured staple goods like grains while more seasonal products were sold at less frequent fairs.

From 1100 to 1300, the population of most of western Europe grew dramatically, and marketing networks improved to accommodate more people and their increased productivity. In England alone, the population grew from around two million in the time of the *Domesday* survey to more than seven million at the close of the thirteenth century.[11] While luck may have been in place, with the climate entering a period of warming and stabilization, clearly knowledge of farming was also improving across Europe. These two factors—weather and know-how—allowed farmers to convert seasonally used high pasturelands to intensive pasturage and tilled fields, marshes to arable land, and woodlands to farmland.[12] Important innovations in fertilization and crop rotation helped restore the vitality of soil that was increasingly tapped by a burgeoning population.[13] Medieval farmers manured the fields and let them lie fallow every second or third year, and they replenished nitrogen in the soil with legume crops. Animals, too, were used more effectively: more bountiful cow's milk began to supplant goat and sheep milk, and horses, which could plow more quickly than oxen, became more widely used as draft animals. In England, wool production boomed and became a valuable commodity that was traded to Europe, and grains were shipped up and down the coast by a complex network of small suppliers.[14] Valuable exports that traveled well—such as grain, cheese, and processed fish—encouraged further specialization of those products.[15] With increased food production, the labor supply also grew, leading to more surpluses, increased trade, and strong networks among market towns throughout Europe.[16]

As their potential became more obvious, European markets became the focus of power struggles among church authorities, feudal landholders, and emerging civic and business alliances. In the town of Bury St. Edmunds in England, the market became the center of numerous debates and grievances over who allocated spaces in the marketplace, who received them, and who had the right of first and discounted purchase. At one point, in an act of civil disobedience, the men of the town lay down naked in the churchyard to protest the market policies dictated by the abbot. A monk in the abbey at Bury St. Edmonds chronicled the struggle in the late 1100s to transition from a direct labor system, in which all residents participated in reaping the grain fields surrounding the town, to a taxation system for residents who did not physically help with the harvest.[17]

Market towns continued to prosper as industry and farming depended less on church monopolies and more on open trade. As always, though, life was tenuous. Seed was broadcast by hand and might be eaten by birds. A substantial portion of each harvest had to be kept as seed for subsequent crops. Yields might be five bushels harvested to one planted, though getting as little as two bushels harvested from one bushel planted was common. And famine did strike. The years 1315–1318 were unusually cold and wet, causing widespread harvest failures and severe hunger across western Europe. In some places as much as 15 percent of the population died of malnutrition in those years.[18]

Growing crops always requires a fair amount of luck. Rain has to fall after the seeds are planted but not just before a harvest, more frequently in the spring and not so much in late summer or vice versa depending on the crops. Frosts have to end early enough for farmers to beat the summer heat and begin again late enough to allow things to ripen. Winters that are warm enough to allow a late picking might not be cold enough to knock back the pest population for the following year. Winters that are too dry can make for a hard spring start, but winters that are too wet can damage perennial plants. Too many deer or rabbits can severely damage a crop, but too few might mean a family at subsistence level goes hungry from lack of animals to hunt.

In the seventeenth and eighteenth centuries, even as Europeans began to understand the chemistry of plants well enough that they could keep some crops and fields under almost continuous cultivation, producing two and three harvests a year, the supernatural was still invoked in songs and stories to explain the vagaries of growing. "God's great and vvonderful vvork" is cited as reward for a grain farmer who sold his harvest to the poor at half price. The following year, "he was recompensed by an extraordinary crop of whet, the like was never before heard; of each stalk of straw having divers full large ears, some nine, ten and thirteen, but generally ten ears on every straw throughout the field."[19] Likewise, warnings about the consequences of poor behavior abounded. In one story about the "Country-miser, or the Unhappy Farmers Dear Market," a farmer sells his corn at market for an "extortionable rate . . . to the great oppression, especially of the poorer sort." The devil then plagues him in the form of a "countrey chap," and he must seek the help of a minister to be delivered from torment.[20]

Luck helps. But growing also requires knowledge. What farmers know about the soil and climate and techniques for cultivation, harvest, and preservation contribute to crop yield and to human health. Better skills mean surpluses can be accumulated. And surpluses can be exchanged at markets, along with news, styles, songs, stories, family bloodlines, innovations, resistance schemes, and plans. In the seventeenth century, farmland was valuable enough in England to prompt its enclosure behind fences, moving pasture and cropland from a common resource to a private one designed for profit. A great migration of country dwellers into the cities resulted. Soon after, in the eighteenth century, the Industrial Revolution geared up. It harnessed huge workforces, among other developments, to improve transportation of food, goods, and people. Canals, railroads, and steamboats moved manufactured products more efficiently to points of use or sale, and produce from farms took these new means of transportation to their urban destinations. By the end of the nineteenth century, markets staffed by producers and growers were in steady decline in Europe.

The Americas had their own traditions of marketplaces. The famous market of Tlaltelolco in Mexico dazzled the Europeans with its size and offerings. It was the market district of the Aztec capital Tenochtitlán, probably one of the largest cities in the Americas, with offerings that had come from great distances. Some of the vendors sold food grown on the *chinampas*, floating garden beds anchored to the bottom of Lake Texcoco with trees. Others, reportedly, sold grains of gold packaged in translucent goose quills, and it bears remembering that the last stand of the Aztecs against the conquistadors occurred at this market, where tens of thousands of Aztec men, women, and children perished in 1521.

The scene before the market's demise was wonderful indeed. Bernal Díaz de Castillo, one of Hernán Cortés' men, recorded the sight in his *True History of the Conquest of New Spain*:

> When we arrived at the great market place, called Tlaltelolco, we were astonished at the number of people and the quantity of merchandise that it contained, and at the good order and control that was maintained, for we had never seen such a thing before. The chieftains who accompanied us acted as guides. Each kind of merchandise was kept by itself and had its fixed place marked out. Let us begin with the dealers in gold, silver, and precious stones, feathers, mantles, and embroidered goods. Then there were other wares consisting of Indian slaves both men and women; and I say that they bring as many of them to that great market for sale as the Portuguese bring negroes from Guinea; and they brought them along tied to long poles, with collars round their necks so that they could not escape, and others they left free. Next there were other traders who sold great pieces of cloth and cotton, and articles of twisted thread, and there were cacahuateros who sold cacao. In this way one could see every sort of merchandise that is to be found in the whole of New Spain, placed in arrangement in the same manner as they do in my own country, which is Medina del Campo, where they hold the fairs, where each line of booths has its particular kind of merchandise, and so it is in this great market. There were those who sold cloths of henequen and ropes and the cotaras with which they are shod, which are made from the same plant, and sweet cooked roots, and other tubers which they get from this plant, all were kept in one part of the market in the place assigned to them. In another part there were skins of tigers and lions, of otters and jackals, deer and other animals and badgers and mountain cats, some tanned and others untanned, and other classes of merchandise.
>
> Let us go on and speak of those who sold beans and sage and other vegetables and herbs in another part, and to those who sold fowls, cocks with wattles, rabbits, hares, deer, mallards, young dogs and other things of that sort in their part of the market, and let us also mention the fruiterers, and the women who sold cooked food, dough and tripe in their own part of the market; then every sort of pottery made in a thousand different forms from great water jars to little jugs, these also had a place to themselves; then those who sold honey and honey paste and other dainties like nut paste, and those who sold lumber, boards, cradles, beams, blocks and benches, each article by itself, and the vendors of ocote firewood, and other

*things of a similar nature. I must furthermore mention, asking
your pardon, that they also sold many canoes full of human
excrement, and these were kept in the creeks near the market,
and this they use to make salt or for tanning skins, for without
it they say that they cannot be well prepared.*[21]

Even after the European conquest, some of the native market locations and traditions continued, in markets such as those in Guatemala held at five-day intervals based on the Mayan calendar. Indeed, some anthropologists posit that the persistence of markets into the colonial period helped to sustain the Indian cultures, serving as places of both integration and cultural memory.[22]

Further north, the so-called Mississippian people founded the city of Cahokia near what would later be the site of St. Louis. With ten to twenty thousand or more residents at its height, between 1000 and 1150, the city played an important role in commerce among villages throughout the middle of the continent. No North American city would be larger until Philadelphia of 1800. The city vanished before a written record could be made, but the archaeological record at the site shows much activity indicating trade. The Cahokia marketplace would have stood among the 120 mounds of the city, the tallest of which rose one hundred feet high. Local foods traded in the marketplace were gathered or hunted from nearby forests or grown on the outskirts of the city in the fertile bottomland near the Mississippi River. Cultivated crops included corn, goosefoot, squash, amaranth, and canary grass. The river also provided the means to move goods long distances. Raw materials such as seashells from the Gulf of Mexico, copper and chert mined hundreds of miles away, salt from nearby mines, and mica from the east made their way via trade into tools, clothing, and ceremonial items in Cahokia manufactories.

Trade was extensive among native groups in North America before European contact and incorporated the newcomers into the system when possible. In the Midwest, the Mandan, Arikara, and the Hidatsa peoples on the upper Missouri River were especially well known to French and other European traders. Miami settlements in Indiana traded corn and other traditionally grown, gathered, and hunted goods—such as melons, squashes, opossum, woodchuck, tree nuts, turkeys, geese, and medicinals—for European-made goods such as kettles, thimbles, bells, and knives. The

"A Cahokia Market" by Michael Hampshire

Miami economic center of Kekionga in northern Indiana was especially renowned for the vast cornfields among its more than five hundred acres of cropland. Until the late 1700s, the Miami were able to maintain their town by negotiating the tensions between French and English traders and their allies, remaining mostly independent of both.[23] In the 1810s, Delaware and Potawatomi people in the Bloomington, Indiana, area frequented at least one "trading house" that stood a half mile from the houses of white settlers. According to the memoirs of James Parks, Sr., who died at 101 in 1882, native families making trades there sometimes stayed the night at his home nearby.[24] Such civilities deteriorated, and indeed ended, across the Indiana Territory as bloody battles between whites and Native Americans included the destruction of property and crops as well as lives. Congress passed legislation for the removal of Native Americans from Indiana in 1830.

European settlers in North America brought their own market traditions with them. Markets flourished up and down the colonial eastern seaboard. The first farmers' market to continue the European model was established in 1634 in Boston by order of Governor John Winthrop. It was open-air until 1662 when a wooden building was added. Markets in other cities followed. Hartford established its first public market in 1643; New York had two markets before 1686 and five more by 1731.[25] In 1693,

DuBois, Pennsylvania, 1940

Philadelphia opened its market twice a week and what had been High Street became known as Market Street, a clue to the origin of a common street name in America. Markets moved with the population, New Orleans opening the French Market in 1779, what would become one of the longest continuously operating markets in the United States, and Cincinnati opening its first market in 1801. As in Europe, colonial American farmers' markets benefited consumers and farmers and stimulated local economies.

Farmers' markets then were the primary source of food for the growing urban population, and products were of necessity produced and consumed locally:

> *To prevent breakage during the rough trip to town eggs were packed in barrels or kegs between layers of straw, chaff, sawdust, or some other readily available material. The consumer always brought a basket to market, in order to have a container in which to put purchases. Eggs were sold loose by the*

Weatherford, Texas, 1939

dozen. A can or jar was usually brought along to carry home the butter. Refrigeration was almost unknown and during the summer months, butter often would be more liquid than solid as it was ladled from the farmer's tub into the consumer's container.[26]

Flours and corn meal were commonly sold, and the produce available was limited to what was in season, except for keepers like apples, potatoes, onions, and processed foods like pickles, sauerkraut, dried fruit, and cured meat.[27] Markets provided an essential means for getting food from the farmers to the public throughout the first two hundred years of European settlement of America.

Even as markets boomed in the middle of the 1800s, however, economic and cultural trends were working against them.[28] Urban populations were burgeoning, and farms were being pushed further and further from the downtown centers of commerce by early urban sprawl. Growers began shipping their produce in by rail, and farmers' markets began to disappear. In the 1850s, in cities where markets ceased operation, such as Hartford and Philadelphia, some farmers opened their own permanent store-fronts. Others sold to those establishments, which were able to offer more variety, quantity, and reliability than any single farmer. In order to compete, farmers on the edge of town shifted their businesses to dairy products and other perishable items that did not transport well. In 1859, the central Philadelphia marketplace, after 166 years, was demolished, dispersing business to neighbor-hood stores.[29]

The remaining farmers' markets struggled. By 1900, about half the municipal areas in the United States did not have farm-ers' markets.[30] New England, in particular, had remarkably few. In Portland, Maine, an 1880 census informant estimated that 90 percent of the food supply came from private stores. In New Bed-ford, Massachusetts, the market house had been converted to an office building, and in Providence, Rhode Island, the area set aside for a market was used "with no great regularity."[31] By 1880, the role of farmers' markets had diminished enough that the mayor of Cincinnati said that the markets there "were decadent and could be demolished with no great inconvenience. He claimed that most of the sellers were hucksters or middlemen, and that the market's original purpose of providing the consumer with cheap supplies was no longer met."[32]

This concern with middlemen's impact on prices was not new. As early as the thirteenth century, the English government had decried the appearance of "forestallers," who "leave the town to intercept such things as come to market and buy them outside the town to sell to middlemen more dearly than those who brought them would have done had they reached the market."[33] Forestall-ers were deemed to oppress

the whole commonality and country. Thirsting for evil profit he hurries out before other men, sometimes by land and sometimes by water, to meet grain, fish, herring or other kinds of goods coming for sale by land or water (oppressing poorer people and deceiving those better off) and he contrives to carry off these goods unjustly and to sell them much more dearly. He circumvents outsiders coming with goods for sale, offering himself as an agent for the sale of their goods and suggesting to them that they could sell their goods more dearly than they proposed.[34]

Top: San Angelo, Texas, 1939   *Bottom: Boise, Idaho, 1941*

However, wholesalers increasingly stepped in as crop specialization and improvements in refrigeration, processing, and transportation systems removed the constraints of locality. Food no longer needed to be produced and purchased near where it would be consumed, and the role for farmer-vendors faded. By the 1920s, modern supermarkets began to appear, and agribusiness producers scaled up to meet the demand.[35]

Most smaller farms could not compete. They could not raise the large quantities at the low prices that wholesalers demanded. As a result, during the middle of the twentieth century, many mid-sized and smaller farms were bought by agribusiness operations, sold to urban and suburban developments, or in other ways passed beyond families who may have worked them for generations. Suburban sprawl meant farmers had to drive further to sell their produce, only to find populations more diffuse and therefore more difficult to reach as consumers.[36]

Even those farmers who remained in business found that their share of the American dollar spent on food was shrinking: "While the retail price of food increased by 18%, in excess of inflation, from 1975 to 1993, the amount of each food dollar during this period that reached the farmer declined from 33 cents to 21 cents," according to one analysis.[37] Children raised on farms, with an intimate knowledge of the hard work and long hours of that kind of life, increasingly found ways to leave the farm. After stints in the army or college, they often did not return to take up the work of their parents, a trend that continues.

As small farms suffered, so did farmers' markets. Between 1880 and 1970, markets made brief appearances, usually in response to economic hard times, but they tended to be short-lived. During World War I, the Depression, and World War II, the number of markets temporarily jumped (from 149 in 1920 to 210 in 1930 and back down to 123 by 1946) suggesting that people were growing their own produce in those lean years and making a little money selling the extra.[38] By the end of World War II, however, as a result of "government regulations, military requirements, shortage of gasoline and tires, inadequate supplies, labor shortages, and other handicaps" small farms produced less.[39] Victory gardens, a war-effort movement in the 1940s, celebrated small-scale vegetable gardening, but they too largely ceased after World War II. Although a few of the most successful backyard gardeners

Top: San Antonio, Texas, 1939　　　　　　　　*Bottom: Weatherford, Texas, 1939*

might sell the surplus from small stands by the house, supermarkets more and more were providing produce for the vast majority of people.[40]

The markets that did persist in some large cities featured only a small number of small-scale farmers, some of them recent immigrants; but mostly the markets were taken over by wholesalers, including nearly all of the markets in New England.[41] Even when individual consumers attempted to patronize these markets, they found quantities too large and quality lacking. Like most of the food industry, these markets had come to emphasize cheapness, availability, and uniformity instead of taste. Only in some rural areas did farmers' markets remain the primary outlet for farmers' produce, and small and informally organized "curb markets" and "courthouse square markets" continued in rural states.[42] In the 1940s and 50s, chain supermarkets ceased to buy their produce at wholesale markets, instead developing their own direct networks with farmers or buying their own farms.[43] As a result, the number of markets plummeted in the 1950s and 60s.[44] By 1970, none of the vendors at the Indianapolis market, for example, which had been in operation for at least a hundred years, produced their own food: they were all wholesalers.[45]

Mass production and distribution made food more available, less subject to the whims of weather or the quality of the decisions of particular growers. However, freshness and taste were trumped by availability, price, and shipping hardiness. Cheaper was always considered better. All of these developments advanced the products of larger and more specialized farms. As a consequence, more small farms failed. More land was sold for sprawling urban centers, further removing the population from rural life.[46] Prime growing land was vaulted under asphalt and lawns. By the middle of the twentieth century, farmers were only half joking when they cited the adage that the only time a farmer makes money is when he sells his land for development.

The food industry consolidated to such an extent that by 1992, six corporations accounted for 46 percent of the total retail food and beverage sales in the United States.[47] Even organic food, which had grown alongside farmers' markets since the 1970s, and which had helped support small and local farms, began to be dominated by the mainstream food industry.[48] A $10 billion sector by 2005, organic food production relies increasingly on big growers steeped in conventional agricultural practices.[49] These larger companies broke into organics by purchasing the smaller, original pioneers, thereby both consolidating and diluting the natural foods market.[50] Whole Foods Market, the self-proclaimed "world's leading retailer of natural and organic foods," grew to 184 stores in North America and the United Kingdom, with one store directly adjacent to New York City's flagship Greenmarket farmers' market. The natural food giants and ordinary supermarkets now compete with farmers' markets by decorating with farm-y trappings and photographs of growers. Sometimes they turn over their parking lots to "farm markets" that feature long-distance produce.

The average distance most commonly cited for U.S. food to travel from farm to table is 1,500 miles. Although that distance rarely comes with a footnoted source attached, much shorter distances have a deleterious impact as well. A study published in *Food Policy* found that moving food as few as twelve miles has greater costs to the environment than growing even non-organic food locally.[51] But the practices of big agriculture do not put much value on the local. Brian Halweil traces the produce of a lettuce farmer in Lincoln, Nebraska, who must first ship his lettuce 225 miles to a North Platte inspection and distribution center before it can come back to Lincoln for sale in local stores:

> *Despite the apparent absurdity of this arrangement, this mammoth distribution center is a state-of-the-art innovation in efficiency from the point of view of the supermarket executive or produce wholesaler. But include the subsidies for gasoline and roads, the effects of smog and global warming, the ecological fallout from the industrial firms that supply the distribution center, and a range of other hidden costs, and the "efficiency" of long-distance food begins to fade away. Because these costs are mostly unaccounted for—not paid directly by the consumer, farmer, or supermarket—the resulting food is artificially cheap.[52]*

Food grown and shipped using "conventional" petroleum-based methods across most of a continent or much of the world simply cannot be sustained in the long term. In addition to suffering a loss of flavor, long-distance food is at greater risk of contamination than local food and requires the use of preservation practices that may decrease nutrients or introduce less healthful ingredients to foods.[53] The resources that make such delivery possible are rap-

Top: Windsor Locks, Connecticut, 1941   *Bottom: Durham, North Carolina, 1940*

idly becoming depleted and the pollution their use causes compounds the degradation of human health. As John Ikerd notes, global convenience may not be the bargain it seems: "the true costs of quick food must include the costs of poor health, lost dignity in work, degraded landscapes, and ethical and moral decay in business matters, including international trade and investment."[54]

By the end of the twentieth century, America had become an urban country: less than 1 percent of the population lived on farms, compared to 1920 when 32 million Americans, or about one-third of the population, were farmers living on farms.[55] The times seemed to be against small farms and the consumers who wanted old foods and traditional foods.[56] Nevertheless, farmers' markets, as it turns out, would hang on to provide fresh, flavorful, and healthful alternatives to mass-marketed produce.

Customer   *Bloomington*

2. New Markets

Although farmers' markets nearly expired in the twentieth century, that period can also be told as a story of their remarkable persistence. Even while innovations in transportation, insecticides, herbicides, fertilizers, preservatives, and mechanization allowed for land specialization that favored large farms; even while dropping water tables, leeched soils, salinization, hard-pack, and erosion drained fertility from the soil; even while people became enamored of the bottomless availability, flawless uniformity, and cheap pricing offered by supermarkets, small growers persevered. And although farmers' markets historically have been disparaged as unfair competition, havens for radicals and misfits, or irrelevant traffic nuisances, some survived. Indeed, small farms and the producer-vendor markets that connect them with customers remain absolutely necessary, for their links to old ways and to alternate ways of organizing for human sustenance. The persistence of markets against the odds of the twentieth century suggests that their traditions of direct contact with neighbors, family farming, and spiritual and ethical engagement resonate with new notions and novel applications, helping to position farmers' markets to become, again, an important site of American culture and community making, environmental stewardship, and economic vitality.

During the Great Depression, weather and banks both foreclosed on farming operations, many of which had become speculative rather than accumulative users of natural resources: agricultural innovations had tended, a contemporary observer noted, "to make the farmer not a better producer of food, but a more expert bandit" of the land's natural vitality.[1] Pushed to the limits of their knowledge by extreme weather, farmers, especially large-scale farmers, found that they had used up their margin for error and tapped out the capital resources banked in the soil. Lenders seized land from farming families in default of their payments and redistributed it to large growers with new methods that further accelerated the consolidation of the agricultural sector. By the time the United States went to war in 1941, significant numbers of families had been displaced from the land and from the traditions of home-grown and farm-fresh food. Recruitment for the armed forces and factory jobs in the northern cities drew even more people out of rural areas.

At the same time, the federal government began diverting many food and agricultural resources to support the war effort. When families felt the pinch of not getting enough fresh food, the government promoted the cultivation of small "victory gardens," asserting that each household with a victory garden aided the military mission by growing at least some of its own food, thus freeing up food for the troops. In reality, the initiative had uneven success, and most of these small gardens disappeared after the war. But in San Francisco, victory gardens gave rise to an unexpected revival of a farmers' market.

In 1943, the founder and director of the San Francisco Victory Garden Council, John Brucato, observed that urban families were not growing enough vegetables through victory gardens to sate their craving for fresh produce. Meanwhile, he discovered area farmers who, intending to take their fruits and vegetables to centralized processing plants, often could not do so before the produce spoiled. Moreover, when the factories couldn't accommodate all of the harvest, the growers were forced to dump perfectly edible fruits and vegetables. The prospect of wasted bounty in the proximity of substantial need led Brucato to propose a win-win alternative. As he tells it, "canneries were paying four cents a pound for choice pears—when they would take them. San Francisco retail price on the same pears range from 17 to 22 cents a pound. Why couldn't the consumer journey to the source and get his pears cut-rate?"[2]

After a trial run, the San Francisco farmers' market officially opened on August 12, 1943. Brucato reports that 1,000 people came to buy fruits and vegetables directly from the Marin County farmers. By the third day of market, a Saturday, nearly 50,000 people bought up the contents of 135 farm trucks. The locally grown food was less expensive and more healthful than what the wholesalers trucked in from halfway across the country. Brucato observed that even wealthier residents began patronizing the market for its health benefits: "The produce there is fresher and more highly charged with vitamins. A prosperous contractor, well beyond his allotted time of three score years and ten, once told me that the Market vegetables not only gave him a new lease on life but also a desire for a tenant to share the lease."[3]

This story from San Francisco suggests just one beginning of what would eventually become widespread dissent from agribusiness as usual. In those days Brucato vehemently protested markets that appeared to customers to be directly benefiting farmers but that actually profited the same commercial merchants and wholesalers that dominated the mainstream food industry. He objected to Seattle's Pike Street Market, which, he said, sought to limit competition to farmers from only two counties adjacent to Seattle. And of the Los Angeles Market at West Third and Fairfax Avenue, a private market founded in 1934, he said, "It is not a farmers' market. The public, though it was unaware of it, was buying from those who didn't know a furrow from a farrow."[4]

At first glance, an unbroken chain from the farm to the consumer may not seem very significant. Direct exchange does not, of necessity, change the composition of the food nor, it would seem, the benefits of purchasing it. But even in those early days of the new farmers' market movement, that connection between growers and customers had several significant implications that continue to resonate today. The San Francisco market organizers recognized a practical and ethical dilemma that a retail grower-vendor market could help remedy.[5] The farmers found that they could sell directly to consumers at a better price than they received from wholesale buyers, putting them in a better position to sustain their businesses and their lifestyles. The customers, too, benefited from quantities of fresh and nutritious produce at competitive prices that were accompanied by an enhanced sense of context and accountability.

Food is a matter of personal and household security, so as people become more removed from the sources of their food, they increasingly rely on any clues about it that remain available to them. The messages that the seller sends—through knowledge about plants, orderliness of the vending stand, type of dress, language, signage—provide hints, intended or not, accurate or not, as

Owen County

to the character and quality of the food. As space-age enthusiasts began envisioning a future that would obscure the sources of our nourishment—compressing them into a single tablet, synthesizing them into previously unknown dishes like "soylent green," or flavor-enhancing them for what Eric Schlosser called a "fast food nation"—a developing contingent was simultaneously embracing "whole" and "natural" foods and the means for growing them as part of a larger social movement.[6]

One foundation of this movement was a renewed understanding of a fundamental element in growing: the soil. Soil had come to be thought of as a simple, neutral medium for suspending plants and nutrients, but it has incrementally revealed itself to be a complex system that coordinates decay, regeneration, and symbiosis in a way not successfully mimicked by manufactured additives. As early as 1940, Sir Albert Howard, a British mycologist in India, recognized that the machine-based and petroleum-based farming innovations of the twentieth century could not be sustained because they do not participate in the cycle of regeneration that allows for soil fertility:

> *The replacement of the horse and the ox by the internal combustion engine and the electric motor is . . . attended by one great disadvantage. These machines do not void urine and dung and so contribute nothing to the maintenance of soil fertility. . . .*
>
> *These [agricultural] chemicals and these machines can do nothing to keep the soil in good heart. By their use the processes of growth can never be balanced by the processes of decay. All that they can accomplish is the transfer of the soil's capital to current account.[7]*

By contrast, Howard noted, traditional farming practices in India complemented the conditions under which plants grow naturally. In particular, traditional Indian composting methods served to restore and maintain healthy soil. These "Indore" compost heaps, named for the Indian state in which Howard did his research, quickly and efficiently broke down raw vegetable and animal matter into fertile soil. They involved layering various material and keeping the heaps moist without being overly wet, much as is still taught today. Indeed, compost heaps became a key contribution to small-scale farming. Howard's work influenced the Soil Association of England, the Rodale Research Center in the United States, and the food politics of Mohandas Gandhi. Howard offered his highest praise for those societies that compost human waste and reuse it in the fields, though not many organizations picked up that particular recommendation.

This recourse to low-tech, natural principles for growing food appealed especially to small-scale American farmers who needed to make the most of the ground available to them. It vindicated traditional practices and lent credence to regional farmers' almanac–type wisdom. Composting, in particular, meant that the poor soil of depleted agricultural areas, neglected urban lots, and intensively used community gardens could be renewed and made productive. Composting became a point of generative devotion for many, supporting square-foot, French intensive, raised-bed gardening, and other high-productivity schemes. All of these approaches accepted the premise that more food could be grown on less ground, a key matter for many of the smaller growers who would come to populate farmers' markets. Novel recipes and tools for composting appeared almost monthly in gardening magazines. Worm farms, drums that could be rolled to cook vegetable matter, watering schedules, wooden or plastic cribs with modular parts, infusions of animal essences—all aimed at getting the quickest, most fertile results, though the rush to innovate could overwhelm the essential simplicity of composting's natural alchemy: given enough time, organic materials rot.

The 1960s and 70s saw a convergence of sorts when traditional farming and marketing practices met innovations that were also integral to newly envisioned lifestyles and their ethical implications. Disillusioned with the prevailing culture, a wave of people sought to live closer to the land and its natural processes. They were a significant surge in American utopianism that includes settlements by the Puritans, Quakers, and Amish, and they found an ethical certitude in growing their own food, building their own homes, practicing animal husbandry, and heating with alternative fuels. In going "back to the land," individuals, families, and intentional communities made a response to the crushing tides of consumerism and urbanism in the United States. Their choices wove strands of self-reliance, pioneerism, and religiosity that borrowed from the Jeffersonian democratic ideal, individualistic adventures like Thoreau's retreat into the wilderness, collective experiments like Brook Farm and New Harmony, and Marxist refutations of

Top: Greene County   *Bottom: Orange County*

material possessions. Latter-day homesteaders, they infused rural communities all over the country with uncounted urban- and suburbanites. Not all would realize their vision of self-sufficiency or utopian community, but their experiences with the land, alternative food aesthetics, and their country neighbors would help to lay the groundwork for the widespread success of farmers' markets.

Many back-to-the-landers considered what they ate, what they bought, and how they lived to be ethical choices. Environmentally sound and self-sufficient living tended to rank higher morally than personal convenience and personal affluence. With close to religious zeal, they made food and other purchasing choices that defied the mainstream consumer culture. They made soap and candles, milked goats, aged cheese and yogurt, and tried their hand at wine and wild meats. The food they did buy was preferably "natural"—uncolored, unprocessed, organic. Such choices were not easy or simple, but "good," as Helen and Scott Nearing observed in *Living the Good Life*, the landmark volume that established them as role models for thousands who went "back" to the land.[8] Describing their lives on a Vermont farm since 1932 and then, when the area became too densely settled, at Forest Farm in Maine, they wrote eloquently about their philosophy of self-sufficiency. They moved to the country, they say, in "a personal search for a simple, satisfying life on the land, to be devoted to mutual aid and harmlessness, with an ample margin of leisure in which to do personally constructive and creative work."[9] Part of a generation older than most of the homesteaders of the 1960s and 70s, they reinforced the idea that looking back to earlier, "simpler" times could be a way of moving forward.

Unlike the government-endorsed homesteading of the 1800s, back-to-the-landers of the twentieth century needed cash to purchase their land. They gravitated, primarily, toward inexpensive real estate, hunting the gold standard of $100 per acre. Small pockets took root along national forests, on the back woodlots of old farms, and in remote valleys after the old folks had moved to town. The result was a seeding of "new people," "flatlanders," and "hippies" into traditional small farming areas such as New Hampshire, Vermont, Maine, Kentucky, southern Indiana, Missouri, West Virginia, Arkansas, Oregon, Washington, and northern California. The integration of the old and the new communities was less than complete, sometimes contentious, and some forty

Greene County

years later remains strained in some areas. However, the convergence of these two cultures became the backbone of the first new farmers' markets nationwide.

Often without appropriate skills or much common ground from which to ask for help, the new people broke ground that had not been tilled in a very long time or that had been farmed out of fertility. They often brought with them philosophical notions of how to work the land. Their ideas of growing arose less from an understanding of seasons and soils and more from a desired relationship with the earth and the food that could be grown on it. So a new gardener's embrace of permaculture, the theory that stewarding perennial and arboreal gardens was more efficient, viable, and in keeping with natural processes than annual cropping, for example, might precede any experience of growing trees. And the notion that hand-digging garden beds would nurture beneficial microbes in the soil might coincide nicely with the economic reality of not having a tractor. Many homesteaders were isolated. Perhaps socially, ethnically, and religiously different from their immediate neighbors, they were also probably pursuing very different trajectories from the rest of their own family. Nevertheless, these isolated pockets exchanged news and knowledge with like-minded people through publications such as the *Whole Earth Catalog, Mother Earth News, Organic Gardening, Co-Evolution Quarterly,* and the *Whole Earth Review,* which became the computer networks of the day, allowing people to share politics, philosophies, and tips for intensive gardening, double digging, companion planting, moon cycles, and biodynamics among the diaspora. Names of bugs and weeds, soapy water insecticides, vinegar washes, herbal remedies and salves, cordwood and fuel-efficient building, and cloth diapers were part of the cultural commons. Borax bug barriers, bread baking, pie tins in the corn patch, sexing of plants, canning, and mulching were rediscovered. Even if they didn't observe them, most everyone knew someone who planted by the lunar cycle or the *Old Farmer's Almanac,* or with a special sensitivity to Gaia. Many advocated ideas that are now commonly part of national conversations: alternative fuels and health care, soy-based foods, global warming, and organics.

It was, indeed, a good life, if not a simple life, full of alternative riches. It meant drinking water out of a seep spring rather than getting a job in order to have city water put in. Self-sufficiency

Top: Greene County

Bottom: Orange County

meant building your own house, by yourself, with only occasional help from generous friends. It meant heating with wood. It meant liking homegrown music, preferably played on a porch, perhaps playing a guitar or singing along. It meant being an environmentalist. Women wore long skirts; men wore beards. It meant swimming naked and smoking pot, or growing it, or just being willing to be around while other people did. If curtains were needed, and mostly they weren't, it meant buying the fabric and making them, perhaps with a treadle sewing machine. If a bench were needed or a shelf or anything else that could possibly be fashioned, however roughly, by hand, then that was done by hand. Flour, blouses, bread, and soy milk were homemade also.

There was a can-do attitude coupled with a generous acceptance of roughness that saw beyond what was actual to what was intended. Thoreau in his cabin, they noted, did not live with all of the self-sufficiency he professed, but he had struck out on his own and tried to make a new way. Thoreau, Emerson, and other utopianist role models had not been able to shake off old and inadequate ways of the past entirely, but they were willing to try to realize new ways of going forward. The twentieth-century homesteaders, likewise, brought their own limitations into their new world. But they were willing to try to recover the best of the old practices at the same time that they pioneered new ones.

Perhaps most significant of all, for the purposes of this history, the homesteaders took up a hands-on attitude toward food and, in particular, gardening. There was a catching-up period, individually and collectively, but over time, many homestead gardens became as lush and productive as those of their more conventional neighbors. Even without petroleum-based herbicides, insecticides, fertilizers, and equipment, homesteaders figured out how to grow big gardens. In all their high ideals and ambitious plans, food figured prominently.

When the first homesteaders moved into the vicinity of Edmonton, Kentucky, in the early 1970s, it was much like countless other small farming towns that would see an influx of back-to-the-landers. As in similar places, the "new people" settling near Edmonton responded to advertisements for land in the back of *Mother Earth News*. It was a modest community, lightly settled, with heavy clay soil that had been unrelentingly farmed. "Locals," by and large, grew a tobacco allotment, worked at the sewing factory, or journeyed thirty miles or more to a better paying job in a larger town. Few retail businesses or professional services existed. The IGA grocery store did not have a produce section, nor was there a farmers' market. Farm stands, too, were absent; everyone grew their own produce or knew someone who would share. Occasionally, a man with a pickup truckload of melons or sweet corn would drop his tailgate on the courthouse square.

Exchange between the homesteaders and the local people was inevitable but slow. The new people mostly dressed, spoke, and held opinions different from their neighbors. The outsiders' cash for land and old trucks was a boon, but also meant family homes and cemeteries went to people who seemed strange and didn't know the old stories. Locals and their equipment hired out sometimes for tilling, bushhogging, or earth moving. What they knew about frost dates, successive planting, and where to get things could be tapped by the new folks. Locals in Edmonton knew that potatoes and peas could be planted in late February and that corn "knee high by the fourth of July" would be far too short for the new hybrids. A longtime resident of Subtle, Kentucky, passed on her heirloom peanuts to new people, along with advice on how to grow them. (Never eat all the peanuts—they are next year's seed. Instead, plant all the best from shells that hold three or four nuts, and over time, the crop will improve.) Another woman shared candy cane (cleome) flower seeds with homesteaders whose gardens were bereft of color. Late in the season, a family might offer a jar of homemade sorghum molasses and, more importantly for those keen enough to pick them up, some hints on how to make it.

But mostly the locals and the new people hailed from different cultures. The homesteading communities had more in common with other new folks in far-flung places than with those who shared their property lines. In many places, the new people developed an alternative food delivery system that suited their tastes. In Edmonton, as elsewhere, they established a cooperative buying club to purchase and share bulk quantities of food that was unavailable locally. Delivered once a month by a truck from the Federation of Ohio River Co-Ops to Lloyd and Tamo Tewksbury's farm, the buying club provided access to flours, tofu, pasta, nut butters, and other foods not sold at the IGA. Organic carrots, onions, potatoes, and popcorn sold in forty- or fifty-pound bags would be shared among several families. Trucks from FORC and other cooperative food distributors were welcome sights on some of the most unlikely country lanes, essentially keeping whole communities alive.

In those days, the food trade flowed mostly in one direction, toward the homesteading communities. Little ever went back into the truck and the cooperative pipeline. But truth be told, few of the new people had the necessary requisites—equipment, good ground, sufficient knowledge of growing, and agricultural business acumen—to make for-profit growing succeed. All of that takes time. Eventually, much like the locals who took their extra melons and a neighbor's early apples to the courthouse square for sale, some of the homesteaders sold their produce directly to buyers by means of the new farmers' markets.

While the cultural groundwork was being laid for renewal on the producer side of the food equation, a complementary shift among consumers brought to light new conceptions of the relationships between food and the environment, politics, spirituality. Rachel Carson's *Silent Spring* (1962) had illuminated the dangers of pesticides. The health of consumers and farm workers, many quickly grasped, was also compromised by what had become so-called conventional farming practices. In response, more people began seeking out "natural" foods that could be found at cooperatives and farmers' markets. Customers widely responded to calls to boycott table grapes to improve the pay and working conditions of migrant farm workers. Frances Moore Lappé's *Diet for a Small Planet* (1971) politicized food choices by explaining their ramifications for hunger worldwide.[10] Since then, the belief has proliferated that one of the most political acts we can do on a day-to-day basis is to eat in ways that responsibly affect farms, farm workers, and local environments.

Vegetarianism, veganism, macrobiotic, and other diets in accord with ethical, religious, or health principles demanded greater quantities of fresh vegetables—often fresher, more local, more exotic, or more ethically or organically produced than what was readily available in corporate grocery stores. *The Vegetarian Epicure* cookbook by Anna Thomas (1972) outlined "ominous and dramatic new reasons" people concerned with health were turning toward vegetarian eating, and *Moosewood Cookbook* by Mollie Katzen (1977) became a bible of sorts for vegetarian cook-

Top: Orange County   *Bottom: Monroe County*

ing.[11] Alice Waters opened Chez Panisse restaurant in Berkeley in 1971 and made her mark by commissioning farmers for the freshest, highest-quality vegetables and meats. Spiritual communities like Tassajara in California, Kripalu in Pennsylvania, and various Hare Krishna enclaves articulated the connections between food and spirit and between the local and the healthful that resonated in the "counter" culture. Deborah Madison came to vegetarianism through the San Francisco Zen Center in the late 1960s and opened Greens in San Francisco in 1979 as one of the first fine-cuisine vegetarian restaurants. Both establishments have long shopped at farmers' markets and continue to advocate for them. Such use of local foods from area farms and dairies helped to broaden the standard American produce offerings to include previously rare vegetables such as arugula, fingerling potatoes, and heirloom tomatoes.[12]

Thus the politics of food—the impact of our choices in growing and buying food—converged with concern for the health of the environment, animals, and people and also with spiritual and ethical implications of those choices. Through a diffuse but widespread movement that was punctuated by a few high-profile advocates, many in the general population came to understand that the food we buy and eat carries with it political, health, and ethical consequences.

Although only a few hundred "farmers'" markets, most of them actually wholesale markets, remained in the United States in the early 1970s, conditions were clearly set for their rebound when Congress passed Public Law 94-463, the Farmer-to-Consumer Direct Marketing Act of 1976.[13] The new law directed the U.S. Department of Agriculture to develop programs to facilitate direct marketing from farmers to consumers for their mutual benefit. That initiative validated the efforts of the few public markets that still featured local growers, such as the Minnesota Growers Association market in Minneapolis, which in 1968 allowed only growers to vend.[14] At once, cheaper, more experimental food gained a viable outlet beyond the compost heap. Organic food, which in the hands of novice growers can suffer bug and disease damage, now had the means to reach a public that increasingly asked for it. Thus markets emerged as one of the few places to find fresh, local, unusual foods produced without petrochemicals, providing an alternative to the consolidation of the mainstream

Owen County

food industry, which continued its quest for consistency, availability, and low price while neglecting taste, variety, and regional character.[15]

After the Congressional act, the farmers' market phenomenon grew like a zucchini in July.[16] In 1970, about 350 farmers' markets operated in the United States. By 1994, their numbers rose to 1,755; to 2,863 in 2000; 3,706 by 2004; and neared 4,000 as this book goes to press. In 1994, about 20,000 farmers used farmers' markets each week, and by 2000, that number had grown to 66,700 farmers who saw 2.75 million customers each week for nearly $900 million in total sales that year.[17]

Roadside farm stands, too, burgeoned. Originally used to supplement a farmer's income by selling in-season surpluses, the new interest in fresh and local food allowed those stands to grow into "one-stop shopping areas" that featured locally grown produce beefed up with trucked-in goods. Wilson's Farm market in Lexington, Massachusetts, for example, grew from its original shed in 1952 to a rambling all-weather building selling year-round produce in the 1970s to a gleaming 8,500-square-foot, showcase barn in the 1990s. The original pull-off area that could accommodate only a few cars was necessarily expanded to provide dozens of parking spaces over that period. Even though the inventory was no longer entirely grown in the field below the barn, the knowledge that some of it was and that the rest had the imprimatur of Wilson's Farm satisfied most customers. Similarly, the Simmons family farm in Columbus, Indiana, in 2005 replaced their old farmstand shed with a gift shop, produce market, and wine-tasting facility that accommodate more customers and reflect the diversification of their business. And in Texas in 2005, the long-lived Arnosky specialty cut flower farm began to reinvent itself as a destination tourist farm, reducing wholesale crops and expanding their on-farm retail business.[18]

Such direct marketing allowed farmers to control all aspects of their business from production to sale. Many took the opportunity to "add value" to their products by turning whole fruits, vegetables, meats, or flowers into higher profit jams, pies, mustards, jerky, wreaths, and so on. Smaller growers, in particular, found that going to a centralized market location meant more competition but greater access to buying customers with the potential of boosting their return as much as 40 to 80 percent.[19] Customers,

Bloomington

too, benefited from direct access to fresh, organic, and specialty foods. Most of those involved enjoyed that the markets, typically lasting for only a few hours, managed to expand a good buying and selling opportunity into a landmark community event.

More recently, farmers' markets have provided communities with a working model for the emerging dialogue about sustainability. A response to the notion that boundless economic development alone will increase the overall quality of life, the tenets of sustainability call for food to be "grown, processed, distributed and consumed in an ecologically and socially responsible manner on a local, community scale."[20] Entering the mainstream discussion in the mid-1990s, sustainability assumes that long-term human survival will require decisions that are "ecologically sound, economically viable, and socially responsible."[21] It acknowledges the limited availability of resources upon which people have so far depended, including petroleum, potable water, fresh air, and fertile topsoil, and seeks solutions to the harmful results of their (mis)use. Some current discussions of sustainability seek solutions, not in the self-sufficiency of the homesteading movement, but in new and creative inventions that could support affluent lifestyles with personal vehicles, disposable items, and electric power. To sustain themselves indefinitely, this thinking goes, communities will need to diversify their skills, resources, and production; moderate their consumption; and improve their sensitivity to local environmental and cultural contexts. Sustainability will require a renewed appreciation for local talents and situated knowledge. It will have to harness both traditional and new ways of organizing human production and consumption, borrowing what works from the past to use with what will be able to work in the future.

Farmers' markets would be a useful part of such a future. Distributed and diversified, this kind of alternative food production and distribution model might serve communities much as similar ones did in earlier times, when people relied on local or regional food systems that were grounded in multifaceted farms using sustainable methods.[22] Post-petroleum organic growing methods would mean smaller and more diversified farming, which would result in more healthful food, greater biodiversity, and cleaner water, air, and soil. With a shorter chain between producer and consumer, such a new system would provide fresher food, improve land stewardship, and reduce the use of fossil fuel in food transportation. As described in a report prepared for the USDA by Integrity Systems Cooperative, a coordinated system of smaller producers would allow greater independence and self-reliance for communities, let them reduce dependence on long-distance food producers and distributors, and pay local dollars to local individuals, keeping more money in the local economy where it can support farms, jobs, and businesses.[23] Such a system links both ends of the food chain through "the bonds of community as well as economy. The landscape, then, is understood as a part of the community and, as such, human activity is shaped to conform to the knowledge and experience of what the natural characteristics of that place do or do not permit."[24] Farmers' markets present a working model that can help us to understand now what such a sustainable community might look like and how it could be adapted for other settings. Moreover, incorporating as they do tradition and innovation, markets can help people to negotiate change from the security of the familiar. Not flawless models, markets nevertheless offer practical insights on balancing the ecological, economic, and social dimensions of life.

Put in more contemporary terms, farmers' markets improve our sense of food security. Although some of the Congressional testimony in the debate over the Farmer-to-Consumer Direct Marketing Act documents a fear that decentralization of the food supply would compromise national security, many now recognize the important role that shorter food chains and direct marketing have in creating food security.[25] Face-to-face exchange at a market means we have a chance, at least, of accountability and responsibility. Identifiable people grow and consume the food sold at producer-vendor farmers' markets. Buyers can see who has cultivated their food and how it has made its way from its origins to their dinner table. One would be correct to assume that growers regularly cook for their dinner table the same food they sell at the market. If the beans have gone tough or a new variety of squash is not tasty, or if the organic consciousness has finally seeped in after years of spraying, the conscientious farmer may not give less-than-desirable vegetables room at the market stand any more than he or she would at the dining table.[26]

In being known and knowing others—in community—there is security. Weekly walks around a market take on some of the significance of ritual.[27] Their regularity, the formalized, even repeti-

Bloomington

tious, exchanges, site-specific sounds and smells, the confirmation of common experience, provide a context for what one market customer calls a new "gathering of the tribes."[28] The many small, routine conversations as well as breaking news of the community reinforce that the individual exists in a larger context inhabited by other people. Seeing a town as little "core" groups clustering at vendors' stands, around street musicians, or by the animal shelter's adoptable dogs makes visible the kinds of interactions and intersections that create a community.

Rather than fostering insularity in those groups, farmers' markets offer ways to bring people together, to bridge their divides so that all feel an enhanced sense of security—in the self, in the home, and in the land. Markets offer a counterpoint to contemporary trends that Wendell Berry describes as moving toward a "postagricultural world" that is also "postdemocratic, postreligious, postnatural." Farmers' markets instead provide a common ground, a trading zone, that relies on the participation of growers and consumers and usually both rural and urban inhabitants—and they put them on the same team. Once in contact, they can help to undo what Berry calls "the old opposition of country and city, which was never useful, [and] is now more useless than ever. It is, in fact, damaging to everybody involved, as is the opposition of producers and consumers. These are not differences but divisions that ought not to exist because they are to a considerable extent artificial. The so-called urban economy has been just as hard on urban communities as it has been on rural ones."[29]

Drawing as markets do on the stability of age-old practices while at the same time accommodating and even facilitating exchange and innovation, farmers' markets help us to refit perennial notions to contemporary times. Grounded in the rhythms of life, they have the potential to be a staging ground from which towns and communities can become what Christopher Alexander calls "live."[30] Growing good food, ethically and to scale, is a way of making peace with the earth, with where we live, with our neighbors, and with other communities that we rely on. The rebounding of farmers' markets and local food in the late twentieth century shows that even today small farmers and direct marketing have a viable role in healthy communities.

Customer, Vendor   *Bloomington*

3. The Bloomington Farmers' Market __

When Dan Cooper moved to Bloomington, Indiana, from San Francisco, he came to the farmers' market almost immediately:

I just knew it was something that needed to be done. It's certainly a very good way to connect with the community, get a feel of what's going on. . . . Particularly if you're living out in a development with row after row of houses all the same. You don't know your neighbors. Coming to something like this does give you a sense of living in a community. . . . We no longer have very many little shops and things where you're going to meet all your neighbors and chat. So this is a very good vehicle that way.

It becomes a bit of a ritual. . . . Saturday morning it's required that I go to the farmers' market almost regardless of whether I need—, whether I have any objective reason for going. It's just what I do.[1]

The Bloomington Community Farmers' Market in Indiana had its start in 1975 when a group approached the city council for permission to organize a market that would "connect back-yard gardeners and small farmers with consumers."[2] A tradition of farmers' markets already existed in this largely rural state. In 1946, nineteen Indiana towns had a market of some sort. Some of the longest lived included Lafayette's first market which had begun in 1826, Richmond's which dated from 1840, Ft. Wayne's from 1850, and Evansville's from 1869.[3] Fifty miles away, the Indianapolis City Market had been in operation since 1821. In 1886, the Indianapolis market was sufficiently established for the state's capital city to build a stone Market House and the adjacent Tomlinson Hall, which provided a mixed-use facility, including an auditorium, a gymnasium, meeting rooms, and retail space. However, after World War II, as was occurring elsewhere around the country, the focus of the Indianapolis market shifted to wholesale commerce.[4] Nationwide, population growth was moving to the suburbs and, as a consequence, many farmers closed their retail businesses. The markets that remained became almost exclusively wholesale. While Indianapolis would have neither the funding and infrastructure in place nor the restoration work completed to reopen a retail market until 1977, down the road in Bloomington momentum was building for a direct-marketing farmers' market in the early 1970s.[5] Its beginning on the first wave of modern farmers' markets and its growth into a city institution make the Bloomington farmers' market an excellent case of this phenomenon.

A small city of 70,000 people, Bloomington is situated in south central Indiana limestone country with its signature karst topography of caves and sinkholes. The rolling ground of this area missed both the leveling and the soil enrichment caused by glaciers that terminated just a few miles to the north. Expert horticulturists, the Miami in Indiana had their largest croplands on rich bottomlands in the northern half of what would become the state, much as later the more mechanized and specialized farms would locate there for the flat expanses of fertile ground. Around Bloomington, the hilly and clay-based soils suited smaller, more labor-intensive farms even to this day, and the area remains substantially wooded. The Miami who lived in the Bloomington area would have supplemented their agricultural harvests with plants gathered from the wild, maple sugaring, and hunting.[6] Likewise, the early white settlers, who first purchased land around Bloomington in 1816, cleared the trees and planted corn and wheat. In 1837, the governments of the City of Bloomington and surrounding Monroe County each contributed $200 to erect a "market house." This building apparently operated into the 1850s as a place "that the townspeople went to barter with the farmers at market."[7] Like the courthouse and homes at that time, this was probably a log building. Like the Native Americans whose ancient hunting tools commonly turn up in the soil of the area, the settlers, too, took advantage of wild game and other indigenous foods, including turkey, deer, and bear. As late as the 1970s, a fur trade persisted in nearby Spencer, Indiana, where the pelts of fox, raccoon, and muskrat that had been trapped in the nearby hills and streams were sold for about 25¢ each during the winter months on the courthouse square.[8]

During the great farming exodus of the twentieth century, many people in the Indiana countryside left for industrial jobs in the cities, including ones in Bloomington at Otis Elevator, RCA, and General Electric. So, as was common in many parts of the country, the acreage farmed around Bloomington in south central Indiana declined dramatically after 1900, with only a quarter of what had been farmed then still being used in agriculture in 1997.[9]

When the Bloomington farmers' market opened in 1975, it happened that the remaining or revived small farms of the area were well-suited to meet its needs. Small-scale, direct-market farming provided—and continues to provide—a good way for individuals and families to meet the various challenges of making a living from the land, including uneven soil fertility and small areas of tillable ground. Going to a market nearby made it possible for farmers to minimize transportation costs, diversify crops to lengthen the growing (and selling) season, and scale their production to a small local workforce with a high turnover rate (often college students).

The City of Bloomington had allowed open-air fruit and vegetable stands on the courthouse square until efforts to modernize between the world wars forced them out.[10] But by the early 1970s, the call for fresh and "natural" produce was finding greater purchase. People were beginning to look with suspicion on mass-produced and "corporate" goods, and cooperation, tradition, and hand-crafting had renewed value, reflecting larger upheaval in the social and political world. The push for a new farmers' market came with the desire of a few organizers to bring the community together around common resources to meet common needs.[11] Much like new markets being established today, the passion of a couple of citizens managed to convince a couple of city council members, and together they organized to "foster both healthier lifestyles and a stronger sense of community."[12]

Their first request for permission for a market, however, was denied by the city. Some people objected to providing public land for private gain. Later, however, Mayor Frank McCloskey got behind the idea. And so, on July 26, 1975, a Saturday, twenty-three vendors assembled in the city's Third Street Park. Customers came, and in the coming weeks, more vendors joined. Twenty-something David Porter, for one, sat cross-legged on a bamboo mat and sold bunches of greens he had learned to love in Thailand, where he spent much of his youth. Another vendor sold cabbages out of the trunk of his Volvo and stood near "genuine" Hoosier farmers with pickup beds full of sweet corn. It was the start of what would become a Bloomington institution and by far the most popular event the city sponsors.[13]

In Bloomington, as in many places, the farmers' market set up in several locations before finding what seems to be a permanent site. The market outgrew its original location and, in 1982, moved from Third Street Park to Bloomington's Courthouse Square. When the renovation of the courthouse made the area more congested, the market relocated to a city parking lot between the old and new public libraries. It remained there from 1984 until 1998. At that downtown location, at the corner of Sixth and Lincoln Streets, the market grew to more than sixty vendors, averaging more than 50,000 customers each season.[14]

A location with all of the prime features represents a kind of holy grail for markets: shade, easy access for vendors, good sight lines to draw customers, and grass or some other surface that does not reflect the midsummer heat onto the produce or the people. Adequate parking and traffic flow, bathroom facilities, and power outlets for coolers, freezers, and cooking devices distinguish the best sites. Covered and year-round facilities are exceptional. The colonial Boston farmers' market waited twenty-eight years before moving into a specially constructed wooden building in 1662. Much more recently, Emmaus, Pennsylvania, the home town of Rodale's *New Farm* magazine, saw its market bounce for fifteen years among various parking lots in town, to a park several miles away, and back "finally" to the town proper.[15] After seeing the booming markets of its earlier years dwindle to next to nothing, recently the City of Hartford built the Main Street Market in 1992 to institutionalize and improve the farmers' market experience. The Santa Fe market, which began informally in the late 1960s with growers selling produce from the back of their trucks, bumped around from place to place until it landed at its current location at the Santa Fe Railyard. The market there has parlayed that investment into a year-round, not-for-profit institution with 160,000 annual attendees and more than 170 registered grower-vendors who saw $1.5 million in direct sales in 2001, making it comparable in size to the Bloomington market.[16]

The Bloomington farmers' market moved to its official home with its significant additional amenities in 1998. More than just another city parking lot, the location this time landed the market two blocks west of the town square right in front of the city office building. Originally built as the Showers Brothers Furniture Factory in 1910, this striking building with a distinctive saw-tooth roof and rows of clerestory windows is a particularly appropriate centerpiece for a city that likes to embrace innovation while also honoring its past. The factory was founded by Charles C. Showers in 1868 and, by the 1920s, employed 2,500 people and accounted for a quarter of the city's total income from taxes.[17] At its height, the factory loaded sixteen train-cars of furniture a day, provided more than half of the country's furniture production, and offered progressive programs for employees such as pensions, interest-earning savings accounts, and insurance policies. In a symbolic gesture that Bloomington remains fond of, the U.S. Census located the exact center of the United States population in 1910 in front of Bloomington's Showers Building.

The furniture factory closed in 1958, but eventually became a key focus of the city's efforts to rehabilitate the less-than-thriving west side. Now renovated, the Showers Building currently holds the Bloomington City Hall and anchors a plaza, what the city calls a "Common." Another side of this plaza is marked by the old train station and a wholesale food warehouse from 1895 that have been renovated for modern business establishments. On the third side stands the old brick smokestack of the Johnson Creamery. Amid these living artifacts, the farmers' market likewise serves to renew a local tradition for contemporary use.

The market is thriving at Showers Common. Used for parking during the work week, it was designed with the farmers' market in mind and functions well in that capacity. It includes four long permanent awnings, several electrical outlets, access to bathrooms and running water, and additional space for parking nearby. Metal sculptures of vegetables fly like standards on long poles above the marketplace. This current, presumably permanent, location for the Bloomington market has space for nearly one hundred farmers plus an overflow area for more farmers, performances, information tables, and a monthly arts and crafts fair. In 1997, at the old site, an average of fifty-eight vendors sold on Saturday mornings between May 1 and October 31. By 2005, after the

Bloomington

move to Showers Common, the average vendor attendance rose to ninety-one. Equally important, the customer count also rose, from an average of 2,500 per week in 1997 to 3,611 in 2005, with more than 5,000 attending at the height of summer.[18]

The Bloomington Parks and Recreation Department and Marcia Veldman, who manages the market for the city, began a rapid succession of developments to take advantage of the increased attendance and more spacious location at Showers Common. In 2000, they launched a juried arts and crafts fair that takes place in conjunction with and adjacent to the market once a month during the summer. Also in 2000, Bloomington's became the first open-air market in Indiana to allow the sale of meat, dairy products, and farmer-processed foods. (Although before then, some farmers brought milk and meat to market and sold them just outside the confines of the market where its rules did not apply.) In 2000, only 19 percent of markets nationwide allowed milk and dairy products and only a third allowed the sale of meat and poultry products.[19] While eggs had been sold at the market for some time, processed chicken and beef were an instant hit in Bloomington. In just a few years, the offerings have expanded to include turkey, elk, pork, lamb, and ostrich, as well as goat and cow milk, yogurt, and cheese.

Efforts to expand the appeal of the market and the incomes of the vendors led, in 1999, to the city adding a smaller market on Tuesdays in the late afternoon. This market, aimed at quick, after-work shoppers and farmers who can use a mid-week outlet for ripening produce, takes place at the same location as the Saturday market but runs only through the height of the season, June to September. Although many of the Saturday vendors participate on Tuesdays, the market has its own seniority rankings and space selection. It remains a significantly smaller market, drawing in an entire season what the Saturday market registers on an average day.[20] In 2003, the city added a "holiday market" on the Saturday after Thanksgiving, which is open to regular-season vendors and juried artists.[21] In 2004, the market season was extended straight through November, drawing 2,200 people during the month, and in 2005, the market opened a month earlier, on the first Saturday in April. The 2006 season continued the new eight-month schedule. Additionally, two grower-initiated markets have helped to extend the marketing season in Bloomington. For nearly thirty years, a private Wednesday morning market has offered fresh produce to the community. Run by vendors, this market invites growers to participate so that there is little competition among their stands. They cap the number of stands at fifteen. The Wednesday market is held on the opposite side of town from the city-sponsored market. Older customers in particular enjoy the nearby parking and less congested, quieter atmosphere.[22] And in 2005, a collaboration of local growers and the Bloomington chapter of the Slow Food movement launched an invitational "Winter Market." Those vendor participants bravely pioneer off-season growing in climate zone five where the temperature can dip to 20° below zero. They set up their booths in the gym of an alternative school, itself a surviving spin-off of the do-it-yourself ethic of the 1960s and 70s.

The new, more expansive location and added resources of Showers Common allowed the premier Saturday market to diversify in other ways as well. It designated one space for a bread vendor and another for a café vendor. Those two had exclusive rights to sell coffee and locally produced baked goods in exchange for 10 percent of their gross market proceeds. This money goes toward direct expenses associated with the market and into a capital improvement fund that has provided such improvements as a drinking fountain, picnic tables, benches, and shopping wagons.[23] In 2006, the city added two additional spots for prepared-food vendors in response to public demand.

A raised and landscaped stage was built into the parking lot to allow for musical acts, cooking demonstrations that use market produce, and other activities. In addition, countless buskers blanket the market, entertaining attendees with various talents and collecting tips. The market area also serves as the focal point for various annual events, including the Asian Festival, a salsa contest, the Breast Cancer Awareness Walk, Earth Day, BloomingTree Week, and Latino Day. Space for table displays of political parties and movements, religious outreach, and other not-for-profit activities run along one end of the market area. The market collects thousands of pounds of produce for the food bank and thousands of signatures on petitions. These activities not only draw potential customers to the market but also "help make the Market a cornerstone in the community."[24]

The Bloomington market seems to be sustaining all these de-

Bloomington

velopments. But the balance is delicate. To be viable, markets must maintain the correct proportion of farmers to customers, supply to demand. Customers must find enough vendors to provide the supply, variety, and competitive pricing that make a trip to the market worthwhile for them. Vendors, on the other hand, must be able to sell enough of their produce at a high enough price to support their efforts. In the early stages, modern farmers' markets tend to have too many customers for the number of growers and what they can provide. That may mean that the farmers sell out their goods, but it also means that the customers have less choice and may leave while still being willing to spend more. In more established markets, the number of growers may increase along with their production and thus outpace what customers can buy. That imbalance can depress prices and prevent growers from making a living wage. The challenge then becomes increasing the customer base and the visibility of the market within the community. In short, establishing a farmers' market takes time—for word to spread, for customers to establish their rituals and rhythms, and for farmers to learn to grow in their climate the quantities and varieties that customers want.

The character of a market depends on the vision and effort of its management to keep the quality of the experience high, particularly in producer-vendor markets. From a vendor perspective, Scott Cooper says that vending at the market in Bloomington "really is not tough. You follow the rules, you sign the paper, bring your stuff, set up. They make it easy."[25] After the city's Parks and Recreation Department took over responsibility for the market in 1997, it increased the time commitment of a full-time employee to act for one-half of her time as the market manager, overseeing all market operations.[26] On the job since the inception of the position in 1997, Marcia Veldman has become known to vendors and customers alike for her patience, fairness, and good judgment, and her ability to put the best interests of the market as an organization ahead of those of any individual. The city also employs a part-time "market master" to supervise the running of the market, a position originally paid on an hourly basis for fifteen hours per week during the peak market season but expanded to twenty hours per week year round, with some benefits. Recently, the market has also added two part-time positions, "market leaders." The market leaders work six hours per week to assist the market master on market days by answering questions, staffing an information booth, and doing set up and break down of equipment. One of the first people to occupy one of those new positions is the son of market vendors, a young man who grew up among the hustle and bustle of Saturday mornings. In addition, an unpaid advisory council made up of vendors, customers, and town merchants makes informed recommendations on a wide variety of issues. All of these people play important roles in creating the tenor of the market.

The Bloomington market and many other of the country's premier farmers' markets require that vendors grow what they sell.[27] The U.S. Department of Agriculture defines a farmers' market as an event that brings together many independent sellers (rather than a single vendor or firm) at a consistent place (which might be along a street or in an empty lot, but would not include people who vend along routes) and at a regular time (daily, weekly, or monthly, but more frequently than annually).[28] About three-quarters of markets nationwide fit this description and are producer-only events, meaning all of the vendors produced at least some of the products they sold. In the United States, farmers' markets typically require that the farmers come from a specific region, that their sales emphasize food over crafts or other hard goods, and that foods that are processed be made principally from locally grown products.[29] Gathered items such as nuts, syrup, and mushrooms must be produced, gathered, or processed in the area by the vendor. Similarly, in Britain "a farmers' market is one in which farmers, growers or producers from a defined local area are present in person to sell their own produce, direct to the public."[30] Britain and California both certify those farmers' markets at which vendors sell food that they grow. The British markets are also, "for the time being," excluding genetically modified organisms from certified markets.[31] In Australia, Canada, and New Zealand, farmers' markets require that the food come from within a specified area and that the vendors be deeply involved in the growing or core processing of the food.

The official guide for the Bloomington market puts its overall policy succinctly: "The Bloomington Community Farmers' Market is open to anyone who grows what they sell."[32] As Veldman,

Greene County

the Bloomington market manager, has said, "Successful markets focus on product that is locally made. Sam's Club muffins can be found anywhere in the country."[33] Thus the Bloomington market rules mandate that "The Market staff reserves the right to verify that all goods are produced in Indiana by the vendor." It protects the flavor of the market by prescribing that 50 percent ("excluding water") of value-added products such as pies, jams, and baskets must be grown or raised by the vendor. Those requirements recognize that the appeal of a farmers' market lies in its connection to the locality and its climates, tastes, and traditions.

The Bloomington market synchronizes with the local seasons by featuring fresh food in the summer season and relegating more hand-crafted items like dried flower wreaths to the fall and spring. In the late 1990s, a woman and her daughter appeared at the market in mid summer with large baskets woven from wild grapevine. They presented a new wrinkle in the producer requirement that raised eyebrows among other vendors. Could wild-gathered materials really be considered "grown" by the vendor? Were the baskets closer to dried flower wreaths that could be sold only in spring and fall or closer to beeswax candles that could be sold throughout the market months? Questions about the baskets were resolved when the market manager and the market board decided they were more like the already-prevalent wild-crafted items like mushrooms and bittersweet, and so would not take the market down the slippery slope toward flea market status.

The only Bloomington vendors who are exempt from having to produce the contents of their products are the four prepared-food vendors among the one hundred market spaces. The market café space has been a subject of debate as to the definition of "local." At the market's mid-1990s location, church groups sold commercial baked goods and coffee from the lawn of the First Presbyterian Church, across the street from the market. For five years, a rotating staff of volunteers brewed coffee and brought in commercial and home-baked cookies, muffins, and cakes, donating the proceeds to good works. When the market moved to Showers Common, the organization of church groups managed the café for an additional year before the city instituted a bidding process that was meant to ensure some degree of fairness in the vending process and localness of the food. The winner of the café bidding that first year and every year since has been the home-grown cooperative natural food store Bloomingfoods. It pledges to sell its own baked good and those made by others nearby and to serve only fair-trade coffee. Those two commitments alone support Bloomington workers, invest in local ingredients when possible, and contribute to small farms in other parts of the Americas. The two newer prepared-food vendors have similar commitments to homemade food.

The imperative to remain local is strong. Occasionally a vendor who is selling produce bought from a wholesaler or otherwise grown by someone else is exposed. One cannot drive two hours south to an orchard and then show up in Bloomington vending what seem to be remarkably early peaches. Nor can a flower grower spice his early bouquets with South American beauties purchased from a floral wholesaler. Both actions violate the rule that vendors must participate in all phases of the production process, from earliest planning and planting, to cultivating, harvesting, and processing. Violators of the Bloomington market rules are warned and, for continued infractions, eventually banished from the market.[34]

The Bloomington market and other farmers' markets warrant this degree of oversight because they provide assets—measurable and palpable—to the communities that host them. Published research suggests that local economies benefit in many ways from farmers' markets.[35] Markets circulate money within a community, draw tourists, provide primary or supplemental income to vendors, and cultivate business skills in new entrepreneurs. They help move people from "personal interest to hobby to business" in an environment that is low cost and simple to enter and that welcomes "entrepreneurial activity and experimentation with new ideas and products."[36] Money spent at the market circulates within the community, rather than draining out to national corporations. And markets boost other businesses when customers and vendors continue their shopping elsewhere on market days. In addition, farmers' markets may encourage a more business-like attitude toward farming, including diversification, niche products, organic production, value-added production, and other means of increasing competitiveness and profits. In short, with careful management, markets become valuable assets that contribute to local prosperity.

For all their benefits, a successfully managed market is no easy feat. By one count, a third of farmers' markets in California fail.[37] One might say that vendors, customers, and communities invest much in their markets and expect much in return. Markets, therefore, require informed, responsive, professional management.[38] In medieval England, the market management adjudicated quarrels, and the twenty-first-century managers have inherited some of that responsibility. Sometimes complaints arise about vendors undercutting others' prices or selling goods that they did not grow. One July, the Bloomington market manager received a complaint from one vendor that another had brought in eight bushels of green beans without having had a smaller picking the previous week.[39] The sudden appearance of the beans raised the suspicion that the vendor was purchasing rather than growing them. Although this was not much evidence to go on, the market manager drove to the man's farm and made a surprise inspection, as the contract rules allow. She found the right kind of bean plants and enough of them to produce the beans he had brought. So the beans were allowed. Even when such suspicions are widely expressed or submitted to the market management, vendors rarely confront each other openly.

Some of the conflict arises understandably from low-margin businesses being in close competition with each other. And some degree of tension may derive from the vast range of ethnic, political, religious, and social orientations represented among the vendors. In Bloomington alone, the market hosts vendors who grew up in homesteading families, some southern Indiana farming families, and some Amish and Mennonites families. Some growers come out of other professions such as teaching, consulting, or museum curation; others grow in order to supplement their income as janitors, graphic designers, shop clerks, or lawyers. Although the income is crucial for some, others seem not to need the extra income or the extra hassle but have spent years vending at the market nonetheless—one such vendor pitches in at market to help the family's cheese business even though he is a professional, another hands out produce samples on days off from his medical practice, and a husband and wife team of college professors brings cuts of their organic meats to market every week. Some vendors are old-guard homesteaders who have persisted in their vision; others are newer artisan producers with offerings like goat cheese, heirloom chile peppers, and grass-fed milk products. Wildcrafters who bring mushrooms, nuts, vines, and flowers may have a certain monomania, while musicians, politicos, and religious pamphleteers share other passions. Good management encourages civility and cooperation among vendors and customers that are based on mutual goals and mutual respect.

However, good management does not necessarily mean visible management. In fact, customers are rarely aware of all that contributes to their market experience and some don't realize a management system exists at all, assuming that the market works smoothly and consistently on an entirely cooperative basis.[40] One important role of effective market managers is to address some of the persistent misconceptions about farmers' markets. For example, many customers don't understand the relationship between the produce being sold and the person selling it. Sometimes they assume the food is brought in from far away and express amazement on being told, for instance, that it was grown just twelve miles west on Third Street. They may be so accustomed to the endless deferrals of corporate food that they do not connect produce with labor and the person standing just an arm's length away.

Others may expect to find out-of-season produce at a market. Conditioned by the seasonless produce of the big-box supermarket, they may be disappointed at an Indiana market, for example, not to find field-grown tomatoes in April or lettuce in August. Customers are perennially thwarted in their salsa making to find that, in Indiana at least, cilantro and tomatoes do not mature at the same time.

Customers who want organic foods may assume that all farmers' market vegetables are organically grown or that they can tell—based on the vendor's age, religion, or hair length—who grows organically.[41] But anyone who has had more than passing experience with farmers knows that such assumptions are unfounded. In years past, the term "organic" was used informally to indicate limited or no recourse to petrochemical fertilizers, insecticides, or herbicides during growing. More recently, the federal government has regulated use of the term. To date, at most farmers' markets most produce is not organic. Moreover, growers who spray may lack training with agricultural chemicals and certainly lack oversight and regulation. Further confusing the matter, the government regulation of the use of the word "organic," while helpful in identifying unsprayed food, does not acknowledge farms "in transition"—those growers who may be using little to no chemical additives but are not yet "certified organic" or don't plan to be. Only a few markets so far have entered the fray by offering only certified organic or sustainable foods, although some require that paperwork be posted for a vendor to label her food organic. The beauty of farmers' markets, of course, is that the customers can ask. Or, as a recent slogan puts it, "Know your food; know your farmer."

Some customers or would-be customers grumble that farmers' markets are more expensive than grocery stores, and it is true that specialty items (organic raspberries, grass-fed organic milk, edible flowers, artisan goat cheeses) go for premium prices at markets. High-demand produce such as the first peaches of the season, picked-yesterday sweet corn, and fresh eggs fetch more at a farmers' market than their tired counterparts do at a grocery store chain. However, several comparisons of farmers' market and grocery store prices have found little difference in price, with markets underselling chain groceries in many cases.[42] Americans typically pay a smaller percentage of their disposable income for food than they used to—12 percent in 1994 as compared with 46 percent in 1901—and less than people in most other countries.[43] The lower food prices Americans enjoy result from a combination of rising personal income and government subsidies to big agriculture. The small growers typical at farmers' markets, on the other hand, usually do not qualify for such subsidies and so compete with corporate agriculture on an uneven playing field, further depressing their prospects for sustaining their businesses.

Although it is very difficult to compare produce prices, the Minnesota Institute for Sustainable Agriculture found that a family of four could substitute about 25 percent of their annual food purchases with comparable quantities of Minnesota-produced food and save about $135, as compared with the USDA's average of national prices.[44] While non-organic, locally produced foods such as cheddar cheese, flour, and chicken were more expensive, those prices were largely offset by lower ones on such things as apples, pick-your-own strawberries, and bulk-quantity beef and pork. Increasingly, shoppers may find the goods at their nearby neighborhood farmers' markets less expensive, when gasoline costs are factored into the price, than those at the mall grocery store.

At successful markets, the managers help to educate both the public and the growers to alleviate these and other misconceptions about the food sold and the growers' relationships to it. Advertising, signage, informational materials, and other outlets help to align expectations and realities. In Bloomington, a collaboration of the market management and the Local Growers Guild has begun public forums, leaflets, and other outreach to reintroduce the farmers' market to the larger community. In addition, a former Bloomington market master presents a weekly market update on a local radio station.

Regardless of conflicting notions about what is being sold at a market, customers do respond. In 2005, 105,000 people attended the Bloomington market, making it about three times as big as the average U.S. farmers' market.[45] The average weekly customer count that year in Bloomington was 3,600 people. The USDA's latest national customer counts are no more recent than 2000, but they indicate a national weekly market total of 2,750,000 people patronizing 2,800 markets. The majority of shoppers at farmers' markets nationally are female, white, middle- or upper-class, and well-educated, and live within ten miles of the market they frequent. Eighty-five percent live within twenty miles.[46] That kind of proximity means a farmers' market is a local affair and must be responsive to its customers and their traditions and foodways.

The Bloomington market fits this profile. The majority of Bloomington market customers come from the surrounding county and others nearby. The city's largest employer is Indiana University. Of the Bloomington residents, about half have bachelor's degrees and 87 percent graduated from high school. Only 10 percent of the population is of color, with Asians making up the largest minority group.[47] The market favors Midwestern American standards like Big Boy tomatoes, Silver Queen sweet corn, and Red Delicious apples. But it also features regional favorites like pawpaws, persimmons, and wild morel mushrooms. Increasingly, the fare reflects the town's new residents with offerings of tomatillos, Chinese cabbages, Asian pears, and African chiles.

By contrast, a successful market located in an area with a different ethnic base will reflect that population. For example, the Vietnamese Farmers' Market in New Orleans for years has catered to the local population, including immigrants to the United States from southeast Asia. A year-round Saturday market, the purchases there tend toward fish, chiles, okra, lemon grass, mustard greens, Chinese greens, snow peas, and medicinal herbs. Much of the produce is grown with traditional Vietnamese methods, even with seeds brought from Vietnam, on forty acres of open ground near the housing developments where many of the vendors and customers live.[48] The Vietnamese areas of the city were either largely spared or largely inundated by flooding caused by Hurricane Katrina in 2005, depending on their exact location. In the months following that devastating storm, the city pledged to revive this market and others as a way to bring life back to normal, although at the time of this writing, the fate of the market and the city remain to be seen.[49] Market prices, too, must be suited to the neighborhood. In lower income or geographically isolated neighborhoods where fresh produce is likely to be scarce, successful markets tend to feature basic products at reasonable prices.[50] California's West Berkeley Farmers' Markets closed in 1997 after just two years in existence even though it was situated in a neighborhood that had only one supermarket—which did not carry produce. However, an unpalatable location beneath an overpass and a sponsoring organization that promotes (higher-priced) organic food meant the community never felt ownership of the market. The farmers, for their part, did not feel they could lower their prices without first seeing an increase in volume of sales.

On the other hand, not far away, the Richmond, California, farmers' market operates in an area where over half of the population is African American (the overwhelming majority of farmers' market customers nationally are white) and where many people are low-income.[51] That market began in the early 1970s as an outgrowth of a buying club that was addressing the closing of supermarkets in the area. This market was responsive to the community and their food interests, selling produce for cuisines such as Asian, Indian, and African American. The prices also were set reasonably, even with a number of organic foods being sold. The New York City Greenmarket farmers' markets address the needs of lower income neighborhoods by assigning large farmers, those

Bloomington

Bloomington

growing on more than fifty acres, to those venues on the assumption that they will be able to sell at lower prices even in markets with less volume.[52]

Bloomington's per capita annual income comes in at the bottom of the middle class at $25,500, which is $3,500 lower than the state average. Thus many of the Bloomington customers do not have much disposable income, even though they have many of the markers of the middle class, including home ownership, automobiles, and higher education.[53] Nevertheless, the Bloomington farmers' market has characteristics of some of the most successful markets, which are apt to be located near middle-class neighborhoods where customers are willing and able to weigh prices against quality. As mentioned, some perceive the farmers' market prices to be higher than those in corporate supermarkets; however, most regulars will pay what they consider to be reasonable prices given the high-quality produce available directly from growers.[54] Some customers account for higher prices by noting that the small farms that sell at local markets are less likely to receive government subsidies, so their prices more closely reflect the true costs of growing. Others, however, don't understand how prices are determined, even assuming that they are standardized across the market: one customer said that she no longer bothered to check prices once she "figured out" the prices were "fixed." Quite a few reckon that higher specialty prices are offset by lower prices that are available for bulk quantities and in-season food, which they take advantage of by freezing, canning, and buying "keeper" varieties.[55]

In recent years, farmers' markets, including Bloomington's, have become more accessible to low-income people through federal and state nutrition programs: 58 percent of markets nationally participate in such programs. Food stamp recipients can now spend the vouchers with some market vendors, and their use at farmers' markets has reached an estimated $75 million to $100 million per year.[56] In low-income areas food stamps can make up a majority of overall sales at farmers' markets. The Bloomington market, too, has recently begun accepting food stamps. Food subsidies for low-income women, infants, and children, also known as "WIC," have created access to farmers' market products, including in Bloomington. In 2003, 2.3 million WIC participants received vouchers that were redeemable with more than 16,000 registered farmers at markets across the country, for some $24.2 million worth of fresh food. The Poe Park market in the Bronx receives 95 percent of its sales in WIC coupons.[57] Another nutrition program seeks to get fresh, nutritious, and locally grown foods to seniors. In 2003, the Seniors Farmers Market Nutrition Program involved 13,000 farmers at 2,000 markets, 1,700 roadside stands, and 200 community supported agriculture programs. In addition, gleaning programs that collect unsold or substandard food and redistribute it to needy families and nutrition centers operated in about a quarter of the U.S. farmers' markets. In 2005, the farmers of the Bloomington market donated six thousand pounds of food to community food banks and kitchens that in turn made that produce available to eighty-three different agencies from six counties, including childcare facilities, women's and homeless shelters, and recovery houses.[58] The well-being of individuals, families, and communities depends on access to adequate supplies of healthful food. Well-planned farmers' markets can address some of the most common challenges to that prospect through reasonable prices, easy access, and sufficient supply.[59] In return, increased sales from low-income shoppers benefits growers.

In national surveys, customers spend on average $17.30 per week with 66,700 farmers at markets, for a reported retail sales total of $888 million.[60] The Bloomington attendance total for city-sponsored markets in 2005 was 105,000, which puts the total spending in the ballpark of $1,800,000. By other measures, about half the customers spend that much again ($22) per person to shop and eat at downtown businesses on market days.[61] So for every dollar spent at market, another dollar, or more, is spent with conventional merchants in town. Nor does this count what vendors themselves spend after market, when it is not unusual to see groups of them having lunch at a locally owned restaurant.

In Bloomington, 141 vendors signed contracts to sell at the market in 2005, with an average showing of 91 vendors. This compares with an average of 27 farmers selling their wares at markets nationwide, which takes into account that three or four times as many growers vend at the height of the season than at either end of it.[62] By this measure, Bloomington has three times the vendor participation of other markets. The strong turnout of customers and vendors in Bloomington may be a result of the longevity of that market. Founded in 1975, it is nearly twice as old as the national average of fifteen years. More than one-quarter of all markets have been operating for fewer than five years.

Most vendors nationwide are relatively small producers, those close enough to drive in and willing enough to stand in a marketplace personally selling their produce. The average vendor at a market such as Bloomington's makes $7,500 per year from the market. Although the income numbers are self-reported from cash businesses and therefore may not be entirely valid, the USDA's figures note that 35 percent of vendors make less than $1,000 from the market per year, and only 20 percent make more than $10,000.[63] That means that 81 percent make less than $10,000 at markets. On the other hand, the largest vendors, who make up 1 percent of the total, make more than $50,000 per year. Reportedly, a good day at a high customer-count market in New York City can yield as much as $10,000 per day for a vendor.[64] As a general trend, the USDA reports, markets with the largest number of vendors, more than 50 and averaging about 127, make more sales per week to more customers per year—who themselves spend more per market. All of which means an overall increase in income for farmers. By all counts, however, growers work hard under uncertain conditions for what usually amounts to very little return.

The growth in the Bloomington market coincides with the boom in farmers' markets nationally, which increased 111 percent between 1994 and 2004, growing to more than 3,700 farmers' markets in the United States.[65] In Bloomington, as at all farmers' markets, food is the marquee event. People want to sell and buy good quality food at fair prices. But the markets provide more than food.

Customers want more than cheap produce: increasingly they know about the problems of large-scale food production, such as jet fuel pollution in "organic" fields, contaminated irrigation and wash water, mono-cropping that is deadly to beneficial birds and insects, pollution and environmental degradation from excessive transportation, dangerous and inhumane animal practices.

Farmers, for their part, feel more than the powerful draw of retail prices: they enjoy the pride of having grown something that a customer raves about, the social contact after a long week of working alone, the rush of hard work, and the satisfaction of a pocket full of cash.

And, although commercial ventures at base, farmers' mar-

Bloomington

kets ground us in local rhythms and communities. They bring us into a direct trade: my time and effort for yours. They facilitate exchange—food, politics, lifestyles, conversations, and points of contact are all on the table—but it seems they operate on a scale apart from the global branding and commodification found elsewhere. Most market participants, on both sides of the exchange, find satisfaction among the market stalls.

Vendors (*top*), Customers

Bloomington

Part 2. People

The structures of each market—its canopies, art, buildings, vistas—contribute to a signature experience. No market is exactly like another, each taking its shape not only from the material particularities of place, but also from its seasons, soils, foodways, ethnic groups, and histories. Each person uniquely experiences a market and, to a greater or lesser extent, integrates the experience into his or her life. At the same time, markets are a common resource and share a recognizable character. When people talk about markets, patterns emerge. The ways their stories differ from and confirm each other sketch the space that modern farmers' markets occupy.

Vendor Notes_____

*Consider a midsummer dinner: steaming corn on the cob,
a salad of cucumbers, green peppers, and Swiss chard, white
new potatoes with parsley and butter, an omelet with peppers,
potatoes, farm eggs, and goat cheese. Some of these foods we
grew—the potatoes, chard, parsley, and peppers—and the rest
were grown within fifty miles of our home by someone we met
face to face, whose eyes we looked into, whose hands we saw,
dirty or clean, calloused or smooth; someone who gathered the
eggs, someone who would accept our empty cartons back to use
again; someone who had written "organic" in careful cursive
above the last two boxes of cucumbers; someone who had
milked the goats and sliced samples of the valuable cheese and
answered the questions again: How many goats do you have?
Where is your farm? I'd love to see that with my own eyes. Do
you really make this yourself?*

*Those questions are important. And the vendor's answers,
though they may be pat or bore her to tears, are also important.
For it is the exchange that matters: the passing of money, goods,
information, presence, and accountability. My world for yours,
an old currency that has become novel again. With it, we sketch
in parts of the story of our food, our neighbors, and ourselves.
Guesswork, speculation, and embellishment are part of that
story, as are tradition and knowing. And the produce, itself, chosen, sown, grown, tended, harvested, washed, bundled, trundled
off to market, presented and vouched for by the person standing
next to it "carries the inescapable marks of the person who made
it"; she, herself, is infused into the product.[1]*

*The story of the supermarket is one of fabulousness, the
height of the American empire and its technologies: flawless
grapes the size of plums, plums the size of tangerines, tangerines
the size of the old Macintosh apples of our youth. Strawberries,
notoriously available at unlikely times of the year, are beautiful
to the eye but apt to be starchy, bland, and oddly sugary to the*

palate. Oversized, watery, mushy, or pithy, the super produce does not fill us up. Everything, it seems, is always available, always in season, yet none of it tastes quite as looks promise. The supermarket's uniformed employees are few and mostly invisible. Their aspects tell little or nothing of their own lives, and their lives tell none of the stories of those fruits and vegetables. The polish on the floors, the humming lights overhead, the sprays for freshness destroy any history that might remain clinging to the roots and leaves.

Bees and bugs accompany us to the farmers' market. Flower vendors, we carry antihistamine cream for those times the country literally rears up and stings the city. Occasionally a mouse or toad makes the journey to town in one of our produce baskets. Always seeds, leaves, and other effluvia of our rural life spill into the city parking lot on a summer Saturday morning. No wax floors here; the dirt we stamp off our boots buries the asphalt.

What drifts off us is picked up by others and enters their lives. What we provide, intentionally or not, passes to others and then goes on to further removes. And we, in turn, pick up their news and novelty: messages on tee-shirts, reviews of musical shows, stories, language. Comments about the weather or politics overheard in one conversation are elaborated on in the next. The basil from our field is full of water from our deep well and compost made from a neighbor's horse manure and the leavings of what we have bought from fellow vendors. It is grown in soil strewn with the stone tools of ancients. Growing and offering basil for sale, living with it as we do—making the choices we do—feeds us on every level, and when you buy this basil, it fuels you as well: from our stand to your belly and your babies' and then shed along your pathways through the world. We breathe in your stories; you breathe out our basil. Round and round the exchange goes.

Walking through an August Market in Bloomington, Indiana

Bouquets—mixed, field, demi
Globe amaranth
Zinnias
Anise hyssop
Marigolds
Strawflowers
Blue salvia
Statice
Sunflowers
Uncultured wild weeds
Garlic in bunches, braids, bulbs
Tomatoes—red, orange, green, yellow, cherry
Rhubarb
Duck eggs
Hen's eggs
Goat meat—chops, roast, stew, sausage, shanks
Basil
Bread
Focaccia
Baguettes
Honey—sticks, jars, bears, comb
Beeswax candles
Bee pollen
Beeswax pinecones
Cilantro
Parsley
Tarragon
Spearmint
Catnip
Garlic chives
Beans—green, yellow, purple
Arugula
Cantaloupe
Watermelon—red, yellow, seeded, seedless, ice box
Bamboo
Salad mix
Nasturtiums
Okra
Corn
Peppers—banana, Anaheim, hot wax, jalapeno, cayenne, habanera, bell, plants
Squash—acorn, butternut, yellow, patty pan, flying saucer, zucchini
Eggplant

Cabbage
Elk
Butter
Beef
Pork
Veal
Yogurt
Hamburger
Sirloin
T bone
Rib eye
Short ribs
Round steak
Cube steak
Chuck roast
Arm roast
Rump roast
Heal of round
Soup bones
Jerky
Pepperoni
Bacon
Backbone
Sage
Columbine
Tomatillos
Cow's milk
Peaches
Hostas
Ferns
Flowering shrubs
Landscape perennials
Coffeecake
Croissants
Scones
Cookies
Biscotti
Cleome
Shoulder roast
Pork chops
Sausage
Tenderloin
Ham steak
Shoulder
Spareribs
Heart
Liver
Bratwurst
Chicken
Visiting chef cooking market produce
Worm castings
"Plant a row for the hungry," sign-up

Simply Living Fair information
Leeks
Blackberries
Grapes
Swiss chard
Chanterelle mushrooms
Roses
Alpaca yarn
Potatoes—red, white, purple, yellow, ugly
Magic/naked lady/surprise/ Godiva/resurrection lilies
Broccoli
Hydrangeas
Plums
Apples
Cockscomb—yellow, red, pink, orange, plumed, crested, giant
Cosmos
Snapdragons
Hyperion
Sweet Annie
Begonia
Rudbekia
Frozen custard
Cheese—cow and goat, traditional, artisanal, curds
Maple syrup
Kale
Queen Anne's lace
Gladiolus
Baha'i information
"Stop logging in our state forest" petition
Democrats, registration
National political candidate information
State political candidate information
International Humanitarian Committee, sign-up
Monroe County Republicans, registration
Lotus World Music Festival Volunteers, sign-up
Foodbank information
Shitakes
Gourds
Onions
Stone-ground cornmeal

Customer   *Bloomington*

4. Market Customers_____

Price is not the point.

—JANE GOODMAN, customer

Not all visitors to a farmers' market buy. Some have vegetable gardens of their own. Some check in on the eve of vacation. Some find themselves low on funds. Regardless, they may still wander over for the music, dance performances, tai chi demonstrations, shoulder massages, cooking lessons, or any of the other special events at market, all open and free to all. The heart of a market is the buying and selling of food, make no mistake. But people also go for the atmosphere and for the familiar ways of being with a community.[1] The stories customers share about markets are worth telling for their similarities as well as for their differences. When an African American customer at an overwhelmingly white market says with confidence, "I can talk to anyone," she acknowledges the challenge that makes that ability admirable. Still, she and other regular customers say that they make fulfilling connections through the market, to the natural world and to others around them, cultivating through the rhythms of market a sense of belonging, security, and home.[2]

Beyond Price

Bloomington market customer Chris Harter says he knows his food through conversations with the vendors. Similarly, a patron of a Brooklyn, New York, market says that shopping there puts him in touch with the rhythms of the seasons in a locale that otherwise reveals few clues. He judges the time of year from which berries are being sold or whether the "garlic curls," "baby garlic," or garlic braids are on display. Shopping outside and being greeted by vendors who know him, he says, "grounds" him. Customer Katie Levin learns about her environment from what she calls the "turtle stand," growers who actually specialize in rhubarb, eggs, and bamboo but who also intrigue their customers with box turtles and other wildlife they bring to share with the townsfolk.

These customers might agree with Jane Goodman when she says that, at the farmers' market, "Price is not the point."[3] A Bloomington customer, she, like others nationwide, scours the market for high-quality, fresh food, choosing to spend her discretionary income on food she considers tastier and more healthful than what is available elsewhere. As another customer put it, "you can't bargain" if you want the best; even if something at market looks battered, she says, it tastes better than the "cardboard" produce at the supermarket.[4] And a Washington, D.C., resident claims that he shops at his local farmers' market simply because he is a "food snob" willing to pay more for better food. He recognizes that supermarkets, even natural foods specialists like Whole Foods, cannot compete with the freshness and flavor of local fare. Study after study has shown that customers across the country frequent farmers' markets for fresher food that they believe is more healthful.[5]

In addition to freshness in her produce and meats, Goodman seeks out organic food because she, like many, believes that organic alternatives to conventional foods, though sometimes more costly, are better for animal, human, and environmental health. For a time, farmers' markets were the only place to find even a few growers who raised crops without synthetic fertilizers or pesticides and livestock without antibiotics or growth hormones. Though even there, organic foods were few and far between. Now the USDA indicates that about four-fifths of markets include some organic growers, and a few markets feature exclusively organic food.[6] Most food at most markets, however, is not organic, and customers must rely on the integrity of the growers and the diligence of the market administrators.

Although the regulations around the use of the label "organic" are controversial, they are more standardized than they used to be. Growers can legally advertise their produce as organic only if they have been certified by a recognized government organization or independent regulator. Today, certification should mean that animals raised for milk or meat are provided with organic feed that does not contain animal byproducts, antibiotics, or growth hormones and that produce is not bioengineered or produced

Bloomington

with synthetic pesticides and fertilizers. However, in reality, loopholes in the organic regulations exist. For example, growers grossing under $5,000 per year are exempt and can call their produce "organic" without certification. Also, big dairies have been accused of exploiting loopholes in the regulations in order to bring non-organic animals and practices into their certified organic milk operations. On the other end of the spectrum, some growers follow many of the USDA's requirements and may even improve on some of them but are not certified organic. Most of these can be described as transitional organic, near-organic, and uncertified organic. At farmers' markets, these growers often signal their intentions, while staying on the right side of the law, with alternative phrases such as "no spray" or "sustainably grown."[7]

Increasingly, customers who want healthful meats, cheeses, and eggs frequent farmers' markets much as tomato and sweet corn buyers did some years ago. Ominous news stories about the hazards of corporate meat-growing practices increasingly make customers conversant in beneficial livestock practices, such as organically fed, grass-fed, and free-range. They may seek out the smaller growers who frequent farmers' markets in the belief that they farm with practices that afford better human health, more humane treatment of animals, and longer-term environmental sustainability.[8] When customers contract with growers for a lamb or a turkey or part of a side of beef or purchase a package of elk, ostrich, or buffalo, they may assign to the grower a certain degree of accountability for the welfare of the animal and healthfulness of the food they produce.[9] Indeed, a survey of market managers corroborates that customers who preferred organic food "were most likely to exhibit interest in the social and environmental issues within agriculture, such as the relationship of agricultural to human and animal health, sustainable development, water scarcity, environmental pollution, and wildlife protection."[10] In other words, many farmers' market customers, people who shop for fresh and healthy food, are willing to see price in light of other benefits. Customers expect higher prices for this arrangement. As one customer put it, there was no point in comparing the prices at market with grocery chains because the difference in quality makes the products wholly different from each other.

Goodman and other customers in university towns such as Bloomington demonstrate the strongest demand for organics.[11]

The popularity of organic food, along with heirloom and locally produced food, has grown with farmers' markets, and is increasingly featured at markets where the clientele can afford to make decisions based on quality.[12] Markets figure prominently in the growing national dialogue about food quality. While the corporate food industry infiltrates the organic movement with giant advertising budgets, farmers' markets may be able to draw off a few of the customers that advertising reaches. After all, the very qualities that corporate organic touts are already found in abundance at farmers' markets. This development has the possibility of shifting organic produce and meats—and thus the farmers' markets that sell them—toward the mainstream, for organic or conventional, farmers' market foods are inevitably fresher, arguably more nutritious, and certainly more environmentally sound than typical grocery store offerings. Although the 11 percent of American households that the government recognizes as not having access "at times to enough food for an active healthy life" are not in a position to spend more money on less food,[13] for many Americans—the majority of whom reportedly are overweight and spend a lower percentage of their income on food than people in other developed countries—less quantity for better quality may be perceived as a reasonable trade-off.

Goodman frequents a farmers' market close enough to her home that she can walk there on a Saturday morning. Like many customers, she has fond childhood memories of shopping directly from farmers, especially on vacations when the family sampled blueberries and strawberries at farm stands. When Goodman was growing up in Massachusetts in the 1960s, before the wave of farmers' market revivals, no farmers' markets set up close by. Indeed, by one count, only a dozen retail farmers' markets operated in the northeast in the 1960s.[14] She remembers the excitement in her family when a market opened nearby in Wayland, offering alternatives to "canned string beans" and the like.

Now an anthropologist who has lived for extended periods in Europe and Africa, Goodman does most of her shopping at food cooperatives, independent specialty food stores, and the farmers' market. She prefers shopping venues where people know her name, and where she can visit favorite and trusted vendors, and directly support their efforts. The market, in particular, allows her to rely on food that has been "preselected by people who care

Bloomington

about food quality and politics," which helps keep her "connected to that part of myself." Goodman emphasizes that buying her food face to face—being able to see the growers and connect with them as people—allows her a measure of food security. She enters into a partnership with them that rests on mutual responsibility: the vendors account for the quality of their food and growing practices, and she, as customer, literally buys into their business.

Like Goodman and an increasing number of people nationally and around the globe, Bloomington market customers Liz McMahon and Chris Harter have made the connection between local food and healthful food.[15] They, too, reflect the growing segment of consumers who want tasty and healthful food that is also environmentally sound and ethically produced.[16] For them, consuming organic and local food became even more imperative after the birth of their son, Wheeler.

In Bloomington, McMahon and Harter at first brought their young son to the market in a stroller, wedging in around him cucumbers, tomatoes, flowers, and greens, careful not to mash either the child or the produce. As he became more proficient at walking on his own, they felt the setting was safe enough to put him on his feet to totter through the crowd, albeit under a watchful eye. The stroller then became a convenient conveyance for watermelons or bags of potatoes. The boy's addition to the family made the weekly trek to the market for organic, unprocessed food more important than ever for them all. They had little extra money, but they considered better food to be an investment in their own and Wheeler's health.

But their commitment to buying locally goes beyond their own family's health. Like Goodman, McMahon and Harter recognize that family farming is more "fragile" than other kinds of businesses, more subject to weather, economic adversity, and failure. They take seriously the buyer's side of the proposition of local food. Nor are they alone. Surveys show that as many as three-quarters of the customers say that they shop at markets in order to help small farmers.[17] Harter, whose family farmed in prior generations, laments that farms around the country are being sold to subdivisions when they cannot sustain themselves. Once chopped up and paved, that land is effectively lost for generations. He and

McMahon say they respond by taking up their responsibility as customers in the farming partnership: they support local growers directly, whenever possible, using the farmers' market to invest in their family's and the public's future.

Transforming Community

Because a farmers' market is a collective enterprise, it does not depend on any single person to make it happen. Customers may miss the dancer with the old-time band when she skips a day, but the market experience carries on with its own rhythm and regularity. As a result, many customers call market-going a "ritual" or even a near "religious" experience. And like a ritual, it seems to have the power to transform. For many customers, the market alters an individual, slightly alienated experience of where she or he lives into a sense of being a member of a community. Market helps to make a landing pad into a home. One customer who moved from a coastal city to a job in Bloomington assumed that the State of Indiana would be a kind of wasteland, with nothing but cornfields and a few farmers.[18] The market, along with other city events such as art fairs and music festivals, slowly helped her feel at home in a new land. She said that if she could show visitors this "countercultural" side of Bloomington, they would see that "Indiana isn't that bad."

The market helped another customer to transform her sense of belonging in Bloomington after she moved there from Vermont. Katie Levin frequents the market to find a "real world community, a place where regular people went," that could provide relief from the intensity and homogeneity of her work world.[19] At the market she could forge valued connections to people from other walks of life. Like many other market customers, both women and men, she attends alone and uses it to "take care of myself" and be "self-sufficient." Her comments echo those of another single woman who enjoys her Saturday ritual of "time alone" at the market. She says, it "doesn't require me to have anyone" else along.[20] Like going to a museum, a zoo, or some other semi-structured event, Levin says, at the market, "you're part of a community, yet you are passively interacting. It's a place where you can go alone and not feel bad about it."

Levin found that she had to overcome a certain regional bias

Bloomington

when she moved from New England to the Midwest. Despite all of the good feelings that kept her coming back to the farmers' market, when she first noticed that a vendor there was selling maple syrup, the signature product of her home state, she bridled. She did not want to take a sample from nor even make eye contact with a Midwestern farmer who claimed to be making syrup. "You don't understand," she wanted to tell him, "I'm from *Vermont.*"

Referring to herself as an "eco-tourist," she says that she observes the "hustly bustly" market as much as she participates in it. She resisted the idea that some produce—blackberries and certain kinds of apples—had different names in Indiana from the ones she knew back home. And she is aware of what she calls the "culture of politeness" of the Midwest even though she feels she is not really fluent in it. She observes that she is among the type of customer who tends to wander and browse the market, as opposed to those who "clump off" to talk to friends and socialize. She enjoys bantering with the more assertive vendors but fears she will offend some if she doesn't decline to buy their goods in quite the right way. She loves the musicians who perform informally, tucked into empty spaces and corners of the market, but she feels that some people on the official stage border on the "terminally earnest."

Over time, however, she took up what she calls the "ritual" of attending the market each week and broadened her regional allegiances. She found herself drawn toward vendors who are, like her, "imported" from elsewhere. She believes they are "kindred spirits" also making their homes in a new place. She says in the end, "the farmers' market represents Bloomington to me."

Like many Bloomington customers, Levin walks to the market, so what she can carry limits what she can buy. In 2005, she secured a new position in Minnesota, and she regretted, even before moving, that she would not be within walking distance of a farmers' market. Living further from a market would make attending more of an event and less of a ritual, she anticipated, not at all the same as having her own market in her own neighborhood. Customers nationally tend to frequent markets within ten miles of home, and consistent with that trend, Levin assumed she would have to find other ways to make her new city feel like home, though she wasn't sure quite what those would be.

Like many people in the Bloomington area, or indeed in

America more generally, David Morgan is not "from here."[21] In his adult life, he has lived in Oregon, New York, Texas, and the U.S. Virgin Islands. Now in his fifties, he bases his business and his home outside Bloomington, Indiana. As a result, many of David's deepest personal relationships are far away. He had been a casual market customer for several years, but when the terrorist attacks of September 11, 2001, struck, he found the market presented the immediacy and friendships that he needed to cope with that traumatic time. The simple proximity of neighbors near his house did not relieve his sense of isolation, but the farmers' market did provide the comfort of community that he looked for:

After 9/11, I had gone out of the house once. I forget what day of the week it was. I may have gone out of the house once or twice to get food or something, but I didn't speak to anyone. And it wasn't until that Saturday morning of market that I went out and spoke with people. . . .

And I was looking forward to that group, that group, because I knew that, whatever I was feeling or whatever bizarre thoughts I might've had or theories or whatever, I was not going to be outside of the realm of understanding of this group and that their perception would be close to mine, and there would be a great venting and learning and sharing of experience.

And it was. It was fantastic. . . . I was almost waiting, looking forward to that Saturday, knowing that there would be like souls to share with. Because, you know, you have conversations with people you do business with and family, but, but this is a special group . . . just a warmer—I really felt that people understood and didn't judge. It was a heavy day.

What actually happened: I was on the phone with my ex-wife. She called me . . . she still calls me when she's uptight about things. She's a lawyer and would have normally been at her law offices across the street [from the World Trade Center]. She didn't go in that day. She called me from Long Island, and we're on the phone. She was watching on television; I'm watching it on television; and the towers collapsed. . . . She called me because she wanted to talk to somebody. The first plane had hit, maybe the second plane had hit by the time she called me, and so we're talking to each other on the phone, watching the towers collapse.

At that time . . . I didn't have that many people working for me. I was kind of isolated out there. I talked to my business partner up in Canada, and then there was no one else around here that I really wanted to—I know my neighbor, but I knew

Bloomington

also the political point of view [among a circle at market] and that there was a similar, a same wavelength.

And it was exactly what I wanted, what I craved. And there was no one else that I wanted to share that experience with. . . . This is around five or six people, core people, and then people coming in and getting additional information and additional information and additional—over a period of time. . . .

It's like when David Letterman started the show again: it was beginning a normal life again. You know, in quotes, in quotes normal life. But I remember that first night with the Letterman show they had Dan Rather on. And I think, actually, I may be making this up, but my memory is that, I think, Giuliani actually called Letterman and said we need you to go back on. It's important to get a normal flow going again. We're grieving, and we need laughter. . . .

I can't remember exactly, but I don't think it was all doom and gloom [at the market]. I think that it was the beginning of commerce, the beginning of intercourse, the beginning of normal life again. . . . And a pattern too, okay: it's Saturday it's market, it's Saturday it's market, it's Saturday it's market, and we're starting again. . . . Like a Sunday, or like a Saturday gathering that you always have. All this is a gathering of, of the tribes every Saturday, and it started the normalcy again.

The regularity of the farmers' market, its familiar patterns and rituals, allowed Morgan the "venting and learning and sharing of experience" that he could use to process the radical break with normal life that the terrorist attacks presented. At the market, he found among his acquaintances "core people" who shared his feelings and who operated in the same "realm of understanding." He did not need them to agree entirely with his processing of events, but he found comfort that "their perception would be close to mine," on the "same wavelength."

Morgan is able to pinpoint more precisely than most the moment when the market became a site of community for him. His sense of the market as a modern-day "gathering of . . . tribes" roots the phenomenon in the long view of human experience. Rarely formal or clearly defined, the social groups that coalesce from "like souls" at market do not operate in isolation; rather, as Morgan quite rightly observed, they exchange and share across lines, with "people coming in and getting additional information and additional information and additional—over a period of time."

Sharing with, responding to, and learning from each other, small groups at market interact and, taken together, suggest a large and diverse community sited on common ground. Morgan had been out to buy food from a corporate grocery story but found it did not sate the deeper craving he felt. The farmers' market, on the other hand, although sustained through exchange and commerce like a commercial establishment, nurtured relationships in ways that provided the intimacy of community that he needed.

In Morgan's 9/11 story, the market takes on transformative power. Its regularity and repetition, its "ritual," suggests a bargaining of the known and familiar with the unknown and unpredictable. Its return on the Saturday following the 9/11 attacks invoked "a whole constellation of relationships" and "the beginning of normal life again." Morgan's incantatory description of the market's rhythms—"it's Saturday it's market, it's Saturday it's market, it's Saturday it's market, and we're starting again"—suggests the weekly gatherings at market have the power to transform chaotic times into "normal life." He provides a powerful, alternative model of homeland security, with farmers' markets as an example of community that goes beyond simple proximity. The weekly patterns and secular rituals, the extra-ordinary appearance of the market each Saturday morning, like a circus tent rising on an empty lot, the varieties of intimacy that coexist at the market, all make up a reliable yet enchanting space that can enable us to move from the isolation of disaster to the comfort of a community in which, as Christopher Alexander puts it, "people themselves can be alive and self-creating."[22]

Establishing Bonds

If farmers' markets facilitate interaction among groups, they also connect people, one to one. The simple exchange between actual producer and final consumer, on which any farmers' market stands, is rare enough today. When it occurs, as it does at true farmers' markets, growers and shoppers become linked in a kind of mutual obligation rarely found in the deferred purchases of today's highly commodified culture. At market, the commercial exchanges carry additional significance for both parties far beyond what can be had at the local shopping mall. Market vendors in Bloomington commonly accept personal checks, even

Bloomington

out-of-town checks, without corroborating identification, to the amazement of customers. A vendor may loan baskets or containers worth more than the actual purchase to help customers carry their market bounty home. And customers almost unerringly return those essential tools the following week. It is not unusual for vendors to "spot" customers a dollar or two when they are short of cash or to throw in an extra ear of corn or hand a free flower to a child. Nor is it unusual for customers to share news of their cooking successes and innovations. They might even bring a muffin, a cookie, an enchilada, or ice cream for the vendor whose produce made the dish possible. It is downright common, and much appreciated, for customers to bring photographs, CDs, poems, and books to share with market vendors. And vice versa. These gifts and the less tangible ones weave unexpected and unlooked-for networks of gift giving and receiving into the market. Being trusted, being remembered, being the bearer or receiver of gifts makes for a powerful acknowledgment of an individual's place in a community.[23]

Bloomington customer Theresa Ochoa shops at the market to get good food and to support local growers, but she meanwhile weaves her own market networks in such a way that they overturn ordinary interactions.[24] A university professor of education, Ochoa goes to the market "to get knowledge," about which plants grow in the unfamiliar local climate and how to treat any ailing ones she already has. A teacher of future teachers, she says that she recognizes the vendors as "experts" who themselves "become teachers." She says in explanation and with emphasis that she trusts the care and expertise the growers devote to their food because "I am buying *their* tomato." Her message about the market is one of social and intellectual leveling: the vendors' relative expertise and her status as a relative novice bring them all into an "equal relationship," onto even footing from which she can "get to know them." The market gives Ochoa the opportunity to make a "person-to-person connection" with people she would not otherwise know, or not know as well. She says that the market provides the "potential to capture a relationship with a neighbor," as though friendships that would otherwise evade her grasp can flourish in the less hurried, more fertile medium of the market. She checks in each week to see "are all my guys there?"

The market for Ochoa has become a "ritual," "part of the

yearly thing" that allows her to find a sense of community and call Bloomington home. During the school year, she is too busy to attend the market, so she associates it with summer and a transition to different activities and membership in a different community. She shopped at the Santa Barbara, California, farmers' market for eleven years and still says, "It was mine." Even today she misses the fresh lemons and avocados available in California; but now she is equally protective of the Bloomington market. "Little by little it has become my market," she says. She likes the fact that Indiana's seasons force her to go to the market more "religiously" so that she doesn't miss any of the changing produce. And when she has visitors, Ochoa takes them to the market as "a way of making my friends and family know that Bloomington is also my home now."

Gregarious as she is, Ochoa does not find a comparable community at the mall or the supermarket. Farmers' markets are qualitatively different from the surrogate-to-consumer exchanges typical at such absentee-owner corporate outposts. Part of the difference depends on the market's face-to-face connection between producer and consumer. As Bloomington customer Cecilia Hartfield puts it, "I know I can go online [for information about a perennial plant], but it's a lot more fun to talk to people . . . that grow it and experience it and know it."[25] Or as local foods pioneer and chef Alice Waters has said, "In so many places now—the only piece of information exchanged between producer and consumer of food is a *number*—the *price*."[26] At the supermarket, nothing is left of origins or destination but a quantity. Like Ochoa and Hartfield, Levin may not know the names of vendors she enjoys, and they may not know hers, but she says nonetheless that the market "is a very personal thing." In fact, farmers' markets restore personality and quality to the mundane but profoundly intimate experience of food. Or as Deborah Madison, another famous chef and local foods advocate, says, "When you think about it, the farmers' market is really about the only place left in our lives where we can interact with someone who makes something we use. And it's hard to imagine, what is more vital or intimate than the food we consume, for it becomes our health, our pleasure, our nourishment, who we are, in fact. Today it is farmers who are providing the fragile connection that binds us in a meaningful way to our own humanity."[27]

Bloomington

Intimate, indeed. Farmers' markets make part of one person's world available to someone else. According to one study, people have ten times as many conversations at farmers' markets as they do at supermarkets.[28] Those conversations and the many other channels through which people exchange information help to heal the now typical breach between producers and consumers and between simple neighbors. As a performance full of lead actors rather than stand-ins, it opens possibilities for shared histories, dialogue, and interdependence. Unlike purchasable and disposable lifestyles that can be mistaken for communities, farmers' markets do not homogenize.[29] Rather, they provide the raw materials for transformation. The ubiquitous August tomato, taken to different homes, can become the foundation for salsa, spaghetti sauce, barbecue sauce, or a BLT sandwich. That shape-changing tomato, far from being disposable, is comestible, fuel for our own excursions, identities, and communities. It carries an aura of uniqueness, the mark of the hand that made it. And the encounters by which the tomato changes hands also carry with them the diversity of their beginnings. Markets do not so much mitigate diversity as spotlight it on a shared stage.

For many customers, a market "symbolizes the city as it ought to be," sharing the mantle of honesty, health, and hearth idealistically associated with rural life.[30] The colors, vitality, and festiveness of the market serve to "glamorize" the produce, as one customer put it, "seducing" customers into buying and into returning.[31] But that should not be taken to mean that a market is all and always good. Nor is it a nostalgic remnant of a simpler time, if that ever existed.[32] Instead, it is a living performance, with all the complexities contemporary life allows for. Unlike the uniformity of corporate marketing, farmers' markets allow for dissent, diversity, contradiction, and conflict. During election years, for example, differences gain renewed importance. A regular, longtime customer may come into a stand with the "wrong" political button pinned to her sweater. Other customers may wait until after a big purchase buys some goodwill to reveal that they are ensconced on the opposite side of a heated issue. One Bloomington customer spent the election year of 2004 walking through the market with political signs on a tall pole, one of which was a profile of George Bush with a foot-long Pinocchio nose. That same year, a couple of vendors donned unflattering Bush and Cheney

Bloomington

masks the weekend before the presidential election. The following Saturday after the slate was reelected, a white-haired woman wearing a Bush button made her usual purchase and then asked with a sly smile, "Where are the masks now?"

In other regular activities, people may tend to "clump together," as Katie Levin might say, with others like them. At church, in sports leagues, at lunch, at work, people socialize with others apt to be much like themselves. At market, however, differences interface. Assumptions about modesty, dress, affection, religion, politics, and national allegiance intersect, serving to confirm and challenge and, hopefully, broaden who we are.

Farmers' markets can play a civic role in bringing people together in familiar ways that become special. Face-to-face, local, and accountable, markets align with the scale of the individuals—to produce, deliver, and consume food, information, and community. Simultaneously, those individuals can tap into ancient patterns of human interaction through a farmers' market in ways that are potent and timely, reconnecting them to a shared space that confers the sanctity of ritual and the power to make a locality into a home.

Vendors   *Bloomington*

5. Market Growers_____

It's in my blood. I think farming is a genetic characteristic that gets passed down from generation to generation. And that's just part of it. You know the other thing? Warren Henniger told me this, and I think it's true. . . . No matter where they are, no matter what their background, their socioeconomic level, he said, every fifth child born is born a farmer. So maybe I was number five.

—JOHN BYERS, vendor

Growing favors tradition. Knowledge of it accumulates slowly and collaboratively: how the seasons move, when seeds should go into the ground, how not to be misled by early warming, how to prepare for early cooling, where the land lies just a little bit lower in a field so that it frosts last in the spring and first in the fall, where trees shading the edge of a field shelter cool-weather crops a little longer into the summer, how a field of stones or stumps can be cleared over generations, that bug infestations will pass, that technologies—wood, stone, animal, or metal—can make life easier but also have their own costs. Growing remembers better times and worse, and both give comfort. Some of what is to be known can be learned in one person's lifetime, but more reliable knowledge has a longer period of observation through many decades or many lifetimes collectively remembered. Growing requires incremental knowledge of the land that is gained through proximity. Of course much of it can be distilled into books and learned in Ag school, but somehow a simple sweep of the hand, a frost in June, or a ten-year flood conveys much more.

Farmers' markets can fill an important niche for all kinds of growers who want to make an adequate living from the land they cultivate. Some farm as a full-time job, with greenhouses or wholesale contracts to round out their income. Others grow part-time with significant off-farm income to sustain them. Backyard gardeners and hobbyists may harvest just a few perennials or they may tear up the grass and plant the whole yard intensively. Markets give all of these growers access to customers and retail prices that allow them sufficient income to live on, work, and steward the land.

For most vendors, the primary reason to sell at a farmers' market is income.[1] The market provides a broad canopy under which to extend the smaller umbrellas of individual farm businesses. Market stands require little start-up capital compared to traditional storefronts that do business directly with the public, which means vendors have to venture only a little to try their hands at retail. The collective nature of the market provides enough presence to bring customers in but also should outlast the lifetime of any individual business. And that's a good thing because growers come and go. Some move away, some give up the dream, some shift to caretaking children or elders, and, if the market runs long enough, some grow old and die. But through all those changes, the market itself will remain.

Studies consistently show that farmers sell at farmers' markets because they are the best or only place to vend their wares.[2] According to the USDA's 2000 survey of farmers' markets, 66,000 farmers sell via farmers' markets, with about 19,000 of those growers using them as their sole marketing outlets.[3] Although the prices to the customer are not necessarily higher at market than elsewhere, growers can earn up to 80 percent more selling directly to customers at retail prices than they do selling wholesale.[4] Moreover, farmers report as much as 22 percent of their crop would not be sold if they did not have access to farmers' markets. An Amish farmer in Indiana said it succinctly: the market "helps me survive."[5] He farms a grade A dairy and sells his milk through a cooperative, but he relies on the market to make ends meet. He describes his frustration with how milk prices are set as opposed to the peaches and vegetables he vends at the farmers' market. He said, the price of milk "is cheap now. It could be as bad as it's been since we've been milking ten years, the lowest price. Everything else keeps going up. They claim there's too much milk. . . . It's the middleman that wipes the profit margins out. [At market] we set our price. When we sell our milk, they pick it up, and a month later they send us a check, what they want to send. See here [at the market], when we sell, we decide our own price." Without the direct-marketing possible through the farmers' market, this family, like many others, might not be able to sustain their place on the land.

Although the income of big vendors on a good day at a roaring market can soar to $10,000, smaller vendors in smaller markets average earnings of $50 a day.[6] That would mean grossing less than $10 an hour for only the time actually at market, without accounting for, typically, months of time and expenses. According to statistics gathered by the federal government, 80 percent of vendors at farmers' markets earn less than $10,000 in a year from such an outlet.[7] While that would place an individual well below the poverty level as a sole source of income, as one of several income streams, it might make good sense. Even part-time growers, small-scale retailers, food processors, craftspeople, and artisans—those who report getting the most enjoyment from a market—say they go to boost their income.[8]

Vendors who earn little or have short-term forays into market growing still report that they benefit economically from the experience. In addition to the extra income, they can gain business experience, develop personal skills, test-market new products, create options for friends and family, and achieve economic stability through their activities at the market.[9] An established cheese vendor might hear such rave reviews from test-marketing a new recipe at the market that she incorporates it into her wholesale product line. Or a backyard gardener might make just enough to carry him through a tight summer. On the other hand, an idealistic but less experienced grower can save time by finding out quite quickly that the intense labor and minimal profits of small-scale farming do not allow for the life of leisure he had envisioned. Sometimes smaller growers seem to price their goods remarkably high or unaccountably low, grow "niche" vegetables without much hope of high volume, or work someone else's stand without pay or without accruing points toward seniority. These practices are less clearly about money. Indeed, vendor surveys show that farmers' markets serve more than a purely economic function for some growers, accommodating diverse economic and non-economic motivations. Part-time growers in particular were more apt to be vending at market because they "enjoy" visiting with customers and other vendors, but large and full-time growers also note the non-monetary benefits of going to market.[10] Even one of the highest-volume vendors at the Bloomington market says that hearing customers rave about the quality of her produce is part of what keeps her coming back.[11] Market, then, sustains vendors economically while opening avenues to broader worlds.

Diversifying Income

The Amish dairyman is not the first farmer to realize he needed to diversify his operation in order to survive. And he, like many market growers, has used the knowledge of farming that he has developed from "as far back as I can remember" to find new ways of meeting the demands of a weekly retail market:

> We're always experimenting with new things to see what works. You've got to adapt to the situation. If it don't work, we just throw it out and try something else.
>
> Back in '92 I put up a little tomato shack. Back then if you got tomatoes by July fourth, that was early. People would be driving all over the place coming out to buy tomatoes. As the years went on, other people have done that. Now, if you don't have them the middle of June, you're late.
>
> So we've made a new shack this past spring. I put a little bit of roof on it. It's kind of like a portable—you roll [the sides] up. It all comes off but the . . . greenhouse roof. They call it a polycarbonate, real tough, ten-year warranty stuff. . . .
>
> We have tomato patches outside for later. Our idea is that the greenhouse tomatoes should be over before the outside ones start. By the first of August, tomatoes are just like noses, everybody's got one. What we try to do is get our patches over with so we sell peaches while other people are selling tomatoes. Then we have a late tomato patch ready to go in October.

Pressure on midsized farms has increased as food farming becomes more corporate and consolidated. Eighty percent of farms sell less than $50,000 per year, including the 60 percent that sell less than $10,000. But that doesn't mean that these growers are any less dedicated to their farming. Markets are particularly useful to small and mid-size farms that need prices to stay sufficiently high to compensate for having less ground in production. Lower volumes of produce and sales mean that growers have to charge more in order to make their businesses viable. Although the vendors may try to push the ceiling on prices, customer surveys in-

Bloomington

dicate that they feel they get high-quality produce at reasonable prices.[12] When vendor prices are too high, produce simply doesn't sell.

At the Bloomington market, the size of the market delivery vehicle is a good indication of the size of the farm. Smaller produce growers come in small pickup trucks, sometimes without a cap, or even in a hatchback car. Bigger growers may come in a one-ton van, a box truck, a full-size pickup with elaborate racks and covers, or with a pull-behind trailer. The proportion of smaller delivery vehicles at the Bloomington market reflects the size of the consumer base and the quality of the local soil, which tends more toward hilly Kentucky clay than Midwestern black gold. The Madison, Wisconsin, market, by contrast, largely comes in by box truck. And New York's Greenmarket has vendors who move enough produce to gross as much as $10,000 on a single market day. One Greenmarket vendor reported that she grows fruits and vegetables on a hundred acres in Highland, New York. Another family from Shippensburg, Pennsylvania, "used to just scrape by on their three-hundred acre farm: 'It was a real "Green acres" experience: run down and tired with no cash flow,'" until that family leased 250 acres more. What did they do with all that produce? "These farmers' markets were, without question, our salvation," they said.[13]

Although New York's Greenmarket requires that farms be "independently owned," a difference in scale clearly exists between their vendors and the ones more typical of many farmers' markets around the country. In Bloomington, one might argue that the policies of the market are designed to keep vendors relatively small. To sell there, vendors must be involved in every stage of the growing, harvesting, and selling of all the products that appear at their stand (a fact that escapes many customers). One year, a large-scale melon grower from outside Bloomington was forced to withdraw from the market because, instead of doing the harvesting himself, he had hired migrant laborers to do the picking. Another farm managed to finesse the market rules by keeping their commercial crops, produced with migrant labor, scrupulously separate from a smaller, more diversified portion that was tended by the family and sold at the market. Hired labor, interns, mechanization, and high productivity all have a place at the Bloomington market, but the size of the vendors is, essentially, scaled to the capacity of the individual human: the market rules require hands-on involvement by everyone selling at the market in every stage of product production.

The Brenda and David Simmons family cultivates one of the largest farms participating in the Bloomington market, with twenty-five acres in produce production and an additional ten in table and wine vineyards.[14] David's family has owned the land near Columbus, Indiana, for about 120 years, where they have accumulated "a lot of family history." For more than fifty years, they have been growing produce, at one time selling canning tomatoes to a factory in Columbus and fresh wholesale produce daily at the Indianapolis market. Today's generation, however, has found its niche in higher-return, more hands-on retail markets. As Brenda tells it, "David's parents have passed away, so it's pretty much us and the kids now. Five of us that work all the ground and take care of everything and grow the produce. We've got some other people, a few other people who help, here and there. . . . We are all right there, together."

They have been selling at the Bloomington market since the mid 1990s, beginning just a few years after they got married. They feature midseason staples such as sweet corn, melons, and green beans, spiced with popular specialty crops like okra, eggplant, and fancy bell peppers. The work runs year round:

> It starts in early spring. We prune the grapes in March and in May we plant the fields with corn and all the grain crops. By April and May, we're putting produce in the ground. In fact, we're putting it in with the risk of getting frosted or not. We grow so much stuff that we just take the chance on the sweet corn and other stuff, the green beans. We've been out covering green beans with plastic [to protect against frost], and you think, what am I doing? Just beating my head against a wall!
>
> So then we're pretty much all summer long selling produce, picking and selling produce. We start picking grapes actually next week [in late August]. The peak of produce has already kind of been here. So that's six weeks of pretty intense picking. By the time the grapes are done, we're harvesting our fall crops. And in the wintertime we're bottling wine. You can make wine all year round, but we're concentrating more on the wine product in the wintertime as far as bottling, packaging.

It's year-round. There are no gaps. What we do has kind of filled in nicely. You get done with one thing, and the next thing is ready to step in.

Preparing for the market is hard work, but the actual selling provides something of a charge. Long-time customers "come up to the stand, [and] they say you have the best corn; you have the best melons," Brenda Simmons says. And that achievement keeps her coming back:

I just really enjoy this market. Part of it is about making some extra money. But the other part of it is I just enjoy people. We kind of tease among the family [because] we're spread out at three different spots, but wherever my stand is will make two to three times more than any of the other spots. Then they'll say, but you have all the stuff! And I'll sell it all. I'll usually have to take off and rob the other stands. Over the years we've built up that base of customers. And we've had the same customers over and over.

The Simmons's displays are neat and bountiful, and often a line of people waits to make a purchase:

One of the catchphrases I hear all the time is one-stop shopping, and that's what people who come up would like. . . . Part of the market experience is shopping around. You know, people want to spread their money around. And then we'll have some people that just want convenience, who will say, I can get my watermelon, I can get my tomatoes, I can get everything I need right here at your stand. And that's probably what I listen to more than anything. What can I do to make it more convenient for the shopper? I've learned a lot about marketing just being here.

Indeed. During the height of the season in 2004, the family had enough produce and demand to sell from seven vending spots at the Bloomington market. However, they had to adjust their strategy when the market put in place a new policy for the 2005 season that effectively limited vending spots to two per grower. The discussion among the vendors during the annual market meeting set the needs of new vendors who wanted access to the market's limited space against the desire of more established vendors to move larger quantities of produce. At least one vendor commented that larger growers should sell at other markets rather than taking up more Bloomington spaces. Others felt that the overall number of vendors should not increase until the customer traffic could rise to support them better. An ambitious vendor said later, "It seems like there's a limit to what you can sell at one table. And if you don't have it on the table, it ain't going to sell." The proportion of customers to vendors is a regular concern among the growers, and in 2005 during the six-month height of the season it averaged about 5,000 customers to 91 vendors.[15] At either end of the season, when the customer counts drop to around 3,000, competition rises. Some people favor open access and increased competition, believing the diversification and innovation in products will bring more customers, while others point out that currently most vendors, unless they feature highly seasonal, specialty, or perishable produce like raspberries, strawberries, or eggs, do not sell all that they bring.

Like many big growers, the Simmons farm takes advantage of multiple outlets for their produce. Being able to pick and sell several times a week mitigates the capriciousness of the weather and leaves less produce to over-ripen or get otherwise damaged in the field. So the Simmons family, in addition to selling direct at the weekly Bloomington and Indianapolis markets, does an increasing amount of business right on the farm. After adding vineyards and making their own wine, they replaced the old family roadside stand with a new and improved building that houses a produce room and a wine-tasting room:

> David has an agriculture background at Purdue University and a minor in chemistry. Those were the two components that really helped [with the wine business]. We, honestly, never made a lick of wine prior to this venture. That's a story we wouldn't tell back then because we didn't know if the stuff would turn out well. But we're in a hundred different stores across the state with our products now.
>
> He does all the winemaking, and I do different jobs with the business. We both do the produce together. When we built the winery, we had separate rooms [in the retail building]—one we call the produce room. We sell fresh produce on a daily basis right out of what we technically call the Simmons Winery and Farm Market. So we kind of have that component as well . . . the farm market component. The produce business had been established for fifty, sixty years so we already had a customer base going into this. So we just moved up from the farm

Bartholomew County

which is across the street—from an old junky stand to air-conditioning and keeping things fresh. We made the produce part of it a lot nicer.

Their long-term plan calls for continuing to diversify the farm's income and also move it toward those parts of the business that are not quite so demanding:

It is a lot of work. We work hard. I won't kid you about that. And I won't feel bad about saying it either. We start Wednesday in the summer when the kids are not in school. We're usually out there by 6 a.m. Friday morning with maybe a half-hour lunch break. And we're working all the way up until loading the truck at 7 p.m. That's 13 solid hours of picking, washing, packaging, loading. We send the first truck and trailer on Friday evening. And everyone else comes in the next day with another truck.

The family knows produce growing inside and out. It provides a consistent income, but Brenda says, one day they will transition to parts of the business that don't depend on so much travel:

At some point in time, we're going to start scaling back on our produce. The winery is growing at a very rapid rate. We're going to build a banquet hall. We're getting ready to break ground this week. We are probably doing so much with the produce right now for college. The boys are 16, she'll be 15. We'll have three college-age kids. This is just a means to get them through college as much as anything. So probably I think in the next five or six years we'll still go at it. But eventually we'll taper off that part of it.

Farming That's in the Blood

Brenda Simmons, who taught high school math, sounds almost surprised to find herself in the business of growing food. She didn't grow up on a farm as her husband did, and she jokes, "I think I made a mistake several years back when he asked me to drive a tractor!" Still, she finds great satisfaction in the choices she has made: "I think owning our own business, being an entrepreneur, that's what I've always wanted." More and more women have taken up market gardening in the past ten years. Some of them have entered into a tradition that resides in their husband's family. The choice sometimes makes them laugh at themselves, but they nonetheless seem to embrace the challenges and rewards.

Chris Hunter, too, affects mystification when she gestures at her crowded honey stand, "I acted interested when we were dating, and look what I got!"[16] She was introduced to beekeeping when she and her husband, Tracy, first started dating. Beekeeping has occupied his family since 1910, but when they first met, she didn't realize that it would become such a big part of her life:

> We were both attending Purdue University. Tracy had received his first degree in land reclamation and had decided to also get his teacher's license in agriculture with a minor in biology so that he could combine school teaching with beekeeping. Just as his mother and grandfather had. I was getting my teaching certification in family and consumer sciences, so we met when we had several vocational education classes together.

Tracy's grandfather operated between seven hundred and eight hundred hives and also inspected beehives for the Indiana Department of Natural Resources: "With the help of his grandfather, Tracy caught his first swarm when he was 14 years old and has been keeping bees ever since."

Chris Hunter was raised on a farm. She says,

> I never had a fear of bees, and I was raised a farm girl, so I knew hard work and everything involved with a career in agriculture. But, I still was a little bothered the first time that I helped Tracy in the bees. We drove to Petersburg, Indiana, to harvest honey from hives that Tracy had put on the old strip mines. The mining companies would plant acres and acres of sweet clover to reclaim the land. We were pulling supers from forty to fifty hives. There were thousands of bees in the air, and some were even landing on me. I can remember feeling a little uneasy at the time, but I did not have a fear of the bees.

Now Chris Hunter seems immersed in the ways of honey. While her husband stays home to work the shop at the house, she attends the market without fail every Saturday. Her banter with the customers is informative and friendly. Explaining bee pollen, one of the many products she sells, she says:

> It's very nutritious. It has vitamins and protein. Some people use it as a supplement. Some people find that it helps with their allergies; it builds up their immune system so they don't suffer

*as much from the pollens that are in the air. I've even had some
people that actually say that it helps them with other allergies.
You can sprinkle it on food or you can just take it straight. I
take it mostly for the nutritional benefits and for the energy it
seems to give me. It kind of gives me that oomph.*

And she shares with them what she knows about honey, the tastes
that "go from a very mild honey like Basswood or spring blossom
to something very rich and powerful like the buckwheat, which is
almost like a sorghum molasses."

Hunter's exchange with customers is remarkable for the care
she takes to acknowledge them as individuals. She asks, "How are
you *today*?" in such a way that one believes she might remember
how they fared last week. She encourages healthy eating habits
and asks after family members who have been ill. She gets the
news about pets and new babies in a rapid succession of conversations that probably average thirty seconds. Always positive
and sociable, she gives a little singsong greeting of "Hi there!" to
people as they approach the stand.

She says of her marriage, "I help him. We are a partnership."
And she says of the bees, "They just keep doing what they do. It's
all so worked out, each with its individual job in the hive. They
are just amazing!"

John Byers knows big-time farming, and he knows he's not in
that league.[17] Instead, he sells at market because he has an affinity
for growing things that is based in a long family tradition of farming. He enjoys putting seeds in the ground and bringing the fruits
in to sell to the public.

The story of the Byers' family farm is not uncommon for
America in the twentieth century. In three generations, the family farm passed from owner-farmers in the 1930s to leasing the
land entirely to tenant farmers in the present. Early on, the family
added land as it became available, taking risks but managing to
sustain the farm during the Depression. Later they continued to
add acreage until they had what Byers describes as a large "cash-
grain farm in the west central part of the state where there are two
things that are allowed to grow besides a little grass in the yard
and some trees: corn and soybeans."

Byers' parents were committed to the farm, but they were riding the cusp of modern agriculture, where one might live on the

farm but strove not to be of it. As the conveniences long available to city dwellers made their way out into the heartland, they, like other farming families, took advantage of the opportunity to shorten the hours of work:

We didn't even have a garden when I was kid. We grew a few tomatoes. My mom was a city kid, and she was going to town to see her mom all the time and shopping at the supermarket. My dad and mom didn't want to take care of a garden. They were taking care of the rest of [the] farm. It was a time when farms were shifting to agribusiness. When they were married they got the requisite cow and chickens, but time went by, and they had more kids. Then they just got rid of the animals because, you know, they had more disposable income, and it was a heck of a lot easier to go to the supermarket.

In 1990, the Byers' son whom all thought would carry on the farm and its lifestyle was killed in an off-farm accident. Given that farming is perennially one of the most dangerous jobs in America, this tragedy is especially sad. John, one of two surviving sons, for a time took primary responsibility for the farm. Eventually, though, none of the family lived on the land, and it was leased to a local farmer. That arrangement, at least, covers the taxes and makes a modest income for them all. Although he makes his own living as a carpenter in Bloomington, Byers still feels connected to the land and hopes to be able to hold onto it despite rising pressures to sell.

When Byers came to Bloomington to attend Indiana University, "I obviously brought some of my farming roots with me." Since moving to this small city, he has participated in several specialty growing operations that have used the farmers' market as their sales outlet. For many years, he helped his former wife sell unusual and heirloom varieties of chile peppers and tomatoes. Later, he found his own place at the market by growing squash from around the world:

The squash is just kind of something I fell into as a niche. Nobody else was doing it, and they're fun and easy to grow for the most part. And they're really satisfying. When they're growing, they'll seemingly double in size in a couple days. The plants will grow crazy wild everywhere. I've had plants that have had forty, fifty squash. . . . One year I had them clear up in a tree about ten feet high with squash on them.

Every fall Byers pulls a farm wagon filled with specimen squash nestled in straw into the market. Tipped on its axle to create a display, the "Squash-O-Rama" presents a cornucopia of large, colorful, and gnarly squash that are the only ones like them on display. Of one particularly inedible-looking squash, Byers says: "Some friends of mine brought it back from Thailand. They smuggled the seeds back. They grew them a couple of years ago, and they gave me one and said, you've got to try this. It was really good. Then I looked in the seed catalog, and there it was this spring: *Thai muang*. It's very good in soup."

John's goal is not so much to sell the squash as to show them off and talk with people about them. He enjoys the growing of them and the interactions at market, setting his prices "by guess and by gosh. I don't really want to sell them that much." He considers eight dollars for an eight-pound Japanese tetsukabuto to be exorbitant and expects to be able to exhibit it for several weeks at that price. Growing specialty varieties of a misunderstood vegetable means there's not much danger the collection will be diminished quickly: "Most people when they think of squash, they think of the standard butternut or acorn variety. But there are people who know that there are different kinds. There's an English couple that come every year, people who want to try something different and have a little sense of adventure. They'll try something that's all warty or spotty."

After he separated from his wife of twenty years, Byers ceded the market spot she had earned with her sales. But he didn't give up the market. Byers now tows the Squash-O-Rama into another vendor's space and helps with that operation: "the maple syrup thing I do because I like to get out of the house in February when we start the production. I get out, outside in the woods. It's good exercise. . . . I work inside; carpentry is mostly inside for me. . . . I'm not getting any fresh air. And I'd rather be outside if I could be." Besides, growing things satisfies a deeply held part of himself, "It's in my blood. I think farming is a genetic characteristic that gets passed down from generation to generation." That inevitability, he implies, is one that goes beyond his family to a human survival mechanism that makes every fifth child born a farmer. He enjoys recounting a friend's adage, "every fifth child is born a farmer. So maybe I was number five."

Other vendors may not have an evolutionary theory to explain their affinity to growing, but they seem no less drawn to it. On a bright fall Saturday, Kenny Hughes and Gregory Ash stand with an impressive display of blooming mums.[18] Hughes is drawn to the camaraderie and what he calls the flea market atmosphere of the Bloomington market, and so volunteers to help. His friend, on the other hand, is really a grower. For all his passion for flowers and plants now, Ash grew up without much push in that direction. As a child he lived in a suburban house on Main Street in Greenfield, Indiana. His parents did not have green thumbs, but he was drawn to growing:

> I grew up messing with plants, probably from my grandparents and working in their yard. My grandmother was a flower person. So that's what got me started. I went to her house to beg for plants. . . . I had a neighbor who lived two houses down who had a big yard. They had an extra lot, and they were farmers. And they grew a garden, everything. They had a beautiful garden and they would always have, maybe, two or three rows of zinnias or cut flowers. And as a little kid I would go down there. I would see all this, and it was great. And she would maybe give me a bouquet of flowers. That was like home. That was a very good influence, to get me motivated. And it's a memory that I enjoy.

When he was thirteen, Ash ordered a tractor trailer full of plants. It pulled up into the family's yard, and he recruited his parents to help pot things up in the garage. After studying landscape architecture at Purdue University, he opened a design-and-build landscape business. He was good at the work, running the business for twenty-five years and entering display gardens in the annual Indianapolis flower and patio show. But it was the growing that really drew him: "I liked the growing better than the design. I kind of got into the wrong trade. . . . I like dealing with the plants more than the people. I like growing." After figuring out that he "went the wrong direction" in all those years, he opened a greenhouse and now grows thousands of perennials.

The business at the greenhouse is good, especially with wholesale customers who buy large quantities. The appeal of vending at the farmers' market is that he can take his plants directly to the customers, turning over a lot of product in just a few hours: "I'd rather be able to sell out quickly than sit on them." The market also helps build the customer base for the greenhouse trade which has slowed lately. As people from the market learn the location of the greenhouse, they visit there midweek to buy more plants.

Now in his fifties, Ash is less concerned with growing his business bigger and "leans more" to wanting to enjoy himself: "You got to like [growing]. It's something you got to like to do. It's not something you do because you're going to make a lot of money." His helper, too, who grew up on a farm, works the market "pretty much for free." He says, "It's amazing how many people go through here. And it's the same faces. . . . They keep coming back and buying. They are wonderful people. . . . So I come here just to meet the people and 'bag them up'! It's a good day. I like it."

Filling a Niche

Most full-time growers, like Ash, have more than one sales outlet while most part-time growers rely entirely on farmers' markets. The part-timers may not gross as much overall from their operations (45 percent said that they made less than $1,000 per year as compared with 83 percent of full-time growers who averaged more than $1,000), but part-timers depend on the markets more, reportedly making 60 percent of their sales at farmers' markets compared with 35 percent by full-time growers.[19] They are just as likely as full-timers to say they vend at a market because "we want extra income," "our other income sources are limited," and "we don't have the capital to open" another kind of outlet like a roadside stand or store. Almost a third of full-time growers and nearly two-thirds of part-time growers say that their business would be hurt or would close if the market were not available. From a purely profit-based motive, growing for farmers' markets may be tenuous even when they are the best available alternative. From a community perspective, however, "they can nurture local economic development, maintain diversity and quality of products, and provide opportunities for producers and consumers to come together to solidify bonds of local identity and solidarity." And from a personal perspective, they may provide just the right mix for a sustainable lifestyle.

Jonas Winklepleck grew up on a family farm in rural south-central Indiana.[20] He says the family "had a big truck patch. My dad years ago sold popcorn and peanuts to the theaters. They'd

Bloomington

buy direct, the theaters and drive ins. . . . That was years ago. So I kind of growed up knowing a little [about farming]. When I was a kid, every hour you could spare, you'd be out there shelling them."

Winklepleck started selling at the market in 1978, three years after it started. Back then, he says, "I thought it was great! We didn't have near the customers [as now], but we did good. I've watched this market grow." And he has grown along with it. When he first started vending, he knew little about how to price or display his produce, but he quickly learned from other vendors, particularly a man about thirty years his senior who still, thirty years later, makes the weekly trek to market: "Old Harry Fowler, I paid attention to him because he was the first. I paid attention to that guy. I always respect Harry."

Now retired from his maintenance position in a public school system, Winklepleck relies on the market to supplement his income. He grows an extensive array of vegetables, from turnips and patty pan squash to cucumbers, tomatoes, and peppers. In the spring, he and his wife, Betty, feature bedding plants and enormous hanging baskets of flowers raised in their greenhouse near Odon. Winklepleck says he is the sole child of the nine in his generation who wanted to keep a piece of the family farm in the family and in crop production: "It's gone. See, there was nine kids of us. And when you have something like that [farm], you have to sell it. They wanted to sell it all. I wanted to buy some of it. But majority wins." He, alone, carries on the family tradition of growing: "You got to like [selling at market]. Hey, it's work. It's not all fun and games. The reason I like it, I try to outdo last week. It's a challenge. . . . When I quit enjoying it, that's probably when I quit. But when I'm out there working, I'm my own boss. I'm doing it my way."

Bob Wise only had to do the math to realize he would need to supplement his income after retirement.[21] Selling at the market turns out to be a chance to live where he wants, carry on something of a family tradition of farming, and make ends meet: "I just heard about [the market] and thought maybe that's something that I can do. I knew I didn't have enough Social Security pension to live on. So that would help a little on that, you know. That, with the cattle, I get along all right that way, see. If I had to depend on my Social Security pension, I would be hurting."

Growing to supplement his income was a logical choice for Wise. He was born in what is now a wealthy suburb of Indianapolis but what was, early in the twentieth century, a farming community:

> I was born and raised on a farm. I've been on a farm for eighty years. I lived in town about one or two years. All the rest I've been in the country. [The family farm grew] the usual for back in those days—we had hogs and milk cows. We didn't have any beef cattle back then. This was up in Carmel. Dad raised Percheron horses and showed them. We had Berkshire hogs, and we showed them. And of course, we raised the corn and oats and wheat. I was a little bitty kid. I can remember that. . . .
>
> [Carmel was just] a farming town back in those days. That's where I started school. Shoot, you wouldn't even know the place now. It's a madhouse! I wouldn't move back up there for all the tea in China. I like Greene County. Hills and all that. Hollers and everything. It's pretty. It's got all those woods and trees. Back there [in Carmel], it's all flat. It's monotonous.

Wise's experience on the family farm turned out to be an asset when he started growing for market. Much as in the old days, he started stocking his market stand with many kinds of produce before he finally settled on specializing in fabulous displays of gladiolas:

> So I went down to the market one day, and I milked the brains of a couple of vendors to see what I could sell. So I figured, I'll just raise everything I can think of. And I did. And I found what would sell and what wouldn't. And finally those glads, I took four- or five hundred in, and I figured everyone would think I was crazy. And I set them down there, and they were all gone by ten o'clock! A light bulb went off in my head, you know. And I started bringing that many as soon as I could, every week. . . . Then when I got older I cut out a lot of that [other] stuff. I knew it would still sell, but I had to cut down on labor.

Wise developed the gladiolas into a unique offering for the Bloomington market. Other vendors grow a few glads, but he has stuck with them long enough to fine-tune his cultivation. He now plants successive crops so that he gets both earlier and later cuttings than are usually available in the area. He says, "I got so I can plant the first week in April, six hundred every week until the first week in July. I planted twelve hundred the first week of July—I should have had two thousand. See, I'm about out now. [Next year,] I'll plant more the first week of July. I thought those twelve hundred would last me clear through till frost. But they're not going to. Unless we have an early frost. . . . I don't care about that frost!" Wise attends for the income, clearly, but he takes pleasure in the trade: "I enjoy meeting all these people, coming and talking to everybody and everything. And when I get home, I even have a little money to spend."

The Virtue of Necessity

Even at a producer-vendor market, not everyone cultivates what they sell from their stand. Some vendors gather wild bittersweet vine with its orange and red berries in the fall, pull grapevines from the treetops and make them into wreaths, or put a boat out on a pond and gather lotus flowers. Wild mushrooms—morels

in the spring, chanterelles in the summer, the occasional chicken-of-the-woods or hen-of-the-woods—are popular finds in southern Indiana. Native tree fruits like persimmons and pawpaws and nuts like black walnuts and butternuts also find their way to the market.

Tracy Branam is one of the wild-gatherers.[22] He grew up in the woods of south central Indiana where his family "goes back about four or five or six generations. We lost count. My mother's family actually goes even further back in Owen County. It's a very local kind of family roots." When he was growing up, his father taught him to harvest the bounty of the woods to supplement their table. Now a research scientist with the Indiana Geological Survey, Branam gathers local wild foods to take to market, mostly as a way to share what he knows about the native plants and forests of the area. He says, "I grew up living in the wilds of Indiana most of my life. . . . I lived in the woods. I grew up on hickory nuts and walnuts. You know, we could not afford the more expensive nuts, so we ate the native nuts. And I just became accustomed to them and learned that they are really better for you anyway. They have a lot more nutritional value. It takes a little bit of extra work actually [to] get them, but it's worth it."

Branam brings the eye of a scientist to his home country, seeing strengths in the wild varieties. And he always takes the opportunity to educate customers:

> My training is in analytical, scientific observation, so I started researching the background of these things. I wanted to answer questions myself. I thought, I want to know more about this. So I started doing research and ended up finding out more and more about all these different things. I've done that since about 1979. . . .
>
> The native species, the native varieties have a stronger flavor and are resistant to a lot of the diseases. And you don't have to spray them—pesticide free. You don't have to worry about the flavor being hybridized out. So that's why I like the native things—for those reasons: better flavor and you don't have to worry about all the diseases. . . . The persimmons, the pawpaws, all of that, they have a unique flavor that does take some getting used to. But once you do, you can't get away from them.

Like many wild-gatherers, Branam enjoys the hunt as much as the money he earns from it. He says, "You get to clear your mind, when you go out in the wild to gather things. You get the exercise, and you get fresh air, and it feels right to just be able to go out and gather things in the wild. It's almost like Christmas. You go out and you find a tree that's loaded with nuts. Or you find a pawpaw tree that's just covered or you go out and find wild mushrooms. It's just a real treat. It's where I get my thrills."

Branam often teams up with one of his children at market to give them a little business experience. In this way, he is like many others who say a top reason for selling through a farmers' market is to create a "learning experience for children."[23] The Bloomington market has always had its share of children and grandchildren helping behind the scenes and at the family stand. An Amish farmer says, "We wouldn't be here if they didn't help us, our children." And the Simmons family has teenagers who, in the heaviest part of the season, would each operate their own stand, stocking, handling money, and conversing with customers. Like many parents, Branam has involved his children in all aspects of market as a form of business and social education:

> This is a good atmosphere. I like the variety of people. And my daughters are usually with me. I've wanted them to come learn marketing and business, and at the same time learn the different cultures that you encounter from people from all over the world who come here. I was talking to a couple who bought some persimmons from me that was from Bulgaria. So it's really neat, the different people I talked to. . . . I got into an argument with a guy from Australia because he swears up and down that my pawpaws are not pawpaws. Well, that's because in Australia they have a different fruit. It is a papaya type that they call a pawpaw. And I keep telling him that that's not a real pawpaw, but he insisted it was. We just let it go at that!

And the education that Branam hopes to bestow on his children goes beyond giving them business skills and a knowledge of the wider world. It is also a way for him to convey a sense of rootedness to them, to pass on to them something intangible but of infinite value that comes to them from being themselves locally grown: "They're learning about all the native things in Indiana that you can live off of. So they're learning about the wild trees, the wild edibles that you can live off of, and how the Indians lived before them and the pioneers. It's sort of getting in touch with their roots, their heritage."

That kind of knowledge he would like to share with his customers as well. He says, "My whole goal is to educate people about the things they can find" and that hinges on an understanding of how things connect to each other, how they are part of larger systems. According to Branam, people understand little about even those things they value highly. For example, he sells the prized morel mushrooms at market. They are a delicacy in the area, appearing only for a few weeks in the spring in seemingly unpredictable places. Everyone has a theory about where to find them, near dead elm trees, among mayapples, under pines. But mostly they remain elusive. It's not unusual to hunt morels for hours and come home with an empty bag. A spring season that is a little too dry or too cold or that warms up too quickly can make these mushrooms even scarcer.

Branam laments that people know far too little about mushrooms because they know far too little about how the whole ecosystem fits together. Fungi and plants are all integral pieces in a large, complex system. To understand wild foods, he says,

> You have to know a lot about the hydrology of the land. You have to know the runoff of the land, the surface features, and where the soil moisture is retained a lot and where it dries out because that is where you find the different varieties of trees. Some trees, like the butternuts, they kind of like water but they don't want to be soaked. And of course, you know pawpaws like the understory, but they like a moist understory not a totally soaked one. They like it dry.
>
> And it's very important for mushrooms—hydrology—especially morels and chanterelles. . . . I gave a talk at the Geological Survey I called the geology of mushroom hunting. Well, people thought I was going to talk about rocks and mushrooms. But what I really talked about was the hydrology and about how the trees are found in certain hydrologic regions, and mushrooms, since they have certain relationships to trees, would then be found in these areas. And elm trees, which morels are also associated with, and river banks. . . .
>
> I've been hunting morels since I was five years old. . . . I'm actually on a life quest. This is a unique story for me. Most people when they go out they are just interested in finding any morels [at all]. My very first time, we found 15 pounds under one tree. I've never seen so many. I mean, they were everywhere. I've been on a quest to try and repeat that. I've spent my entire life trying to find that same kind of scenario again. I haven't yet. It's haunted me ever since because I still have in my mind the image of all these mushrooms, everywhere, as far as you can see. And I have not come across that ever again. I've seen some impressive ones. I've come across a 5–6 pound finding with big, big bright yellow ones just standing up, but it just wasn't— It was exciting, but it just wasn't the same. And I've heard stories of people still finding those big ones, but I haven't yet, so I'm still looking. . . .
>
> [Mushrooms are] actually being over-harvested. And the land is changing the hydrology, the development of the land is changing it. When you timber an area, you remove a lot of the ability of that land to hold moisture, so it dries out rapidly, and you don't get the mushrooms you used to get. It dries out too fast.
>
> So a forest like that, a managed forest, is going to ruin the mushroom harvest. I hate to get on a political thing here, but when they talk about managing forests, they don't mean to help a forest overall. They mean a healthy timber forest. If they would just say that, that would be fine because that's

Bloomington

what they're managing it for, for a timber harvest. They're not managing it for an ecosystem because I've seen what they've done, and the trees that grow, when they cut them out, grow too close together for anything to properly enjoy the environment and live there. . . . The hardest hit are the mushrooms. It really hurts the mushrooms.

Farmers work much alone, so the weekly trip to market can figure large in their lives. Love affairs and marriages can begin in what one vendor calls the "good dating pool" that the larger market community affords; and news of the world small and large circulates there.[24] Growers bring much of the intensity that allows them to succeed as growers with them to the market. Silent types, athletes, scientists of formal or informal training, loners, family-fanatics or -exiles, they are, if by this activity alone, slightly out of step with the larger culture. Yet they can gain a kind of status at the market, becoming teachers, experts with advice for backyard gardeners.[25] The markets give farmers access—to ideas, to companionship, to income—allowing them to do what they could not as individuals. They incubate farmers' businesses and their relationship with the land. The founder of the San Francisco farmers' market said in the 1940s that "the farmer is the world's greatest gambler."[26] Of course, the secret is that the more a grower knows the better his or her odds will be. Market farmers help the rest of the community place a few good bets.

Customer   *Bloomington*

6. Market Generations_____

> There were old beat-up pickup trucks and old farmers in their
> work clothes. It always seemed that we went really, really
> early. Seems like you went on a mission. You were there to
> grab those eggs and the very best stuff. And you went early. It
> seemed like the sun was just coming up, and you were freezing.
> [Attending the market now] is a much more casual experience.
> There's no pain involved.
>
> —DAN COOPER, market customer, on attending as a child
> with his grandmother

Farmers' markets carry on traditions and push toward an ever-
emerging future. When J. D. Grove talks about how she "wants to
go back" to work the farmland of her great, great, great grandfather in Greencastle, Indiana, she talks about doing so "in a new
way" that uses the wisdom of earlier generations along with her
own contemporary sense of the right way to farm and to live.[1] She
describes her approach as "going back as a way of looking at the
future." Farmers' markets figure large in the future she envisions.
She anticipates that selling at markets in Greencastle or Bloomington or Indianapolis will be the best way to sustain a life on the
land, reaching customers with the freshest-possible produce and
flowers at direct-market prices.

The special connection that farmers' markets have to food
and place, tradition and promise mean that they evoke something
of the old even while they partake of contemporary tasks. Folk-
lorist Henry Glassie defines history as "a canny series of recursive
acts, of little revivals, as people go back to go forward."[2] Society
moves into the future, he says, only as it simultaneously references
the past. At a farmers' market, the past, the present, and inklings
of futures stand side by side. In Bloomington, morris dancers keep
alive a May pole dance and vendors in old dress grind corn and
wheat with a noisy steam-powered mill. Meanwhile, Amish and
Mennonite vendors sound chords of a different time even as they
find their place in the milieu of today, some negotiating the world

with cell phones, trucks with drivers, and savvy business practices. Old ways resonate in leaf-covered goat cheeses and unbrushed wool fleece even as they coincide with iPods, face tattoos, and spandex bike shorts. Markets stand in this cusp. Not wholly nostalgic nor an unrooted vision of the future, they instead enact a going back to go forward. They straddle the diverse directions participants come from and the multitude of directions they head off in.

Vendors and customers who discuss the farmers' market and how their lives intersect with the market reflect on the past in order to tell stories of the present and future. "I can remember, because I'm close to sixty, I can remember when I was growing up we used to have butterflies all the time," is how Cecilia Hartfield prefaces comments about how much she is looking forward to her buddleia (butterfly) bush in the coming year.[3] In many market stories, the market plays a role in bridging the past and the future, helping people to create continuity across generations.

Inheritance

Dan and Tom Weber inherited the family tradition of maple sugaring about forty years ago. Their family's sugaring in Vigo County in south central Indiana follows a regional practice established long ago, Dan says, by Native Americans who processed maple sap into sugar for easy handling. The concentrated source of energy provided a boon at the end of a long winter. Settlers, too, learned to tap the trees. According to Weber, in Indiana's early years:

> *Everybody made maple syrup who was a farmer, just about. If you were a farmer, you didn't have anything to do in January, February, and March. If you had some maple trees, it was an easy way to make some money. You're not doing anything else.*
>
> *There was a camp as recently as five years ago less than a couple of hundred yards from where our camp is now. A guy named Cornbread Burns ran it for eighty years. Then his son-in-law ran it for a while. It was a real cute kind of rig. You couldn't stand up in the sugar house. He had the wood stacked on the side. It worked! It worked. It was him and his wife. They'd sit over there, and they'd drop eggs in the boiling syrup and poach them. . . . They were good that way.*
>
> *There was a lot of syrup made in Indiana back in the old*

days. Most farmers at the turn of the century and maybe on into the '20s, '30s, and '40s made at least a little bit. Because they were farming ten acres or twenty acres, and they had maybe ten pigs and twenty cows. You could feed them by eight o'clock in the morning, and then what are you going to do all day? . . . I would imagine that something like half of all little farms had a little bit of a maple syrup operation. Well, sugar was more expensive in relation to syrup than it is now.

A good stand of maples meant a valuable asset that was more quickly renewable than walnuts or oaks that were typically cut down to harvest the timber.

At the family's maple sugar camp, the brothers learned how to distill the sap, and they also learned how to become part of the community into which they had been born, though not without some false starts. The operation requires tapping leafless, seemingly dormant trees in the dead of winter. When the trees are ready, just as the sap begins to rise in the trunks, the taps divert a portion into plastic tubing that feeds by gravity into large containers. The sap is collected at a sugar camp where it is then boiled down to concentrate the sugar. The result, as most people know, is sweet golden syrup. Says Dan:

When I was ten years old, my great-uncle, he had twenty-six acres, and he had about a hundred trees on it, and he had a little building that was his camp. And he called it the Hideous Hideout. So he said, you boys want to go out to the camp? And we said, sure. We didn't burn anything down, but we made real bad syrup. We used a storage barrel, about a 200-gallon wooden stave barrel that we got from Doxsee Foods, and it had been used to ship olives from Italy. We rinsed it out real good: salty, olive-flavored syrup. We worked harder on that than anything in our entire lives, times three. And we got, like, two quarts of dark stuff. And then we got it done and got it home and said, come on, Mom, let's have pancakes. She said, this is terrible!

Lesson number one: When you're concentrating something sixty or seventy to one, you can't have salty olive flavor. It was worth its weight in gold as a lesson. No, you can't do that.

Those few weeks a year working the sugar camp still stand apart in Dan Weber's mind from other more ordinary childhood experiences. Being at the Hideout and suffering the trials of the enterprise bonded him to the practice of sugaring. He says,

It's just like something that gets in your blood. . . . Just going out there. It was the first time I was ever outside in February all night. The shack had gaps between the boards that big, so it was essentially like sleeping outside. And the experience of being with my brother in a real cold place with not very good clothing and lying on the shelves that were along the walls, trying to get to sleep and freezing to death and finally giving up and sitting sort of in close to the fire. And it was like that night lasted about thirty days.

Since then, except for a hiatus in their twenties, the Weber brothers have made maple syrup. Along with some extra cash and a reason to get up on Saturday mornings, syrup vending has given them license for all manner of zaniness at the farmers' market. There, the Weber brothers, brother-in-law Dick, and friend John have a rollicking time ribbing each other and joshing the customers, juggling, sneaking cigarettes, and generally carrying on. Their stand is a modest affair, a small card table with jars of syrup and a clutter of handmade cardboard signs proclaiming "World's Best Beans" and displaying the latest clean drug test that Tom needs for his heavy equipment operator's license. To customers they proffer a plate of small sample cups of syrup and during the summer months push Dan's green beans. In years when the trees don't provide much sap, Tom sells yearling ginkgo trees in pots ("guaranteed male") and inedible buckeye nuts for 25¢ apiece to provide visual interest and stretch out the syrup. They try to bring something most weeks, even the preposterous, because the spaces at market are allotted on a seniority system that is based on the number of days vendors sell. Neither of the Weber brothers relies on maple syrup for his primary income. For Tom, a heavy equipment operator, February is a slow month, and he may defer jobs until after the sugaring season. Dan is a lawyer in Vigo County and has been known to schedule proceedings around the running of the sap, exercising what he refers to as his special "exclusionary period." Clearly, though, they both enjoy the market.

Pints of syrup go for $11.95 each, and one year each Mason jar on the card table had a nickel for change on its lid. That convenient place to store change developed into a betting game among nearby vendors and a few customers. Every morning, they put a dollar into a pot and wrote a number on a secreted piece of paper that made their guesses at how many times that day customers would ask what the nickels were for. Each time a customer asked, the nearest maple syrup man would triumphantly ring a bell and make a mark on a tally sheet. At the end of the day, whoever had guessed the correct number of nickel questions won the pot, with a tie carrying the game into the following week. At one point that year, the pot rose to $80. Some customers looked a little abashed when a simple question was answered with enthusiastic banging on a bell and cheers and moans from the back of the stand. But most took the hoopla good-naturedly. They saw they were the butt of a joke, suddenly rubes out of their element, but most willingly enough suffered that temporary reversal.

For Weber, the market marks not only who is in-the-know and who is not, but also how far he and his brother have come in their own understanding of maple sugaring. They learned syrup making nearly forty years ago following the lead of their grandfather's generation, but since then they have improved on the operation immensely:

> My great-uncle just kind of gave us a quick lesson, I suppose. I can't even remember [how I learned to make maple syrup]. He had a flat pan about this wide, about six, eight feet long. It was the crudest possible method. And he just sat it on some bricks he had in this building. He just built a fire under it, and he had a chimney. I mean, it was really crude. And then you had to boil it, boil it, boil it, and hold it up and kind of pour it off the corner into a jar. It would spill! So it was much more difficult for us to make one or two quarts of really horrible syrup then than it is to make a hundred and fifty gallons now.

Weber's stories about the early days that he and his brother Tom made syrup frequently mention how hard and inefficient the work was and how mediocre the product was. They are, in essence, stories he tells on himself, self-deprecating but offered to show by contrast how well the business runs now.

Sometimes the comparison of quality of the syrup and the effort expended in making it shows best against others and how they operate. Weber tells a story about going with his brother to New England to see the renowned maple sugaring operations there:

> One year they burned our barn down, in 1990. They burned it down on Easter Sunday morning in 1990. So the next year we

Bloomington

are out of business, and Tom and I decided, OK, if we're going to be able to do this all over again, let's do it right. This will be the perfect year since we are not going to make any [syrup]. We took a week or nine days off, and he and I just drove out to Ohio, Pennsylvania, New York, Vermont, New Hampshire, and a little bit into Massachusetts. We just drove around in March and April. It was their season. It's a little later there. And we'd get on the smallest road we could find, and when we saw some steam going up, we pull up, and say, Hey guys! You know, Are you using buckets or what? We're from Indiana, what should we do?

What we saw mostly was the wrong way to do it. They had pans that were leaking and rats running around. They were trying to make bigger amounts, but they weren't making good syrup. We came back and said, Here's how we want to design the camp. For example, the guys that were making syrup that would let us have a taste that were using oil burners: the smell was in the syrup. You can't keep it out. . . . [We decided,] we're going to do it the hard way with wood. Even if there is a little tiny bit of wood smoke flavor in the syrup, at least it's a normal, natural smell. That was one of about fifteen things we realized. That and how to market it.

Playing on their outsider status as Hoosiers, knowing that the New Englanders would mistake them as newcomers in what that region likes to consider a proprietary activity, the Webers were able to gather useful ideas and discard poor practices. Most importantly, they confirmed that the business would be more profitable if they retailed their products themselves rather than selling to a wholesaler. They saw that the syrup operations they visited were selling by the barrel to wholesalers, getting a couple of hundred dollars for a barrel "after doing the hard part," rather than packaging and selling it themselves to make many times more.

Not long after that, they found the Bloomington farmers' market. There they have built a customer base eager for homegrown syrup and willing to pay the going price for it. Like many of the farmers' market vendors, they found that a little more work adding value to a product yielded quite a bit more profit in the retail price.

Syrup has become a passion for them, which is a good thing because maple sugaring is a steward's enterprise. Like field farming, this crop depends on natural rhythms, climate, and weather for its viability. It also requires long patience with the trees, as they grow to appropriate size and as they come slowly back to life late each winter. A sort of alchemy, syrup making calls for old knowledge of gravity, fire, and distillation to coax ordinary sap into sweet gold. The tough outdoor working conditions and the further transformation of exchanging glass jars of syrup and the nearly inedible "moople" byproduct for greenbacks are signs of a social alchemy these brothers work at the farmers' market. Their games, jokes, and banter all contribute to the transformation. Weber's sugaring stories, too, are all about alchemy, as something ordinary or less than valuable is always being transformed into something miraculous: the dormant season into the production of food, winter idleness into work, sap into syrup, boys into success-ful sugar men.

Looking for the Future in the Past

Dan Cooper is a long-time market-goer who allots part of most Saturday mornings to visit at the vending stand of a friend he has known for decades.[4] He is not a big spender, having his own intensive vegetable garden at home. But he enjoys the market experience and looks forward each week, as he puts it, to "taking up station with the lads." From that vantage point, he enjoys camaraderie and the myriad market goings-on. The stories Cooper tells suggest that he especially values the connections that the market allows him to make and the bridges it allows him to build across past, present, and future—from his family history and childhood, through his relationships with his friends and con-temporaries, and, speculatively, into the future.

Cooper first frequented the Bloomington market some 25 years ago while a university student. After graduation, he lived for many years in San Francisco where he did not regularly shop at a market and where, coincidentally or not, he did not feel like he was much a part of a community. After he returned to Bloom-ington in the 1990s, he immediately reacquainted himself with the market. He says returning to the market was "something that needed to be done" to give him a sense of place and "more connec-tion to the land." Like many customers he comes to the market be-cause, as Wendell Berry says, he knows "that things connect—that farming, for example, is connected to nature, and food to farming, and health to food—and they want to preserve the connections."[5]

Greene County

Cooper says succinctly that, through the farmers' market experience, he feels "connected to the process" of life. Formerly a professional illustrator, Cooper continues to draw and paint regularly and so recognizes the beauty of the market: "Market is a very rich visual experience. All the produce and plants, mixed in with all the people and activity is very engaging. All the colors and shapes and sounds. That's pretty rewarding for me."

The market allows him to connect, also, to his family roots and the memories he holds of his childhood and his grandparents. Like many Americans, Cooper's immediate family did not farm, though his grandparents farmed for much of their lives. As a child, he attended markets in Middletown, Ohio, with his grandmother. He describes going to the market at the local municipal parking lot with her as a ritual of arriving early in adverse weather to get the pick of the crop. The physical challenges and sense of a "mission," similar to what Dan Weber describes, offer elements of initiation. Cooper's memory of the market as between times, "really, really early" as the sun rose, marks it as special and potentially transformative. As a child, he got a glimpse of the world of men there. And now a man, he wants the market to help him look forward into the future.

Cooper, like many in the baby boom generation, seeks models for the possibilities for growing older as a man. As he himself ages, he feels the dwindling of the generations ahead of him. He says he misses the early days of the Bloomington market and the connections to people of other times and other values. He laments what another customer calls the market's "gentrification" over time, feeling that some of his ability to "connect" through the market has worn off in the "professionalization" it has gained through thirty years of operation.[6] In earlier days, he says,

> There was an old guy that sold his transplants out of flats. He would just tear them out of there. I like that. I like that real, casual, utilitarian aspect to it. You know, everything put in a little cup just doesn't have the same appeal to me as that old guy with his flats of tomato starts. You know, "How many do you want?" And he would grab a big wad full of them. That feels a little more connected to the process.
>
> Now, I don't think most people would care about [that, and in] the end it might put them off a little bit. There's an aspect of commercial production, prepackaging that we see in all of our stores that also affects this market. So everything is

Bloomington

neatly and tightly bundled, and that tends to isolate one from the product and from the experience. Part of the reason we go to farmers' markets is because they do give you more connection to the land and the food. And when you package anything off really nicely, it isolates you. Now it's just a product.

Creeping commercialism threatens to obscure, for Cooper, the more direct, visceral experience that he seeks at farmers' markets. He recognizes the homogenization of commercial culture that "tends to isolate" customer from product, customer from experience, and customer from customer.[7] Indeed, large commercial ventures depend on those qualities as much as on standardization and mass production. In shopping malls, racks of seasonally changing merchandise create the discomfited feeling of being left out of a desirable community while simultaneously offering the means for buying one's way back in. We are especially vulnerable to their allure when social networks and stable communities break down.[8] While perhaps threatened with the easy community membership that can be purchased through fashionable trends, the folksy version of private consumption that occurs in the context of farmers' markets is, at base, optional to membership. Free and open, farmers' markets require no purchase to participate. Cooper rarely buys anything, and he still fully partakes in the non-commercial aspects of the market:

People watching is great fun. Of course it's always nice to admire all the attractive women. It just makes you happy to be alive. I was just commenting about how it is to see a young woman go by with her children. And there [is] something very attractive about that. It's just nice. A very pleasant experience.

The market's very uplifting. What's the French term? Joie de vivre. That's probably my biggest sensation about coming here. Market is something to look forward to. Even if you don't spend a dime, you feel like you've had a worthy experience.

He values the contemporary community of the market—it's "a good place to connect with people, see what happened last week"—while he also appreciates the connections it gives him to earlier times and future possibilities.

When Cooper started attending twenty-five years ago, the market was held in a small city park on Third Street where he remembers old farmers setting out their goods. He misses them

Bloomington

now, in part because his own age has advanced and he would be hard pressed to find someone actively farming who is more than ten or twenty years older than he is now:

> *If you were on the parking lot you sold out of the back of your truck. Then there was another aisle and park side where you had to bring everything in. In earlier days it had a, what would you call it, less professional quality than it does now. As people get better at it, the quality goes up. Their presentation improves. How they deal with their customers generally improves.*
>
> *But there's something nice about an old farmer in his overalls and seed cap selling you tomatoes. And that's not here anymore. We were just saying about the missing older generation. I look around here today and there aren't any whiteheads around. And that's a loss because you get to know them and they are always full of stories. And I like those stories. I used to listen to them from all my great aunts and uncles and my grandparents. You get the same flavor from these old farmers. So their absence is a loss.*
>
> *We're getting close to that category. . . . I'll be sixty in eight years. The old guys, the ones who can tell you about Bloomington in—during the Depression, things like that. During the war. But all those guys are getting really ancient, near the ends of their lives. . . . I wonder about the old guys because Jeff and I aren't quite in that category and we also don't have the early connection to Bloomington. So that's a segment of history that's lost. They can tell you about running through the back alleys of Bloomington when they were 13. It's just not in our experience. . . . I have the experience of dealing with produce certainly. I have some experience in dealing with my relatives. I know their stories. But if some kid came up to me and started asking me about, well, What was it like in Bloomington? You know, I can't tell you what it was like in Bloomington.*

What does it mean to grow old without having an earlier generation as guide or a younger generation that could listen and remember? In times of small and transient families, close connections and models are apt to be far away if not entirely missing. Cooper tried and then turned away from "career and all that . . . the models I'd been brought up on. It takes a long time to find your own way and unlearn a bunch of stuff." He welcomes the company of his peers, while at the same time missing models for growing older. The farmers' market, straddling past and future, provides one place ripe for reflection upon this predicament.

Bloomington

Emerging Traditions

Neither Amalia nor Steve Krecik had ever made maple syrup before they bought one hundred heavily wooded acres in Jackson County, Indiana.[9] But through trial and error and some help from neighbors they learned, literally, to tap that asset of their land.

Steve grew up in heavily populated Lake County in northern Indiana where there are few trees. He knew from family camping trips as a child, however, that some people "wore Smoky the Bear patches and got paid to go on vacation." Now a forester by trade, he never thought of making syrup until one winter when he looked around at all the maple trees on their new land.

Amalia grew up in the big Indonesian city of Jakarta, where she "had no exposure whatsoever to agriculture." She met Steve when they both worked for two years on a telecommunications project in Borneo. When that project finished, "we moved here to the middle of nowhere in Indiana," she says. The transition was significant. The first night that she arrived, she was frightened by the sounds of coon hunters and their dogs hunting nearby: "It was scary! In Jakarta, if there's a gunshot, somebody's dead."

She found work at a health insurance company and soon settled in. Despite long hours working at her job and on the farm, she says: "This is a nice life, the farming part. A really nice life. I learned it, and I love it. It's beautiful. The people are nice. The peacefulness I like. We live on property where we don't have close neighbors. When you go outside, you hear the birds."

It took a while to learn the farming part, however. Amalia says that she could not do much when Steve first began tapping the trees because she had so recently come from the much warmer climes of Indonesia: "I had to adjust myself for the winters here. . . . The first two years, I didn't even come outside to help him. He was doing everything by himself. I couldn't handle going out to stand in the cold winter! I would just stay in the house and look out the window."

She says now, "The last two years, I've been helping. . . . It's a pretty simple job. It's just tapping and gathering and adding the firewood. It's just a lot of time and a lot of work." Still, they both laugh at the number of times they burned the syrup just before it was finished boiling. Eventually, they say, "We learned."

Bloomington

Although they met in the South Pacific, they now call Indiana home. In the Bloomington community, a forty-five-minute drive from their land, they find a customer base that appreciates the unusual varieties and Asian vegetables that they want to grow. From the vendors they learn growing and marketing techniques. The market experience, Steve says, "is inspiring and builds on itself." Their land now hosts two thousand blueberry bushes, and they hunt wild ginseng in the woods to sell at market. They are ready to move into a new house custom built for them and expect their first child around maple sugaring time. The little one should be ready to accompany them to market when the season begins, having inherited the tradition by birthright.

"So finally," Amalia says, "things have fallen into place."

As a site for making new traditions and carrying on established ones, the farmers' market provides a sense of constancy and expectation for both vendors and customers. Inevitably, past and future, tradition and change reference each other—the pristine quality of today's pre-washed market produce in tidy displays implicates earlier days of dusty potatoes heaped in the back of a truck or tomato plants scooped roughly out of a crowded flat. This year's golden maple syrup evokes stories of wonderful syrup-poached eggs of olden times. Traditional families serve as contrast for newer configurations. This circling around of history provides firm ground from which to reflect on the "options and constraints of human possibility."[10]

Top: *Greene County*
Bottom: *Bloomington*

Part 3. Harvests

Farmers' markets are about harvests. Food makes up one harvest, and social exchange, entertainment, discovery, friendship, and an occasional wedding form a few of the others. Markets also, in their presentation of many of the myriad ways of living, broach a harvest of possibilities for people as they make their own distinct choices, as individuals and as members of groups. And insofar as they point out options, markets help point to constraints. The stories that emerge here illustrate a few creative and alternative paths that market participants have started down. Their revised relationships to food, community, and the environment test the potential for individual and collective action to make a difference.

Vendor Notes _____

Last week was the biggest farmers' market of the year. The cockscomb is in full color—rose, fuchsia, burgundy, yellow, gold, and orange, plumed and crested, large fasciated crests like roman topknots, and giant brainy rounds. The sunflowers came out small but have rebounded from deer damage better than we expected. The broomcorn blackens beautifully. The blues in ageratum, spirea, and trachelium vibrate against the red cockscomb. The weather on Saturday was clear and not too hot, with a pleasant breeze. So the bumper market we expected really did come to pass. Our stand was radiant, and people stopped to photograph family members in front of the baskets of mixed bouquets. Those outfitted with zoom lenses and bulky bags leaned in for close-ups. Other stands were glorious with peaches, apples, tomatoes, and cucumbers, fruits of late summer in Indiana. We had our year's highest take. Lots of give-aways, too.

We have heard about your grandmother's bleeding hearts and the way the butterflies have come back into your garden. We know the joke about your brown thumb. We see how your children have grown and that you're old now like your parents used to be. We have known you through our own strength and now into latter days. We can tell you more about this watermelon or honey batch or coreopsis than you have time to hear. Your activity, the pace of your life, the colors of your world play out for us as we, no doubt, gray in your eyes, lean more, bend less, tell our repetitive stories. After thirty years of market, the old vendors are ancient and we who were the younger ones are now old. Some have died. Some are tired or have lost the husband, the wife, or the spark that made the market worth it.

The market is thinner today. Not noticeable to some, perhaps, but more people are going home early. The corn man didn't come at all. The big growers are back down to one stand. It was a terrible year for tomatoes—far too dry through much of the summer then the tremendous rains in mid-August. Heavy fogs in September just about finished them off with molds and other diseases. The heat, unrelenting even now into the second week of September, fools some of the customers. They are shocked that the corn is gone or that the basil will end soon.

We knew, during the cutting a week ago Thursday, that the season had peaked. The full-on color does not deceive us any more. Brown lies just underneath, the walnut leaves drop steadily, a yellow tinge shadows the willows, and hints of orange tell of fall in the sassafras. The plants are giving out, the dogwoods are decidedly red, and the walnuts, always shockingly early, have lost nearly all their leaves. This is fall. We can warm the planet a few degrees and spread around chemicals that boost life or maybe hasten its end, but the earth, so far, moves along its track unhindered. The novice growers look shocked and embarrassed that their gardens are tapped out, but really it comes at about the right time. Fall is now.

Here we are at the start of the cold. Into the market bag goes a wool hat, an extra shirt, some socks. The dried flowers are ready, but we'll hold off bringing them until the fresh are gone. And that will be soon. September 21st (yes, September 21st, we must repeat to customers) is our average frost date. So frost could come any time. Any time. A big wind knocked over the broomcorn and the deluge that followed spread a lot of disease. We're about done here. How long, anyway, can we expect to go on?

Vendors   *Bloomington*

7. New Farms, New Farmers_____

For farmers' market vendors, those few hours a week in the public eye can make or break the viability of the home-grown business, the ability to remain on the land, and the possibility of dreaming and testing alternative visions of life. Not every would-be farmers' market grower will stick it out and not every market vendor envisioned that particular weekly trek as part of the bargain. Many farmers prefer solitude, making them well suited to that life, finding their animals and the quiet of their growing things preferable to the noise of people. Many growers settle for a lower income rather than spend more time interacting with potential buyers or tethering themselves to "desk work." How many people dream of living on the land, providing for themselves and their loved ones from its fruits? Which of them make the move to new territory? What makes those who persist stay? How do individuals adapt when the dream meets reality? How do they weigh lifestyle, income, inclination, and commitment? Whether they channel their passion and drive into new outlets or more singlemindedly adhere to their plans, all test the possibilities in interesting ways.

Nationally, midsized farms are dwindling while the number of farms under one hundred acres grows, 60 percent of all farms sell less than $10,000 annually and 80 percent sell less than $50,000. Suffice it to say, hardly anyone is getting rich off farming. And few are inheriting the profession from their parents. Instead, a breed that author Gene Logsdon calls the "ramparts people" populate the land.[1] As he describes them, they live at the edges of society where they can expand and protect its mainstream. They explore the alternatives, reminding people of what they would forget or hailing what appears off on the horizon. One can debate whether they make up backwater or the leading edge of a new wave. We would argue here that their revisiting of old notions and imaginings of new ones help to keep us all afloat.

The trying on of dreams, that ducking in and ducking back from compelling but less-than-familiar possibilities, offers much to how individuals make up their lives. Even short-lived experience with an intense commitment to the land, even small-scale acts of contrariness can resonate through a lifetime and, potentially, with collectivity, from there through the culture. The exchange that happens at a farmers' market has larger ramifications than coins for cucumbers. Markets help to metamorphose imaginings into possibilities. New growers are envisioning new ways of being in the community and on the land.

Dreams

The increasing number of small farms reverses a population trend that had been depleting rural communities for much of the twentieth century. A Bloomington vendor and the son of a large-scale farmer notes that the "trend is starting to reverse not so much in agribusiness land but in places like this where the economy really isn't based on agriculture, where people have an opportunity to be a part-time farmer. Where, you know, you're working nine to five but in order to have some *connection*—say, if you're a computer jock or something—you turn to farming."[2]

Pam Kinnaman is one of those who moved away from town life.[3] She says she had "always, since I was a little girl," wanted to live on a farm. She grew up in rural New Jersey, in an area where other families, though not her own, lived on farms and kept animals. But it was not until much later that she would realize that dream: "It took until I was 50 years old to get it, to fulfill that vision." The specifics came clear to her, however, only when she and her husband Tim were in the process of moving to Indiana from Florida:

> *Tim was already in Indiana working, and I was still in Florida working. I knew I wanted a farm. I knew I wanted a farm, and I knew I wanted farm critters, but I didn't know exactly what yet. And I really wanted something that I didn't have to kill, my pets.*

So I was watching one of those early morning news shows while I was getting ready for work, and they had a woman on there that was an investment banker or something from New York and dropped all that out of her life and ended up buying a farm and getting sheep and learned to spin and weave and was making afghans and selling them for an extraordinary amount of money. And I thought, I can do that! And that's how I thought of sheep.

They purchased a small farmstead in Greene County, Indiana, near Bloomington, dubbed it Wee Sheep Farm, and began "figuring things out."

Kinnaman says she planned to retire immediately from the wage world to focus on the farm. Indeed, Department of Agriculture statistics show that more than a quarter of active farm operators are age 60 or older—compared with only 13 percent of the overall workforce. Some farmers extend their working years into their late sixties and the rest begin farming late in life.[4] Not yet 60, Pam Kinnaman, if she continues with sheep farming, would straddle those groups. Her scheme did not unfold as neatly nor as quickly as she hoped, however, because she and her husband, a postal worker, suffered a series of illnesses. She says, "We had a slow start, but we're getting there." After her own health rebounded, she found work as the director of a not-for-profit in Greene County, but she continued to learn about raising her Shetland sheep, processing their wool, and marketing the farm's products. Everything was new and much of it difficult; "It's been trial and error on things," she said.

After four years of building her herd up to thirty-four head, Kinnaman believes the farm has survived its difficult launch. That means, however, that soon the business will have to earn its own keep, and how to do that is the conundrum. She enjoys vending at the Bloomington market and hopes it will have a place, perhaps along with an internet site, in making her business viable: "We've got to get out there with this [business] or it's not going to do anything." On occasion she carries a spinning wheel, fleece, and yarn to the market in hopes that the novelty will draw people into her stand: "Even if you don't make any money, it's still a nice morning, sitting out here and enjoying the crowds, the atmosphere, and the music. I wish I could make money on just the demonstration part because I have fun with that." In the meantime, though, she is hoping that the relationships they are building through the farmers' market will pay off in sales months or even years later.

Kinnaman likes counting her sheep as pets and had resisted the income to be gained by selling them for their meat. But recently the financial realities forced her to reconsider: "I [now] know why meat-sheep breeders do that—because you make more money on that because you can sell the meat more regularly. . . . I am sending my first two to market tomorrow. . . . So I'm going to make about $140, and that's a lot more than I made on two pounds of wool last Saturday at $10 a pound." Kinnaman is committed to the business. Her brochure says the farm is "A Dream Come True" where she can "experience the change of seasons, beautiful spring flowers and the opportunity to have my critters." She and her husband stick with it despite cruel realities and the mystification of their family: "Our kids don't understand, but they can just *not* understand!"

Adaptations

Harvesting the meat of sheep one had hoped would be pets seems a harsh readjustment to have to make. But though their ambitions may start as dreams, farmers don't dwell in dreams long. They work hard, they make little money, their businesses are fraught with threats from disease, creditors, rain, drought, bugs, deer, and more. It's not unusual to find that a puppy you brought in to protect the chickens has taken a liking to killing them or that a goat has managed to hang itself from an electrical cord or that the remnants of a hurricane a thousand miles away have knocked a beautiful crop flat. Lore has it that highly successful, highly diversified organic farms can gross up to $25,000 per acre, compared to less than $200 for a conventional corn or soybean acre.[5] But those high-value acres are few and far between. They require good ground, good know-how, and good luck.

People may move into farming for the romance, but they quickly experience the hard and unrelenting work and the insecurity of investing all up front for a return not to come in for many months or even years. Even when people find the conditions too tenuous for their risk tolerance, they may not abandon their goals entirely. Instead, a number of would-be market gardeners rechannel their efforts to support local food and community in ways

Greene County

that better suit their talents and proclivities. Their redirected efforts can be powerful drivers to new partnerships in sustainability, bringing other resources and other ways of organizing one's time to create a good life with good food in a healthy environment.

It didn't take Art Sherwood long to learn that growing vegetables for market was not the most valuable contribution he could make to the supply and accessibility of wholesome local food in south central Indiana.[6] He and his wife, Gwen, sold produce at the Bloomington farmers' market for one year before they redirected their efforts. He says,

> *I think I got involved for idealistic reasons because I believe in local food and I believe that it's not fair that only rich people can eat well. I just don't think that if you have food that doesn't have chemicals all over it that that should be a niche product. That should be everyone's product. Because it used to be that way. . . . We've forgotten that we're supposed to eat natural stuff. Large-scale farming is what made us all forget that organic farming was what was done throughout the history of the world.*

Although he had grown up on a small farmstead in rural Wisconsin, Sherwood found that growing more food than would supply his family of four was a challenge. Moreover, fitting even a small-scale farming business into a life already brimming with a full-time job and the children's school, music lessons, and sports proved untenable. Still, he and his wife threw themselves into the task.

They relied substantially on what they could learn from books, trying to implement strategies that sounded good in theory but that came up short in practical application. Trying one organic method that has been very successful elsewhere, they mounted a chicken coop on the back of a wagon so that it could be wheeled to different places around the farm. In theory, the chickens peck around the wagon, feeding on weeds and bugs, fertilizing the ground, and developing bright, nutritious eggs that can be marketed for a premium as "free-range organic." The work for the farmer is light, simply waiting until the chickens bed down in the coop at night and shutting the door. The next morning, he wheels the wagon to a different spot to spread the benefits around. Sherwood laughs as he tells the story of his own real life experience:

A free-range chicken is a dead chicken. I'll tell you! Who are these people who free-range chickens? They must sit with shotguns outside the coop. We went through hundreds of chickens! It was terrible! We had raccoons, dogs, hawks, everything.

Okay, [we said,] lock them up!

We did all these interesting, theoretical ideas. . . .

Here's what happened. The chickens are in the cage. I come out in the morning, and one more chicken's gone. . . . There are no holes, [the predators] haven't dug underneath, nothing! All we can find is, outside the cage, the two claws and the head. Outside the cage! The body's gone, but the chicken wire's fine. I can't figure this out. So I ask everybody I can find. Finally I got an old farmer book, and I find out that raccoons will grab a chicken and pull it out piece by piece—and eat it. And that's what was going on.

And then we had the Valentine's Day massacre by weasels. There are no weasels in Indiana. How did I get a weasel? I had it all blocked off, and he somehow crawled in and killed every single chicken. It was terrible.

It's such a bloody thing being out in the country.

When things went wrong for the Sherwoods, they shifted tactics and tried again. But as relative newcomers, they had too much to learn all at once and few ready sources of help.

Part of the reason they didn't simply quit when things went wrong was that they had committed themselves to supply a community supported agriculture cooperative, known as a CSA. In these agreements, customers purchase a season's worth of groceries directly from farmers. The customers may pay in advance to provide the growers with start-up capital and to secure a share of the harvest for themselves. They then collect a grocery bag or more per week of fresh-picked produce. The contents change with the season. In May, the bag might contain mostly greens, herbs, asparagus, and perhaps free-range eggs; in July, it might have cucumbers, tomatoes, corn, and flowers; while in September, it could feature squash, apples, and potatoes. In a thin year, the customers share the risk and vagaries of the harvest, and in a plentiful year, they share in its bounty. Nationally, the number of CSAs remains relatively small at approximately two thousand.[7] But the theory seems like a win-win collaboration and CSAs are growing around the country.

Acting prudently, the Sherwoods did not form their own CSA

but joined a cooperative. The idea is that having a group of farmers benefits customers with more variety in their produce and growers with more backup so that they can focus on a few products that they do well. A crop failure by any one grower won't doom the customers to a summer of only, say, spaghetti squash. In practice, however, Sherwood found that joining a CSA did not return all he expected. Because he lives in an isolated rural area, he had to drive more than a couple of hours each week to where the grocery shares were assembled. When he figured in gas and labor, Sherwood found the business just wasn't making any money from the CSA. And toward the end of the year, when the local climate turns very dry, the crops simply started petering out: "By the end of the season, it was terrible. We were committed to the CSA to give them food. And in the end, we ended up having to buy food so *we* could eat fresh food because we were giving all our food to the CSA! . . . We said, This isn't right. Let's go back to principles. . . . Why are we doing this? We want fresh food, we want to serve our community. . . . But this doesn't make any sense." They enjoyed the festivity of the farmers' market, and they made money on their produce there, but even taken all together, the income from the farm simply did not amount to enough to make the enterprise worthwhile. Although they had ambitiously jumped into the idea of growing for market, they didn't have enough experience with the local climate or the target quantities to make the project work.

Fortunately the Sherwood family had other resources. Art's position as a business professor at Indiana State University where he studies small business development meant that they didn't rely on the market or the CSA for income. It also meant that he could not ignore the bottom line when he tallied the farm's books at the end of the first year. He believed strongly in the goal of a local food system, but he realized contributing as a grower was not the best he could do for that worthy cause.

Sherwood's academic research told him that, while the CSA did not benefit him economically, cooperation among small businesses can have powerful results. So he became involved with a new organization that seeks to make farming in the area more economically viable by helping growers work together to expand the markets and resources available to them. Originally led by the local food cooperative Bloomingfoods, which itself was founded at the same time and from impulses similar to those that launched the farmers' market, the informal gatherings became a not-for-profit called the Local Growers Guild. Much like the professional guilds of the Middle Ages, its mission is to build communication and education among farmers and buyers so that they can collaborate to build local food systems in ways each could not accomplish alone. Sherwood contributed his skills in business analysis and planning, grant writing, and education. He also helped to plan and facilitate a public forum that brought representatives from restaurants, hospitals, and schools together with farmers to discuss the merits and logistics of farm-direct food. In addition, he heads up the guild's effort to educate the public about the benefits of having each family buy just $12 worth of local food each week. That commitment, he maintains, will be a good start toward making local farming viable.

Sherwood is realistic about the challenges before the guild and local food, more broadly. He knows that the guild must develop broad-based, grassroots leadership to carry its various projects forward. For farmers, that goal presents even more of a challenge than it might for another group. The occupation calls people who prefer to operate alone, who follow their own schedules or the weather's, and who involve themselves in every facet of the business. Regular meetings in town can pose a problem. Sherwood notes that, for the growers, "Even getting customers became less of a priority once it was clear all the things that needed to be done" off the farm in order to realize their plans. Many vendors would rather spend their time doing what they love, growing plants and animals and spending their time in beautiful settings, than developing contacts, drawing up contracts, and making deliveries. They simply are not in the business to strike it rich. Sherwood also observed that some small business owners who perceive a limited customer pool may be reluctant to cooperate with their competitors. Success would mean more for all, but success is not assured. Says Sherwood, "I think some people saw this whole concept as threatening. . . . Idealism clashes with the practical business of the marketplace."

The Sherwood family no longer grows more food than they and a few friends can consume, and the production beds have been planted in raspberries as an experiential business education for the children. But they learned from their partners in the CSA and continue to enjoy those friendships. Art maintains that this new arrangement has allowed the family to move closer to their goals of connecting to and enjoying the land than they were able to during the year when they grew for market:

> *One of the American ideals, I think, is to go out and farm.*
> *That will get us close to nature and each other and everything*
> *else. And we found that in a lot of ways the opposite was true.*
> *We weren't spending time in a way that we wanted to with*
> *our kids. We weren't spending time in a way that we wanted*
> *to with each other. And we certainly weren't taking advantage*
> *of what we had worked a long time to acquire. And so we*
> *changed the plan to enjoy a little. . . . [Growing had become]*
> *an obligation versus something that you want to do.*

Not abandoning those other ideals of community and sufficiency, Sherwood now contributes his significant talents to them in more effective ways. Through the guild, he works toward making local food more available at the farmers' market and elsewhere and generally more practical and realizable: "It can't rest on a few people's shoulders forever. . . . Things get done because someone starts making it happen."

Bobbi Boos, too, worked her passion for country living into a presence at the farmers' market and then into activism beyond it.[8] As a single mother without many financial resources, however, her efforts to realize her vision have been complicated. For eight years, she worked as an employee of one of the most senior vendors at the Bloomington market. She lived in the rough-and-tumble old house on the farm as part of her compensation and enjoyed being able to walk out the back door to go to work. Her daughter was born in that house, and Boos liked being able to take her along to work and school her at home. She helped supervise activity on the farm and participated in planting, cultivating, and harvesting crops for market. Rhubarb, garlic, bamboo, herbs, and greens were their specialties. The pay was low, but she had room for her own chickens and goats, so they provided food, satisfaction, and some income. On Saturdays, Boos trucked the farm's produce to market and made the sales. Most market customers couldn't have known that all the food she sold, except for the eggs, came from a farm she did not own. In fact, other than an informal agreement with the farm's owner, Boos had no stake or security in the business at all.

Greene County

But for many years, that fact didn't matter much to Boos. She grew up in farm country in Michigan and has tried many of her adult years to establish a rural life for herself. Having little money and knowing she needed to throw in her resources with others to make a go of it, Boos years ago bought land with a friend in rural Greene County west of Bloomington. That experiment did not go well. A friend who was staying with them was prosecuted for growing marijuana, and later her land partner simply left. Bobbi tried to persevere on her own with her small child, but she felt desperately different from her rural neighbors and terribly unwelcomed by them. Her house was broken into, ransacked, and looted. Her dog was shot twice, the second time killing him. After her goats were stolen, she realized that she and her daughter were in danger. And so she left. "I don't want to *not* know my neighbors again," she says now.

In 1996, she moved into the house on the farm and began her work there. It felt like home in a rocky period. As her daughter got older, she helped with the farm tasks and learned to identify wildlife and handle money. The arrangement was a good one. But as time went by, Boos found she was unable to save any money. Nor did she have any lease, contract, or long-term agreement with the owner. Any improvements to the house, the outbuildings, or the fencing meant investing in something she didn't own. Boos tried to strike a deal with him to secure some permanent stake or profit-sharing in the business. But that was unsuccessful. When he suddenly fell ill and died, she was, just as suddenly, left with no job, no savings, no severance, and no equity in her home or the business she had worked in for nearly a decade. She was on her own again.

Rather than be deterred by these experiences, Boos tries to learn from them. She thought that moving to the country alone would never be financially or practically viable for her. Instead, the connections she established through the market are making it possible for her to buy five acres on her own on contract. She plans to build her homestead on this ground. Her ideal job at present would be to one day manage a cooperative "incubator kitchen." This would be a commercial-grade kitchen certified by the health department and available for rent at a modest fee to market growers, home gardeners, and others. It incubates in the sense that people can use it to launch small businesses with little up-front investment. There, for example, a market vendor with surplus apples could process them into more valuable pies or butters. Alternatively, a small urban gardener could use the kitchen to stretch the value of just a few extra tomatoes into premium hot sauce. Selling those higher-priced, value-added items at the summer and winter farmers' markets and to local groceries could provide a fair income to small entrepreneurs. The famous precedent is the Brown Cow yogurt company, which began selling at the Ithaca, New York, Farmers' Market in 1974. Twenty years later, they had become one of the largest regional yogurt makers in the northeast.[9] A local not-for-profit has expressed interest in the incubator kitchen idea as a way to help low-income people develop their own small businesses, and Boos can envision herself managing the kitchen and using its facilities to finance a life in the country.[10]

The challenges Boos finds to living in the country are not unique to her. Rural communities don't provide many jobs, and many rural dwellers logically turn to farming. Yet many of the challenges she faces hit women particularly hard. Nationwide, only 5 percent of all U.S. farmers were women in 1978, and twenty-five years later, their portion still made up only 13 percent. Moreover, much of that small increase in women farmers is the result of fewer male-operated farms rather than in a big change in how this high-investment, high-risk, traditionally male occupation is viewed.[11] Boos, though, hopes to help change that profile by making farming a more viable profession for all farmers, women and men. Like Art Sherwood, she has become deeply involved in the Local Growers Guild. Elected to its board in 2006, Boos sees in it the possibility for networking growers, customers, and services in ways that boost the prices farmers receive enough to keep them in business. She also recognizes that the hard work of farming becomes lighter with more hands. Once a month, she participates in cooperative work parties that the guild sponsors, helping to put up a trellis, build a barn, skin a greenhouse, or dig a root cellar.

Moreover, the farmers' market has allowed Boos to develop her own network of resources. Even faced with losing her job, leaving her home, and relinquishing her livestock, Boos feels some security because she has joined a community through the market that is much bigger than the Saturday goings on available to casual participants. For her, the market has opened possibilities.

She learned about incubator kitchens and has joined in the planning process for a local one. She joined the Local Growers Guild, which has introduced her to new people and a side of herself that looks a lot like an organizer. She got a lead on a new farm from an acquaintance at the market who heard about her plight. She has even begun to speak at agricultural extension conferences around the state about her experiences with growing for markets. Losing her foothold on her employer's farm and disrupting her identity as a grower could have presented far greater problems for Boos than they seemingly have. Instead, she hopes the investments she was able to make through the market—in networks of people, new knowledge, and new skills—will position her for greater opportunities.

Harvests

The challenges of farming are real. Yet some people do persist in it. They find a niche. They eschew comfort and convenience. They are willing to work long hours and bring their time and creativity to the most unlikely tasks. They experiment. They track the influx and outgo of money, but their primary motivation lies elsewhere. Their visions may be no better and no bigger than others'. But they hang on—maybe not forever, but for now.

Maria and Scott Cooper's vision involves feeding people.[12] When they make a pan of lasagna or a big pot of chili ("you can't make a small pot of chili, you know"), they hang a red flag on the mailbox to let their neighbor and his 16-year-old son know they are welcome for dinner. At the farmers' market, their intention is the same, to get good food to people at reasonable prices. They certainly vend to supplement their income, but their words and actions indicate that they want to help provide for people's food security.

Their commitment arises from their life experiences. The Coopers met while they were serving in the army, and after retiring, they moved back to her home state of Indiana. Maria puts it simply, "I come from a big family. I can't stand to see anybody hungry." Maria's family worked a small farm when she was growing up, and she shares with Scott what she learned in her childhood. Together, though, they adapt that knowledge to new varieties and methods and now to vending at the Bloomington market. They keep as close to organic as they can, "without letting the bugs eat everything," and try to recover the old ways of growing. As Scott says, "That's knowledge that comes from years ago that we've lost track of because of all the hybrids and everything else. The older people knew that stuff." Maria tells their story:

> My parents always had a garden when we were growing up, and we canned for the winter, and gave stuff away, and had it fresh all summer.
>
> So, when we got married, we were in the service. We didn't have a garden. When we moved back home fifteen years ago, I had a little garden, just enough for us. And then he took over the garden, and he didn't know how to garden, and we had twenty-five tomato plants for two people! So we had excess, couldn't give it away. . . .
>
> We stopped one day [at the Bloomington market] and walked around. It was an early market. There wasn't a whole lot. The prices were kind of high. So . . . when he had all that excess—I mean, when you're talking bushels of excess—it just come into my mind that we could do it [have a farming business]. So we showed up, and they said, sure. . . .

For the first few years, the Coopers did not have enough seniority to rent a permanent vending space where customers could find them every week. Season-long spaces are awarded on a points system and are perennially hard to come by. By-the-day spaces are more available but not predictably so. As newer vendors, the Coopers had to arrive early for every market and wait in line to secure a space for the day. During the height of the season, they might arrive on Friday night, sleep in their truck, "get up at 4 a.m. to get in line and then wait till 7 to get a space." In addition to the physical discomfort that entailed, it meant that their location always changed and customers did not know where to find them. Says Scott, "You know, if you grow something in particular they want, they've got to look for you." By diligently attending every market, however, they steadily accrued the points that allow them to have a well-positioned, permanent space.

Maria holds a job in town, so she provides much of the family's income while Scott has chosen growing for market as his primary occupation since settling in Indiana. But they both enjoy the connections that they make with vendors and customers "from all walks of life." They tell stories about how their produce figures in the lives of the people who buy them—about a woman whose children would eat no green cucumbers but only their lemon cucumbers and how they started growing a particular melon because a customer from Armenia missed it from back home. They establish long-term relationships that entwine their lives with their customers'. Maria tells this story:

> I have one customer that, two weeks ago, he made my day. His wife has been ill. And the first time I ever brought flowers—it was the second year we were here, I brought irises—he stopped and bought a bouquet for his wife. He said, she's not well, and I'm going to take her flowers. So he came back the next week, and he bought her some more. And so I asked how she was. I don't know what it is, but it's a long-term thing. And so for all these years I can't wait to see him every spring to see how his wife is doing.
>
> Three weeks ago, I guess, I had a bunch of little bouquets left, and that's all I had. I saw him wandering around, and I said, I'm just going to bag these up for his wife, and he can take them home to her. You know, maybe she'll enjoy taking them apart and putting them back together again. But she was here!
>
> He says, I'll bring her to you; she wants to meet you. So he brought her over and introduced me. And I don't know his name, but I know her name [now]. And so now I can ask how she's doing. And he comes to see us every week. It doesn't matter if I have flowers or not. He comes to see me, and let me know how she's doing.
>
> And I mean that's part of [the draw of the market]. After I got home, I called my mom, and I said, Mom, that man whose wife is sick brought her to meet me today. It just flabbergasted me! It really did. But it made my day.

Rippling out from a small purchase of flowers come human connections that can extend well beyond a simple exchange over the vendor's table. The customer's wife and the vendor's mother, unlikely to ever meet, become part of the same story. That interweaving is part of what keeps the Coopers coming back.

The anchor that they have set in the market hinges on fidelity—to each other and to their goal of feeding people. As Maria says, "A lot of it with us is, we can grow it cheap. We don't have any labor but our own. We can keep our prices where we know people are happy. We see a lot of the same customers every week, the older people. Maybe they've only got ten dollars, but ten dollars buys a lot from us." In the double-voiced way they typically tell stories, they describe their vision,

> *Maria: Sometimes we get in trouble . . .*
> *Scott: This spring we had tons of greens. We sold them all for a dollar a bag. You know, we're happy, and the customers, I think, are happy because they kept coming back.*
> *Maria: [In past years, other vendors have come by saying,] You know, don't you think your prices are too low? . . . But if I won't pay it, I'm not going to set [the price] there.*
> *Scott: We try to stay close to the grocery store. You know you can get a little bit more [at the market] because it's fresh, it's local. But like lettuce, a head of lettuce is perhaps going for 89 cents in the store. You should be able to get a dollar a head out of it [at market]. And you do for some of it. . . .*
> *Maria: For us, we're happy. If I go to the grocery store and I see a price on something and I don't like it, I don't care how bad I want it, I'm not going to buy it. And I don't want people to come up to our table and say, I'd like that, but I'm not going to buy that. . . .*
> *Scott: Well, too, I think we both understand the actual theory of the old farmers' market. If somebody had excess or planted excess for that. And back then, it was because people in town didn't have the space, didn't have the time to grow a garden.*
> *Maria: And people were hungry.*
> *Scott: It gave you a little extra income.*
> *Maria: We get those few customers that can afford to pay more that buy from us. But we get a lot of customers that really can't afford to pay more.*
> *Scott: We figure as long as you're happy—you are getting what you want out of it and your customers are happy—*
> *Maria: That's what the market's all about.*
> *Scott: As long as they're happy, it's all right.*

Eventually, the Coopers would like the farm to earn enough that they could both stay home to work it. That will mean meeting the competition and sticking to their prices despite pressure from other vendors. Scott admits, "It's a lot of work. . . . You've got to try to stay one step ahead of everybody. Now what am I going to do next year different so I'm ahead of them?" Maria is ready for the challenge. She says, "We want to be where we can spend our time together doing this. And if it means that we have to be big enough to do Saturday market and Tuesday market and maybe Wednesday market in Indianapolis, then that's what we're going to do. So five years from now what we hope is that we'll pull in here on Saturday morning and I'm not going to work someplace else. Then we can spread the joy a little bit."

Anthony Blondin's Sun Circle Farm is unusually quiet.[13] He has swapped out the typical farm's ubiquitous gasoline-powered machines in favor of equipment that can be run with the engines of horses and humans and fueled with what sun and rain and labor can coax from the ground. He uses a scythe to cut the grass, and he plows and tills with draft horses bought from an Amish farmer. When he works the ground, no sounds can be heard but the horses' hooves in the soft ground, their breathing under load, and his calls to them to gee or haw. He walks along behind, very straight, holding the reins, a team of three. A Great Pyrenees dog, not on deer duty at midday, lies in the shade of a crimson amaranth. The only sounds of motor vehicles come from the road up on the ridge.

He lives in a small octagonal house, tucked into the woods past the "tool shrine" hanging with dozens of specialized knives, saws, axes, and hoes. Not hooked up to the power grid, he heats with wood and carries water. When he has help, the interns live in another hand-made house out of sight of Blondin's own. Its second story has a sleeping loft that is walled on only three sides and looks onto a dense forest that falls away into a hollow. The interns' house also comes sans electricity, but water flows by gravity to an attached produce sorting and washing station from a holding pond above the field to a spotless stainless steel sink. The whole scene could not be tidier, more organized, or more peaceful. It remembers the best of the old ways and clearly poses new ones for the future.

Blondin wasn't raised to farming, the son of a factory worker and a carpenter, yet from somewhere he calls the tenacity to stick with it and with the land. He first fixed on farming while a student at the University of Michigan, where he got a bachelor's degree in biology, including several courses in entomology. His epiphany came when he went on an alternative spring break to The Farm in Tennessee, an intentional community founded in the 1970s. At its height, as many as two thousand people lived at The Farm, though when Blondin visited there in the 1990s it had dwindled to fewer than two hundred. Still, something rang true for him.

Greene County

After college, he returned to The Farm for two years to help set up an internship program, with himself as the "guinea pig intern." Later, he worked on a family homestead perched on the side of a mountain in Tennessee. Not a production farm, they grew food in beds with flowers and annual vegetables in among the perennials. It was an organic operation, everything done by hand on narrow terraces along the mountainside. As he tells it, the farm was idyllic but not set up to grow more than a subsistence living.

When Blondin's path led to a horse pasture on the Lazy Black Bear outside the village of Paoli, Indiana, he took what he had learned in his internships and set up his own organic farm for larger-scale production. It's not a big farm, but he makes the most of the area he has, planting high-value crops that can be marketed directly to the consumer through the farmers' market. He uses "bio-extensive" farming methods that trade space for fertility. In this system, plants are given more space than they would have ordinarily so that their root systems can grow to take advantage of the nutrients from a larger area of soil. The space in between plants is covered with crops that protect the soil from erosion and attract beneficial insects and birds. As a result, about two-thirds of his vegetable-growing area supports cover crops, which are themselves tilled into the soil to add to its tilth and fertility.

Blondin is committed to organic farming, which means he must deploy knowledge and management skills that other methods don't require. Research suggests that organic methods are more complicated to use than conventional ones and that farm management is especially important for crop yield on organic farms.[14] Organic growers must understand plants and insects in ways that nonorganic growers don't. While a conventional farmer simply has to recognize a pest is present in order to decide on an application of pesticide, an organic grower may have to learn about the entire lifecycle of the insect in order to find a way to disrupt its impact. Organic farming also requires time to observe local soil systems and weather patterns and to devise creative ways of working with the challenges they present. Blondin's college training in biology—the knowledge base and observational skills it provided—together with his personal trait of meticulous organization no doubt have contributed to his success as an organic farmer.

An idyllic setting, yet Blondin founded Sun Circle Farm as one of four friends who shared a vision of a sustainable farm here on an isolated farm on the edge of the Hoosier National Forest. After only a few years, the others pulled up stakes and left, yet Blondin digs his own foundations in deeper. He is the only one who remains. What makes him the one in four who stays?

Perhaps an answer lies in the rising structure of an enormous, handcrafted barn along the drive into the farm. While Blondin's original farming partners were building a very sturdy, very necessary, but also quite modest "loafing shed" to shelter the horses, Blondin had started what looks to be a century barn, one to last a hundred years or more. The massive post-and-beam building goes up slowly, even now, as time, labor, and funds allow. But it is a pace in keeping with the rhythms of the place.

Blondin helped cut many of the big beams with a friend who logs with horses. And they build the barn together using old ways. Already fully imagined, when finished the barn will include several horse stalls, some of which horses will be able to go in and out of at will, another that the team can stand and rest in during a work day without being unharnessed, and the rest of which can be leased to recreational riders who use the national forest. The ground level will also hold a root cellar and a produce processing room. On the expansive floor above, he plans a warmer vegetable room for produce that keeps at sixty degrees and an apartment. Up in the rafters at the top of the tall building will be storage for the hay. The multipurpose structure speaks to Blondin's precision, his vision, and his commitment to this land.

Meanwhile, his Sun Circle market stand features many-hued potatoes and sweet potatoes, elephant garlic, and other specialty crops. Blondin sells most of his produce in Bloomington where people and sometimes restaurants are willing to pay premium prices for organic, heirloom, and unusual varieties. Even though rising gasoline costs eat into his profits, he drives by at least two markets on the way to Bloomington to get the prices he needs. Because he lives so far from town, finding labor is tough. In the past eight years, he says, he has had about forty interns, most short-term. He advertises now for an apprentice, someone who would bring more skills and make a longer commitment than interns do. However, his postings in the trade journals go mostly unanswered; in his no-frills operations, the pay cannot be much more than a lovely place to stay and the satisfaction and knowledge gained from a season's hard work.

Right now, Blondin feels lucky to live where he does. Having fared successfully without many of the modern era's "improvements," most changes in his chosen lifestyle would smack of the first unacceptable steps on the slippery slope to compromise. His health remains strong, and his housing adequately secure. He has plenty to keep him occupied and plenty more to learn. Many projects are just beginning to show fruit. He sometimes ponders who will succeed him in stewarding the farm. Only in his thirties, he seems young for that worry, but then, most everything he does takes in the long view, back and fore, as he finds the fertile middle ground between the two.

"Sometimes I think I'm a madman," Jeff Evard says while surveying a holding tank of vegetable oil destined for conversion to biofuel and banks of newly tilled garden beds.[15] He and his wife, Melissa, have come to farming with a vision to do their part to change the footprint their community makes on the earth. More specifically, they have taken on the mission of providing good food and a model of an integrated, healthful, and sustainable local food system. For new visions of the human relationship with the earth and new technologies to support those visions to catch on, Jeff says, "You're going to have to have models, models for people [to] look at. This is the thing to do. . . . This is how we go about doing it."

Both Evards attended Purdue University, a storied agricultural and engineering school. While Melissa studied materials engineering, Jeff took an agricultural track. After graduation, he "followed the money" into a business that cultivated turf for golf courses. The business boomed, but the more he thought about what he was doing, the less satisfied he became:

> *Jeff: I got fed up with the way I was taught. I'm not trying to put a political spin on it or anything, but there's no organic farming initiative [at Purdue] where you can learn how to be an organic farmer. They teach you how to buy chemicals, basically.*
>
> *Melissa: They don't have as much funding for organic endeavors as they do for chemicals. So all the research is sponsored by companies who have money.*

Greene County

Jeff: Millions and millions of dollars, so that's the program that gets researched. So that's what brings me here today— You don't hear crickets on a lot of other farms. You really don't. . . . I got sucked into the world of plants, I guess. You know, I had every intention of being a businessman or business marketer of some sort. And I just moved on, met Melissa, and remembered what I was supposed to be doing.

He admits that, even with a degree in agriculture, he started growing organically from a knowledge deficit: "Every year I learn something new. I mean seriously, as far as growing plants, [at Purdue] I concentrated on growing turf grass. And a lot of it carries over . . . sunlight, water, soil. But I learned most about soil. And I just play with it and do some experimentation. [With the vegetables now,] it's all a big experiment. I know that manure helps a lot." What he didn't learn at Purdue, Jeff acquired "from keeping my ears open and being open to information. I hear about things and explore them."

Jeff's first big garden was on their suburban home lot in Greenwood, just outside of Indianapolis. The first year they had four tomato plants and the second year, "he just went nuts," Melissa says, expanding the garden to two thousand to three thousand square feet. After selling at the Greenwood farmers' market, they decided to pull up stakes and try somewhere different: "We were trying to stay there for several years, but we just couldn't stand it anymore. The whole area had grown up quite a bit. It was country when we moved there, or fairly country when we moved out there. And then suddenly we were surrounded by these massive neighborhoods. . . . Once you get that fever, you just can't not do it."

The Evards began seriously farming in 2003, on an old horse pasture in Morgan County, Indiana, about halfway between Indianapolis and Bloomington. When they plow the ground for their vegetable, corn, and sweet potato crops, they keep an eye out for the grave of a previous owner who fought in the Civil War or any sign that Tecumseh really did camp nearby. The ground is eroded and seeded with horseshoes and arrowheads, but the tired condition of the land makes for part of their vision: "This hillside was barren, even when they didn't do anything with it. So I took it upon myself to kind of fix it," Jeff says. Soil takes time to regenerate from years of conventional farming practices or even the benign neglect of a horse pasture.[16] And when growers, even those with the best intentions, switch from conventional to organic farming, their crop yields tend to drop for several years. In fact, one wonders, if customers knew that farmers' transition to organic methods was also, essentially, making a commitment to lower yields, would they be more willing to pay prices to support that effort? The Evards have responded by firing on several cylinders at once.

They have established an extensive system of garden beds along with a few acres of selected row crops. They are not vegetarians, but they try to eat "lower on the food chain" as a contribution toward overall energy savings. "The idea," Jeff says, "is to get permanent beds going. . . . zero input other than what my two hands can do." The plan is to avoid the pitfalls that accompany loans that banks are all too willing to extend to farmers who want start-up money for expensive equipment, land, and labor:

> You have to have collateral. A lot of those farmer banks, they specialize in these huge lines of credit. So you've got a year: they give you $250,000, and you've got one year to pay it back. So that's your seed money, that's your equipment money, leased land or bought land. Now you have to grow crop to pay back however much you withdraw on that line of credit.
>
> I go by a dollar per square foot. And if I can make a dollar per square foot from a crop, it's worth my time. And if you do the math, that's one acre for $45,000. So these beds, this might be the third crop in here this year. You've just got to keep pegging thirty-five cents per square foot and make sixty more. That's how I do it. So by those calculations, growing row crops is ridiculous. Because those people still don't make any money, unless you've been landed for generations. . . .
>
> There is so much push behind the chemical companies, the huge input companies. This is the way we've done it for a thousand years, and boom—they've got to make their money, they've got to patent their seed. And their seed works well in these huge input systems. . . . It doesn't make sense to me.

Understanding that such conventional investments do not respect the actual pace of the growing world, Evard favors a permaculture model that combines perennial plantings and animals in symbiotic ways, so for example, ginseng is planted in the woods by the house, and ducks lay eggs while grazing the peach orchard. He says, "You can see a little bit of what I'm trying to do here. We've got the orchards on the outskirts. The crops that don't take any time out there [away from the house]. These [high-maintenance] crops in close. You have a sustainable system that requires me to do the least amount of work. I really am lazy! But getting it to that point takes time." In 2004, the Evards opened a restaurant on the Bloomington courthouse square called Roots. It features vegetarian and local foods. Jeff cooks "on Saturday nights, for fun mostly," does the bills, and picks up compost, in addition to growing some of the produce they use. Their business partner, Ryan Dauss, oversees the cooking end of the operation. Consistent with the Evards' vision, the restaurant makes a special effort to purchase locally produced foods—including eggs, fruits, bakery items, salad greens, and the makings of their renowned sweet potato French fries. Melissa and Jeff make pesto with basil from local growers, mix organic teas, and freeze their own produce to be used in wintertime concoctions at the restaurant. With a central location and quality food, the restaurant is picking up business, albeit with some false starts on how to make it cost effective and efficient. As Jeff says, "We do everything from scratch. No preservatives. We're not opening up a can to make this $20 entrée. We're working hard to make a $10 sandwich." He believes good, quality ingredients will be a profitable investment in the long run.

Ideally, the waste from the restaurant becomes part of the profit. Or more accurately, it becomes incorporated into the food system as part of the cycle of generation and decay. Jeff trucks vegetable waste from the restaurant out to the farm for composting with earthworms, and fry grease becomes the foundation of a bio-diesel fuel project. Although there isn't much to show for it yet besides tanks of French fry grease, these Purdue "boilermakers" plan to create useable fuel from this byproduct. The process entails a settling and distilling process that uses a retrofitted hot water heater, lye, methyl alcohol. Jeff's plan is to run his tractor and perhaps even his diesel pickup truck from this biofuel. He estimates that a single forty-gallon batch will run the tractor for a year. The byproduct of the process is soap. Melissa adds scents to mask its fry basket origins and sells it at the market. They hope to sell the French fry windfall to several interested farmers they have met through the market. At a dollar or so a gallon, they may indeed find buyers.

Still, for Jeff and Melissa and their partner Ryan, Roots is as much about making a difference as making a profit. "We're helping Anthony, with his farm and what he is trying to do. . . . And we'll all be getting good food" because of the partnership. They "try to be mindful," as Melissa puts it, that there are other growers who would like to be able to sell to their restaurant. So they use the market as an outlet for their own produce to leave room for the restaurant to purchase from other local growers. They also canvas the market for produce that the restaurant needs:

> *Jeff: I stand behind the booth on Saturdays. But I also spend a lot of time talking to people that are trying to sell their products to places like restaurants. Getting Yergerlenger cheese into Roots is our most recent accomplishment. . . . I'm trying to find a way to buy their food—buy local food, serve local food, and sustain the business.*
>
> *Melissa: He also makes sure about the growers, to make sure we're not bringing something into the restaurant—*
>
> *Jeff: Sometimes I talk to somebody [who says], "Yeah, I sprayed the eggplant this morning after I harvested it because there were still bugs all over it!"*
>
> *Melissa: OK, we don't want to eat that!*
>
> *Jeff: "I don't need anything today. Thank you." And I go to the next place. I talk to the people to find out how they're growing stuff before everybody eats it. We're doing our best.*

And doing one's best usually requires adequate time. Melissa, who grew up in the suburbs but inherited the ingenuity of generations of coal miners and engineers on one side and stockyard operators on the other, spends her week as a material scientist at Rolls-Royce. Her income gives the family breathing room. Even so, she wants to participate in the farm. She works the market stand on Saturdays in Bloomington, takes care of the composting worms, grows herbs, and minds the chickens. And she takes on various projects around the farmstead, though she admits, "I eventually lose track. We give me things that, if I'm going to be gone for a week or something, it's not a big deal. I like to feel like I'm a part of it and in charge of some things." Jeff, meanwhile, devotes himself full-time to the farm-related businesses. Spending about half the week on cultivating the crops, Jeff spends the other half selling them:

> *Here's what I do. On a Thursday night and a Friday, I do markets. On Friday afternoon, about two o'clock, I go to the Traders Point Farmers' Market. And I sell at the Traders Point*

*Farmers' Market. And then I come back, and load the truck
for Saturday market [in Bloomington]. Melissa gets up early
and goes to the Saturday market. I follow suit, a couple of
hours later because, on Saturday night, I close the restaurant.
So I can't go from 4 a.m. until 1 a.m. anymore. If I ever could.
That's just my one, busy, busy, busy day.*

The markets are an important piece of the sustainability pic-
ture for the Evards, even beyond having retail outlets for vegetables. The market experience creates a way for them to go public with their philosophy and network with others. Through the
market they offer not only produce but "the face of what we're
trying to do," says Melissa. The Evards have high hopes for the
future—for their farm and for their impact on society and for
reforming the system of agriculture currently in use. They hope to
purchase ten or fifteen acres closer to Bloomington where they can
follow a variation on the Chez Panisse model that brings together
food production with restaurant services, sustainable energy, and
holistic medicine—to, as Jeff says, "Just bring it all together for
everybody." Perhaps then people will understand that vegetables
have seasons and choices have consequences: "I'm into organic
growing and making organic farm systems more viable. So I go
talk to people, like I'm talking to you people today. I'm just trying to build my farm, build my restaurant, build a better farm
system."

They know that their farming operation is still small, still
emerging. But they plant and pick and eat what they grow. Melissa says of her family: "I remind them a lot of my grandpa who
was a farmer." But she knows, "I'm technically not really [a farm-
er] in our society. I'm just a gardener. People don't take this very
seriously. You have to have two hundred acres and a big tractor to
be a farmer in Indiana." Still, they continue to move beyond what
they call their "past lives" into an emerging new vision of sustainable, holistically integrated, local agriculture.

> *Jennifer: It's a great vision.*
> *Jeff: I'm saddled with it.*
> *Jennifer: Is that how you feel, that you're saddled with it?*
> *Jeff: No, I think it's funny. I enjoy it. I've got to do some-
> thing because this is what came to me. I don't have a choice.*
> *Jennifer: How did it come to you?*

Bloomington

Jeff: It's more of an acceptance that what you see is actually wrong. We are saying that you should not just go along with it. It takes a lot of work to do what is right.

Melissa: It's kind of like that expression, be part of the change that you want to see.

Jeff: Yes.

Melissa: The responsibility, once you realize what is going on, you can't just turn back. . . . That's just the way it is.

Customer   *Bloomington*

8. Market Futures_____

On a bright market morning, when money, wisdom, and wit are flowing around a market, it is easy to forget the tenuousness in the proposition of growing for market. If, like a language, the skill to bring seed to plant to harvest to table could be lost in the matter of a few generations, then the future of smaller farms and farmers' markets in America and abroad has special importance to an industrialized nation that depends on that knowledge even while it rewards the alternatives.

On May 7, 2006, a group of people gathered to speculate on the future of farmers' markets. They met on a cool spring evening in a barn on Hart Farm, two miles from the crossroads called McVille, in Greene County, Indiana. The spring had been cool, and many plants—cockscomb, sunflowers, basil, snapdragons, dianthus—were lined up to harden off before transplanting into the field. The people who gathered have made long-term commitments to local food. They represented varied perspectives and personal experiences, but their range of relationships to a farmers' market suggests their conversation was not unique, that it might unfold in much the same way in the context of many markets around the country. The views they expressed, when not evoking scenes of post-gasoline apocalypse spurred by rising oil prices and war in the Middle East, erred on the side of hopefulness, while also remaining realistic about the challenges that make small farming in the United States a difficult endeavor to sustain.

They sat among the tools of a flower farmer's trade—wooden bushel baskets; an assortment of dibbles and a widger; wooden and plastic flats; swan hoes, stirrup hoes, grubbing hoes, collinear hoes, and a wheel hoe; hand seed sowers, a push seeder, a broadcast seeder, and a drop spreader; wheelbarrows, a garden cart, and wagons; rotary tillers and tractors. The assembly included:

- a market manager in her forties who had brought a promising city market along to bursting success;
- a long-time customer of farmers' markets and retired biology professor in her fifties who speaks and consults around the country on genetically modified organisms and other contemporary agricultural issues;
- a customer in her twenties who works in a not-for-profit that serves low-income people;
- a single mother and former tenant grower who has remade herself into an organizer for local food;
- a woman in her thirties who has inherited a family farm (that is being rented to others) and plans to establish herself as a flower and vegetable farmer. She currently works in an apprenticeship with a more experienced grower;
- a grower of six years, in his thirties, who specializes in vegetables and who plows with horses and lives without electricity;
- a ten-year grower of vegetables and flowers in his forties who had earlier experience in his family's greenhouses and now has committed to working full-time on his own land; and
- a long-time market grower, now in his sixties, who has specialized in ornamental plants, cut flowers, and herbs, for twenty-nine years.

On the assumption that, as one participant put it, "the seeds of the future are always in the present," these participants were asked to speculate from their individual perspectives about what the future of farmers' markets and local food will be and what major challenges they foresee.[1]

The group begins by introducing themselves.

Marcia Veldman: I am the market manager for the two City of Bloomington farmers' markets. Also I am a grower and sell at a private market on Wednesdays. I guess life is full of interesting twists. I was working in California at an environmental education site, and someone I was working with was putting out a big garden with the goal of becoming a market grower. I thought, "Ah, that's an interesting concept!" It never occurred to me that would be something I would be doing in life. I remember our first night after tilling this big field, putting out plants, drinking a beer. I thought, "We're on to something here!" And then when Steve, my husband, and I moved back to Bloomington, I applied for a position with the Parks and Recreation Department, that was, in part, working with the farmers' market.

Marti Crouch: I have been going to the market since 1979 as a customer. I started out by trying to eat all of my food locally, having everything that I eat come from the local environment, which is a bit of a challenge. But the farmers' market made it a lot easier to do that. I am interested in how agriculture and nature interrelate, how people use the land for food, and how that impacts and interacts with wild nature. The farmers' market, although it has mainly cultivated foods, has some connection to the wild through berries and nuts and mushrooms.

About ten years ago, the city decided that selling wild mushrooms was too risky. They were going to ban mushrooms sales from the market. At the time, I was teaching at the university and taught a class on biology and food systems. I was concerned that this link between wild nature and the city—that was represented by the exchange of mushrooms at the market—was going to disappear. So a group of us got together, restaurant owners and people who wanted to maintain mushrooms at the market, made a proposal to inspect the mushrooms and to limit which ones were sold and to have people sign waivers, and to give them information sheets. We floated it to the lawyers, and they went for it. I was a mushroom hunter for a long time and knew a lot of different species. I then, essentially, appointed myself as "mushroom inspector," and I have been mushroom inspector at the market ever since. As far as I know, I am the only one in the country working at a farmers' market.

So I am fascinated by what probably will become the inevitable, that we are going to have to eat locally. And wouldn't it be nice if we figured out how under less stress than necessity.

Bobbi Boos: I have been a grower for about ten years now. I first started working with community food issues with Mother Hubbard's Cupboard [a food pantry open to anyone who needs assistance], trying to rescue food and redistribute it to people who need to eat. But more recently, I have been elected president of the Local Growers Guild. We help small and local farmers become more sustainable, both economically and environmentally.

Jessica Williams: I worked at the Rise, which is a low-income transitional housing facility. I volunteer at the market. I have talked to the women at the Rise about it, and I have taken my Little Sister to the market.

J. D. Grove: I grew up watching farmers around me go-
ing out of business, seeing how harmful agricultural practices
could be to the land. I've watched deforestation. My family
has moved away from farming, and I want to go back in that
direction in a new way. I am trying to start a farm on my
great, great, great grandfather's land and do it in a completely
different way than people have recently. More in the way that
he farmed. So I'm interested in kind of going back as a way of
looking at the future.

Anthony Blondin: I have been at market for six years now.
To some people I am known as "the Potato Guy." Though
I'm not sure I want to be known as the Potato Guy. I am cur-
rently trying to transition my farm from tractor power to horse
power. I am trying to end my reliance on fossil fuels as much
as possible, trying to get things back to solar power or as close
to that as possible.

Pete Johnson: This is my tenth season at the market. I got
into the business at a family farm in the Boston area in the
late eighties, working in the fields and in the wonderful glass
greenhouses that they had. I really liked the work, but after
five years working there, I decided that the chemicals and the
growing of the disposable bedding plants wasn't what I wanted
to do. When I came back to Bloomington, discovering the
farmers' market gave me an idea for a new way of staying in
the business, while getting away from the things that bothered
me. I could grow food and cut flowers with a minimum of
input and using organic methods, which just seemed a lot more
worthwhile way to make a living. My wife, Leslie, and I just
moved to a new piece of land down in Washington County,
and this should be our first season both working full time
there. We've got a lot to do!

J. A. (Jeff) Hartenfeld: Welcome to our farm, Jen's and
mine. This is my twenty-ninth year of field-growing cut flowers
at market. The market is thirty years old. I don't know if you
can realize how fast thirty years go, but, man, it goes fast! All
of a sudden, it is going to be sixty years old. I am really curious
as to what it is going to look like then. I am seeing Anthony
having to leave on Thursday to make a two-day trip to town
with the horses. (Laughter) I am serious! I see people huddled
in big masses around open fires in the towns they are passing
through. He probably has to have Jessica riding shotgun to
keep marauders off from trying to get the produce. There is no
oil, or gas is fifteen or twenty bucks a gallon, maybe more. It is
going to be really different.

In my lifetime of farming, the weather has changed. We
are having many more violent thunderstorms. Weather science

Greene County: (clockwise from left) Veldman,
Boos, Blondin, Grove, Crouch, Hartenfeld,
Johnson, Robinson

*has been saying for two decades that erratic fluctuations are
going to be one of the first signs we see of global warming.
So growing now, being an outdoor grower, is a real challenge.
Everybody is not going to be able to have plastic-covered
greenhouses, that plastic is going to be too costly or won't be
available at all.*

*About a month ago, I had this big delivery of organic fer-
tilizer I am buying from Pennsylvania, and bags of dirt that I
get from Indianapolis that comes from God knows where. It's
not really even dirt. So, in one week, I have a thousand dollars
of stuff coming in that is not from here. That's not sustainable.
Right now you can kind of skim by and make enough money
to pay for those expenses and sort of ignore the ramifications,
but in thirty more years, when J.D. is old and at the end of her
days, what's it going to look like? It is going to be a harder
dance for the younger growers than I think it was for me.*

*That is the down side. The up side is that local food is not
going to be a movement. Local food is going to be a neces-*

*sity. You know, one hundred years ago, every major city had
its own farms. Down in Louisville, the knobs, up high above
town, were settled by Catholics who had a lot of kids. They
grew vegetables for the people in the city for years and years.
The south side of Indianapolis was the same thing. Settled by
the Dutch and the Germans, big families, they put out vegetables and brought them into the city. Looks to me like we are
headed back in that direction.*

Who will the new farmers be?

After thirty years, the farmers' market has become an institution, which means that the farmers will turn over and the customers will change but the market will remain. The question then
is who will populate the next generation of growers. The children of market vendors, almost inevitably, don't want to carry on
the family business. The director of New York City Greenmarket
notes that only a quarter of the "old order" farmers have children
willing to take up the business.[2] Perhaps the percentage is not
even that high. One successful Bloomington market grower says
that one of her sons frequently makes comments along the lines
of, "Mom, when I get out of this house, I'll never pick another
green bean! I'll never pick another tomato!" An Amish farmer
faces the same resistance in his children. He hopes that they will
come back to the family trade of farming, though he has no guar-
antees: "They always don't like what Dad wants them to do. As
they get older, they'll want to make a living, and they'll look for
something they know how to do."[3]

Growers who have large families say they benefit greatly from
their help. The two farmers mentioned above say, respectively,
"The kids, as they've gotten older, have just been a tremendous
help. It's just like having three extra adults, to be honest"; and,
"We wouldn't be here if they didn't help us, our children." But
even the self-generated labor of children does not last for long.
Children simply do not remain at home for very long.

Growers who don't have large families must pay for help or
find volunteer interns. Some of the growers participating in the
barn conversation use unpaid interns and apprentices as a way
both to pass on what they know and to bring desperately and
perennially needed help onto the farm. It is an old model and a

mutually beneficial one when the people involved and their expectations match. Two of the discussants had been interns themselves. But the growers disagree on how much commitment and skill they can expect from someone who is essentially a volunteer and whether it is optimal, or by implication even ethical, to expect someone to work for only rudimentary room and board.

Boos: I am hoping the future looks kind of like an hour glass. At one end are a number of older people who have retained farming skills because they were part of their family. There aren't very many people my age who have skills like that. But as I get to be in the middle now, I am starting see a new wave of young people who have these interests and are trying to hold on to them. A few years ago, the average farmer was over sixty, and it looked like we were in trouble. But now it seems to me that, hopefully, a new, younger generation coming up behind me is recognizing the value of that kind of knowledge and holding on to it.

Blondin: This area doesn't have the apprenticeship scene that I experienced in Ann Arbor when I lived there. There were probably thirty or forty people every year who worked on farms throughout the Ann Arbor area. And a great number of those people have gone on to start their own farm.

One of the most exciting things for me is when interns actually harvested something that they had planted the seed for and had cared for along the way. It was the first time that they had actually harvested something that they had planted. It brought joy to that person to do that. And that was a pretty well-educated person who was concerned about food issues but who had never actually grown their own food.

Grove: Growing is such a complex skill I feel like I'll spend my whole life learning it, but it is also intuitive.

Blondin: I have listed my farm on a website for an apprentice this year.[4] The way the website is set up is as a map of the United States, and you click on the state where you want to apprentice. But who is going to click on Indiana to do a farm apprenticeship? (Laughter) There is no way that my farm is going to be located by someone unless I am in Oregon, Washington, California, or New York.

Boos: There are a lot of people who think they really want to farm, and they don't get very far before they realize how much hard work it is. And then they're gone. Interns come and go. You put effort into training them and teaching them, and they're excited, but they don't stick with it. Internships are a good way for them to learn if that's the right thing for them.

Hartenfeld: I have people work here as paid farm workers. J.D. and I have an informal apprenticeship relationship, but I pay her. I'm not asking her to subsidize my business.

Grove: Yes, we have that kind of relationship.

Hartenfeld: This is her second year working here. She's learning a lot of different things. It's very much an apprenticeship. But it happened by chance, and I don't have someone after her who's going to want to learn the skills of growing.

Grove: I traveled with migrant farm workers in this country for a couple of years. I try to remind people, when these apprenticeships are academic and professionalized, that there's also a pool of skilled farm labor in this country, and there has been historically. And talk about poor people who are committed to farming! People who live in tents year round and travel where it is warm enough to do that. I feel like those are the people we need to be finding and finding work for. They are people who are committed to such an extent that they are willing to live in ways that are uncomfortable.

Blondin: I have a problem with people mixing up internship and apprenticeship. An internship is what you are talking about where people are experimenting. [An apprenticeship is when] you make the decision that this is the lifestyle that you want, and now you are trying to acquire more skills.

Grove: I have several years of farm work, serious living in a tent and working in the fields. Year-round farm work. If I had come out of college or had been on a college internship, that would be different. I went to Antioch, and a lot of Antioch students go on internships to organic farms. And they think, wow, organic farms! And they do it for a while and find, oh, it's not so romantic. That's an internship.

I agree, an apprenticeship is different. Jeff and I definitely have an apprenticeship relationship, where I need real, focused, direct professional skills, and I can only get that with a professional farmer. I need someone I can call to ask if feed oats are okay to substitute for regular oats. It's a very different dynamic. Jeff's farm is the closest farm I've ever seen to the kind of farm I imagine for myself.

While college students, traditional migrants, and social dissenters represent one pool for the next generation of market growers, the discussants also talk about the promise of other groups who seem poised to repopulate rural America and establish vibrant urban gardens. In recent years, for example, several Asian-born vendors have joined the ranks of the Bloomington market. Most are town dwellers and accomplished enough with standard and specialty varieties to sell all summer what they can grow in their yards. Amish vending stands, too, have multiplied in the past ten years, setting high standards for productivity and quality. Both approaches—town and country—have the potential to keep farmers' markets alive and well in the future.

> *Crouch: When you drive through the depoperate parts of the Midwest, it's now all Hispanic, the places where the economy has faltered and the towns are declining. I always drive the back roads to go up to northern Indiana. And a lot of those towns used to be dead, and now they're all lively again with lots of young people, and lots of farmers have bought up the cheap farms. They're from Guatemala and Honduras and Mexico. They're growing home vegetable gardens, and their young people are learning. That's happening right now. It looks good to me. It's like rural America is rising from the ashes but speaking Spanish!*
>
> *Veldman: My parents are immigrants from Holland, and when my dad came over here, he was a migrant farmer. They both grew up on farms in Holland. But their goal was to get off the farm! They think I'm absolutely nuts that I'm interested in it.*
>
> *Johnson: My maternal grandmother was the last person in my family to farm. She said the one thing she knew was that she wanted to marry a city man. But she's happy to see somebody in the family getting back into farming. She's given me some financial help that has been invaluable.*
>
> *Blondin: There are a lot of people coming into our area [of Orange County] now who are Amish from Pennsylvania. Their numbers are actually increasing. They can sell a farm there, and they're able to afford three farms here. So they're buying a farm for themselves and two for their kids.*
>
> *Crouch: That's another real success story for rural America.*

The group expresses admiration for people who manage to pass their commitment to the land from one generation to the next, recognizing how difficult it is to compete with the allure of fancy gadgets, Technicolor culture, and the sensory rush of city life. They marvel at the success that the Amish have had in retaining their children in family businesses and a plain lifestyle. The group acknowledges that the strong communities that the Amish build are crucial to their success in rural life. The growers in the group, in particular, lament their own very isolated attempts to build integrated lives around agriculture. The larger culture, they say, does not offer viable, contemporary models for living life on a farm.

> *Johnson: It's encouraging to see that it can be done, but there are certain aspects of the Amish success that are difficult to recreate if you don't have the help of a community.*
>
> *Grove: I don't know if the social structure in general is trending in that direction, toward having big families with a lot of community support. I don't see myself as that far out of the norm for a thirty-year-old farmer. But I don't see myself having a husband. I see myself maybe having a baby alone, maybe with a structure of women around me.*
>
> *I think things are really changing in terms of not having that same kind of heterosexual nuclear family structure associated with farms, which I think is great. But there's not necessarily a model to replace it. A lot of us are gay. A lot of us aren't married, so we are going into this completely alone and in rural communities where we are not likely to meet someone.*
>
> *I look at Bobbi and think, how is Bobbi going to farm while she has a daughter? If I could see a woman doing that, I would think, okay, it can be done. But it's hard to imagine.*
>
> *Boos: It's hard to imagine. I'm still wondering how it is going to work for me. From my perspective, a single person on the farm is different from having two adults there. In that case, one person can actually work off the farm or both of them can work half-time off the farm. That allows for one low-wage job to balance a higher-wage job to make ends meet. But when you're one person alone, you either have to work part-time or choose.*
>
> *Blondin: I ended up with a couple that didn't have kids, and they got to choose who they wanted to take over the farm. They said they kind of shopped around until they could say, you have the ideals that we have, and we'd like you to inherit. I think that there are a lot of couples out there that have land, that have knowledge, but they don't have anyone to pass it on to. We somehow need to connect that group of people with the people who have acquired the skills and the desire to do it but who don't have the start-up capital.*

Who should farmers' markets serve?

Occasionally amid all of the celebration of farmers' markets in the popular press, a contrarian opinion will emerge, charging farmers' markets with being elitist, overpriced, and untenably

nostalgic. The group gathered in the barn at Hart Farm talk about the tensions and trade-offs that exist between creating an openly accessible and affordable market and one that allows growers prices sufficiently high to provide a living wage. They discuss the dilemma of growers with little capital or experience who might, with help from subsidies, benefactors, or education, be the sustainable and sustaining market vendors of the future.

> **Johnson:** *It is important to me that the farmers' market phenomenon reach outside of the college towns and larger cities where it seems to have made the greatest strides in recent years. I really think it is important to grow staples and provide them at affordable prices, but you know, it seems hard to do that side by side with the Wal-Mart phenomenon of "the lowest prices at all costs." I don't want the farmers' market movement or organic agriculture to become a boutique phenomenon that is only for the affluent.*
>
> **Veldman:** *I was going down to Dubois County for a conference and saw this truck outside Wal-Mart—$9.95 for fifty pounds of potatoes. OK, you can't compete with that! But,*

people see those sale prices and think that is what the price of produce is.

The subsidy in agriculture is cheap oil right now. It keeps food prices low. I think there is a misconception that the farmers' market is expensive. I have recorded prices at the market and then have gone to the supermarket to take a look, and on many things the farmers' market is quite a bit less expensive. It is just the different ways things are packaged. You see those bags of lettuce that look kind of big, but there is really not much in there, and some of it is already going bad. So when you compare that to the market, it is actually cheaper at market, and it will last two weeks in the refrigerator. I do think that, as oil prices go up, the farmers' market actually becomes an even more affordable place.

Johnson: But it strikes me that a lot of younger growers accept a very thin margin to live on, and if a new generation of growers is going to replace the older farmers, I think it's going to have to be a little more attractive. You are not going to have to make a great living, but you can't be on the edge of ruin all the time. I think that for so many people who are trying to start a farm, if you don't inherit one and have to start from scratch, it means long years of living on very little money and having very little, very little to fall back on if there is a bad year or some other sort of financial set back.

Blondin: Market is becoming pretty gourmet. That's how we all are making a living at it. I drive by three markets on the way to the Bloomington market in order to be able to sell potatoes for two dollars a pound. There is no way that I could get that price fifteen miles away from my house. No one would support that because they are going to Wal-Mart to buy their potatoes, as you say. I would love to be out of a job at the farmers' market selling eight different varieties of potatoes. Who needs purple potatoes, when you come down to it?

The tension between good food and cheap food, of course, becomes more significant as people's resources become more limited. If choices must be made between premium-priced local or organic food and quantities of food, people may find they are less able to have discretion in their purchasing choices, particularly those with lower incomes. Moreover, the more class-based a farmers' market becomes, the more that class will set the market's tone and priorities—and prices. The discussant who works at a not-for-profit warned against complacency.

Williams: *I work at the Rise, which is a low-income transitional housing facility. What I found was that a lot of people who could use their WIC vouchers [for low-income women with children] there don't feel comfortable entering the environment of the market. Not that the market itself is inherently discouraging, but the other people who go to the market and things like that are. Some of them were really surprised at how cool I thought the market was. Some of them had been and didn't want to go back. It just wasn't a comfortable environment for them. There are a lot of people [at the market] who are trying to make food affordable and accessible, but there are still a lot of barriers.*

Veldman: *That is interesting because I always think of the market as being a really welcoming place and pretty available across the board, economically.*

Johnson: *We might like to idealize it as being egalitarian, but from the outside, I think it probably looks very different. Looking from outside of Bloomington, not just the market, but Bloomington itself looks very different.*

Veldman: *Yes, I know! Some of the vendors who come from the outlying counties say, "I had to bring my Mom up here so that she could see what was going on!" Like it's a freak show!*

Crouch: *Which is a traditional function of a market. It's where you go to get your fortune told.*

Hartenfeld: *The market is seemingly one of the few places in the community where anybody can go that doesn't cost anything. And I know that we do have some vendors who are concerned about keeping their prices down, and they take real pains to move produce. So if people are uncomfortable, it might be that they think farmers' market is expensive—these same preconceived notions we've been talking about.*

I see a lot of kinds of people at market. I see a lot of poor people at market. I see a lot of working-class people at market.

Grove: *The Greencastle market right now is completely different from the Bloomington market. It's, like, two guys with a pick-up truck, sitting at a picnic table, and their produce is spread out on the picnic table. They just sit there. One of them smokes a pipe. It is not intimidating for class reasons, but it is intimidating in other ways!*

Veldman: *There are a lot of [government food] vouchers used at market. Plus, the Growers Guild and the market just submitted a USDA grant that in part involves accepting food stamps. I think that, even if the grant doesn't come through, somehow we will find a way next year to be accepting food stamps at the market. It would be better if we got it through* *a grant because it would come with a lot of money to do the outreach and the marketing and get the word out. But one way or another, I do think that will happen.*

Most small growers know they cannot compete with heavily subsidized agribusiness operations and loss-leader products sold below cost by large retailers. So they try innovative ways of cutting costs to broaden the customer base, they appeal to a smaller segment of consumers willing to pay higher prices, and they prepare for a future in which they might serve a more crucial role in feeding greater numbers of people.

> **Blondin:** *Myself and a lot of other horse farmers are trying to take the small-scale production up to a larger level where we can actually sustainably produce larger amounts of food and feed larger numbers of people.*
>
> *I think that it is feasible to farm without using gasoline. The Amish communities around us are already doing it. They are feeding themselves and also have excess. All the Amish folks around us are a huge resource. But that type of agriculture is a community of agriculture. I'm trying to do it by myself, and there is no way that I can do that by myself, especially providing staples. You can eat a lot of potatoes, but it is nice to have some grains every once in a while.*
>
> **Grove:** *I am going to be farming in Greencastle where there isn't a solid community that supports sustainable agriculture. There is not that consciousness. What I like is the idea of using the nonprofit sector in this country to draw some resources into rural communities that would allow farmers— some of the older guys who are already farming—to make that change toward sustainability. I think that is something that is untapped and might be a possibility for the future.*
>
> *I think there is a lot of potential to use some of the USDA money that is available right now to set up farming cooperatives, grower skills, farmers' markets in small towns that do not have the support that Bloomington does. Use that as a way to create a market for people who have been excluded from this model because they are different. They are the ones who could be growing the [staples like] carrots and potatoes.*
>
> **Veldman:** *The number of farmers at the market using sustainable practices has really increased. I think that there is value in developing an interest in something other than the very standard varieties. You know, heirloom tomatoes are a niche crop, but there is the value in promoting that diversity, the desire for the flavor, and the integrity of something that has*

been carried through the years. I think that is really neat that the farmers' market does that.

It certainly costs more to grow an heirloom tomato because the productivity is lower and that sort of thing, but I am happy to see more and more of those being grown. And I think to look toward the future, we need to look at the world's largest seed company being bought up by Monsanto, and you start wondering if all these hybrid seeds are going to be owned by huge corporations, so that one day they are going to raise their prices. Then it will be really good that there are people out there caring for the open-pollinated seeds, for the diversity, and looking to small seed companies, so that it doesn't all get held in the hands of large corporations in the future.

Blondin: [Niche markets allow you to] gain your skills as a grower, to gain experience at that same time. If someone had to start off making what traditional conventional potato growers make, anywhere between a penny to three pennies a pound for potatoes, there is no way that someone could do that without a niche market—unless you have huge acreage, and then you have to grow two hundred acres of potatoes just to cover your costs. I think that the niche market is a really valuable tool at this point. People are out there gaining skills and teaching other people and new people are getting into growing. I see a lot of new, young growers at market, and that is really encouraging to me. And it is even more encouraging to see that the new growers are organic growers.

The farmers' market appears to be a going concern. The growers express their perennial concern about the proportion of vendors to customers and how it can be nudged in favor of higher incomes per vendor booth. That issue balances, however, with the continuing concern by a community organizer in the group that the food get to the people regardless of vendor profit.

Veldman: The Parks Department did a survey of the community in Monroe County that said that 50 percent of the population attended the Bloomington market. It was a significant survey. I thought that was a really high percentage.

Boos: Maybe. You are saying half of the people go at least once a year, in the count. And we only get four thousand a day over twenty-six markets. Maybe we need to look at how to get repeat customers. Because that means a lot of people are only coming once or twice or not often. How can we encourage people to come back more often?

Crouch: I bet there are lots of reasons. I don't think it is necessarily a bad thing. I mean, not everybody likes to spend several hours shopping. Not everybody likes to get up early on Saturday. A lot of people work on Saturday. I know some older people who get tired walking through the market. People have trouble finding places to park. They don't like to see tattoos. A lot of people don't cook with fresh vegetables very often. I would guess that there are lots of reasons why people wouldn't come.

That is why I like the idea of a thousand markets blooming [on every street corner as they do in the Third World] because then you create social spaces for [an] exchange of goods where you feel comfortable. I don't think that we necessarily want to replicate Wal-Mart at the farmers' market by having it get bigger and bigger and bigger.

Hartenfeld: We are a long ways from Wal-Mart!

Crouch: I know, but what I am saying is, having everything in one place, and have it be everything to everybody. I don't think that is necessarily a model to go for.

Boos: We keep talking about being vendors and how are we going to sell our produce. I think we need to ask, how can we get more people growing in urban gardens? One of the programs that we've tossed around while we are dreaming up plans is to be able to sell in small quantities. You know, if you are going to market your goods, you are going to have to be able to grow enough to be worth marketing. But if you are small and gardening in your back yard, people don't want to grow very much because they don't want to have excess. People don't know what to do with it. That's where an incubator kitchen comes in, to start small food businesses.

But what if there were more options for those people to sell small quantities? That might mean multiple farmers' market days with room for more vendors who have smaller quantities. I think more people would grow their own food and grow as much as they can because then they'd have a place to sell it. Markets now are kind of limited. You know, you can be small on the big scale, but you can't be too small, or it is not worth going at all.

Will farmers' markets continue to thrive as more outlets for local food become established?

The group discusses the viability of some of the alternative models for selling food locally. Several customers and vendors have been involved with community supported agriculture (CSA) arrangements, in which subscribers pay a fee in advance for a

Greene County

weekly share of a farm's produce. Also, several growers have sold in bulk to retail businesses, a strategy that local food organizers advocate as economically sustainable.

> ***Crouch:*** *I remember there was a group of people interested in setting up community supported agriculture about ten years ago because it was spreading all over the country. Several farmers came to the meeting at the public library, and a handful of farmers decided to try it. But because the farmers' market was such a reliable place to sell produce in Bloomington and because they could basically sell anything that they grew and sell out at the farmers' market, the incentive wasn't there to work with all these fussy consumers who didn't know how to use the rutabagas or who didn't know that strawberries weren't in season all year. A couple of the farmers I talked to who had tried it and quit said that it was too stressful because there were too many expectations put on them. Whereas at the market, they could just show up with whatever they had and sell it and be done with it. So because our market was so good, it didn't succeed here.*
> ***Hartenfeld:*** *I think you are exactly right. I have sold*

wholesale, retail, and in all kinds of ways, and if you are selling something that someone can't see exactly, there is a lot of pressure to make it really, really good. At the market, you can put it out there and if they like it, they buy it; and if they don't like it, they go to the next guy.

Along the same lines, wholesale contracts with restaurants are great, except look at the turnover in restaurants. You can have a great client, and he goes out of business. I have sold wholesale to grocery stores for a long time now, and when they go out of business or change hands, I've lost huge wholesale accounts. One was bought by a company who had a policy of not buying locally. Another just got sold. I think they sold it to a company who is holding it and selling it to another company. I don't have a clue as to what is going to happen there. So I like the farmers' market. I know that it's going to be there every Saturday. I know there will be customers. The customers know there will be vendors. That is really advantageous.

While the challenges to small farms and locally grown food are substantial, markets that put producers into contact with consumers offer both stability and promise.

Hartenfeld: The thing I have realized in doing this book project is that, in this last thirty-year stint of farmers' markets, they have become an institution in our culture. Which is really cool. Even after everybody is gone, the next group of growers and town people will continue the market. This is a valuable thing to pass on and to have as a part of our culture.

It would be great if the market were year round, an indoor-outdoor situation, where it was comfortable for people. It would be great if we had ten thousand people coming through market. I know there is a fine line between increasing the growing side of market, bringing in more and more and more vendors, and getting more on the customer side. If we don't have more than five thousand customers in a peak season, and get more vendors, everybody walks with less money. We are tapping just a few people.

If I were advising somebody just starting out, I would say, support your market. Educate people to come to the farmers' market. Small growers can make a living selling directly to the people. There are potentially plenty of buyers compared to only a few growers. Both groups benefit greatly.

We can effect change locally. We can take care of ourselves and those in our community.

Johnson: That's all we can do.

Vendor, Customer   *Bloomington*

Conclusion_____

We're doing more than just growing vegetables. We are creating biodiversity and protecting water, as much as our small farm can. And I just enjoy being able to take it to the market. I enjoy interacting with people who eat it, appreciate it, and enjoy it. I meet a lot of neat people there, doing a lot of neat things. It's kind of inspiring. You get tired, oh gosh! But you go there, and you meet all these other people who are doing these amazing things. And I think, I could do more! Who am I kidding? I'm not doing anything!

—MELISSA EVARD, vendor

One might view farmers' markets as places of *in*convenience. Most are held out of doors where customers experience the vagaries of seasons, their shortages, and their inundations. Visiting a farmers' market may mean journeying to neighborhoods unknown to hunt for parking, walk too far, and carry awkward loads. The growers, for their part—after a week of bending over, carrying buckets, slopping stalls, hoeing, cutting, rescuing animals or putting them down, working in the sun or the wet—arise earlier than usual, wait for the crowd to materialize, and hope that they sell all that will not last until next time. Despite all this, farmers' markets are springing up in parks, parking lots, and empty lots all over America, bringing renewed life to an ancient human institution.

For customers, the weekly trek to the farmers' market provides a shopping experience unlike others. If their goal is to find fresh, quality food at reasonable prices, that is likely achievable. In other ways, too, the market experience contrasts sharply with the interchangeable and exchangeable nature of many more mainstream commercial shopping experiences. While goods on sale at a typical mall, for example, may convey only a fleeting sense of belonging by gracing the consumer with the current (soon passé) style, the farmers' market offers the raw materials for self and belonging.[1] In this way, markets offer *not* a purchasable lifestyle that can be mistaken for community but rather a community that takes into its scope the American predilection for the consumer experience.

For vendors, a vibrant market has the potential to rewrite the place of growers large and small in the community. They stake out a clear space for an independent business, and they enter into a social network of trust, accountability, and reciprocity with fellow vendors, customers, and others. Farmers using sustainable methods, in particular, should be regarded as assets to and stewards of their communities.[2] Wendell Berry says that being a farmer can take a lifetime to learn.[3] And communities will benefit from investing in their success.

The convergences in the stories that vendors and customers tell describe the common ground of farmers' markets. They bring people into proximity so that they have the chance to create "mutual and simultaneous histories" with those around them.[4] Each of their stories is new and unique and yet familiar, and together they reveal patterns, showing a means to bridge the permeable borders of old and new, individuals and group, and town and country. They provide space for individual creativity among the lingering, talking, observing, editorializing, gossiping, brewing up of critique and dissent, and creating of bonds that sustain communities as surely as foodstuffs do. Not spectacular events, farmers' markets are nonetheless special ones. Like festivals, rituals, and other cultural performances, markets encapsulate a culture so that it is on display for itself and others.[5]

Challenges loom for markets even in this boom time. Long a bastion of organic food, farmers' markets face the entry of Wal-Mart, the world's largest retailer, into that sector. Organic food at the mega-scale brings into question its assumed association with local, ethical, and sustainable practices. Rising petroleum prices will further squeeze the small and midsized growers. And as much as markets prosper from the differences they incorporate, the intersections of those differences also threaten market patrons. In the United States, we have been lucky to be able to assume that our markets are, by and large, areas of safety and peaceful co-existence, but around the world, markets regularly suffer violent political action and protest.[6]

Farmers in the United States are aging and traditional prac-

Monroe County

tices worldwide have been replaced by Western notions. Because farming and its practices are constructs of culture, they must be passed on or forgotten. Once gone, they must be reinvented. Even now, farmers work to recover ways in common practice before the "green revolution" introduced and quickly dominated other ways of knowing about agriculture. Fertilizers, pesticides, machinery, transportation, all shifted rapidly—in just a few decades of the millennia of farming—to a petroleum-based system that overturned tradition. Knowledge, development, discretion, and power moved out of the hands of the growers.[7] And innovative ways quickly became "conventional" such that knowledge of the old ways became suspect, and the skills and plant varieties that incorporated them dwindled like an unspoken language.[8]

Wendell Berry has identified two "complementary efforts" that must be undertaken for small farming to survive all the various cultural, political, economic, and environmental onslaughts against it:

> *The first is entirely up to the farmers, who must learn—or learn again—to farm in ways that minimize their dependence on industrial supplies. . . . The second effort involves cooperation between local farmers and local consumers. . . . The long-broken connections between towns and cities and their surrounding landscapes will have to be restored. . . . What we must do is simple: we must shorten the distance that our food is transported so that we are eating more and more from local supplies, more and more to the benefit of local farmers, and more and more to the satisfaction of local consumers.[9]*

Farmers' markets are the logical site for such partnerships to take shape. They can create a place of bonding that helps to rebuild local crop diversity, shift diets toward more healthful and fresh foods, restore the ecology and beauty of local landscapes, and boost local economies. Markets can help communities rebuild their capacity to control their own food security, shifting power away from the handful of corporations that now control the vast majority of products in grocery stores worldwide and "return it

Greene County

to the public."[10] Indeed, this is the other homeland security, locally based, secular, mutual, and in scale with the individual human endeavor. As we go to press, we hear about new farmers' markets in American cities and towns of every size. Not the only site on which to build a renewed sense of community, they are a particularly apt one—grounded as they are in history, tradition, climate, and the ecologies of culture and place, tapping as they do that most primal drive for food and combining it with the sustenance of social organization and place.

No one at market can build a permanent structure. Like bazaar purveyors on the streets of regional cities worldwide, the vendors create the institution each day from scratch. Every one makes a look for his stand, choosing signs with movable letters, a chalkboard, or a word-processed price list. Some display their farm names on a banner, a piece of carved wood, or spray painted onto the side of the truck, a cooler, a T-shirt, or a nail apron doubling as cash pouch. Some vendors offer paper bags or plastic, display in white tubs or blue ones, load their wares into baskets, buckets, or bowls. While seed companies are claiming ownership of fertility itself and hogs are grown to specifications that fit the disemboweling machines and commercial growers plan to laser cut their logos into every tomato's skin, farmers' markets remain idiosyncratic. One might say that branding at a farmers' market is more like bonding. It happens most clearly in the one-to-one moment of exchange: the stories a customer can tell about getting a deal, finding a sought-for variety, or sharing the fruits of the hunt with a certain friend. The individual matters there—as a unit of production, as a unit of consumption, as a unit of community. At the end of the day, when the vendors and customers leave, the market vanishes. It does not exist without the people. They roll everything up and carry it all away.

Greene County

Notes

Introduction

1. See Berry, "How to Be a Poet (to Remind Myself)."

2. USDA, *AMS Farmers Markets;* U.S. Census Bureau, "Geographic Comparison Table." In 1910, approximately 32 million people, or a third of the population of the United States were farmers living on farms. By 1991, only 4.6 million people lived on farms, less than 2% of the total population, and by 2000, less than 1% was employed in agriculture, fishing, forestry, or hunting.

3. Berry, *Another Turn of the Crank.*

4. USDA, "U.S. Farmers Markets—2000."

5. For one study that shows declining nutrition of conventional crops, see Davis, Epp, and Riordan, "Changes in USDA Food Composition Data for 43 Garden Crops, 1950 to 1999."

6. Both authors write from the perspectives of longtime vendors at the Bloomington Community Farmers' Market and also as analytical observers at that farmers' market and others. The data collection methods used for this book include ethnographic approaches of participant observation and directive and non-directive interviewing. We conducted nearly 50 in-depth interviews over a 2-year period with customers, administrative staff, vendors, and allied purveyors of the Bloomington market and other selected markets, nationally, with countless other conversations along the way. Data collection occurred both on-site at the market or at people's homes or farms (arguably also to be considered on-site) and off-site in restaurants. Conversations were recorded in field notes; as audiotapes of interviews, focus groups, and informal interactions; and in photographs. Some interviewees were known to the authors on a long-term basis and had bonds of acquaintance of varying degrees. Others were encountered in the context of this project. Nearly all of the interviewees agreed unstintingly to full identification in publication, although the authors have chosen to reserve some identities in certain instances. Without exception, all of those we spoke with were exceedingly generous with their wisdom and time.

This study assumes that human society and culture are created through repetition of patterns, which themselves allow for, and are made up from, variation and individual enactment, following theorists such as Mikhail Bakhtin, Erving Goffman, Christopher Alexander, Richard Bauman, and Charles Briggs. We assume that those individual enactments are also informed by the common resources available within a social group.

1. Markets Past

1. Clark, *Onions Are My Husband.*

2. Bromley and Symanski, "Marketplace Trade in Latin America."

3. Project for Public Spaces, *Great Public Spaces.* Descriptions of markets around the world, including some described in this chapter, can be found at this internet resource.

4. Bromley and Symanski, "Marketplace Trade in Latin America."

5. Pyle, "Farmers' Markets in the United States"; Wann et al., "Farmers' Produce Markets in the United States"; Paul, "The New Face of Old McDonald."

6. Wann et al., "Farmers' Produce Markets," iii.

7. Botsford and Robinson, *Hellenic History,* 158.

8. Britnell, *The Marketing of Grain in England, 1250–1350.* For more information about medieval markets, see this internet resource.

9. Much of this paragraph after Britnell.

10. *The Domesday Book.*

11. Hallam, *Rural England, 1066–1348,* 246–47.

12. Muhlberger, "Medieval England."

13. Knox, "Medieval Society."

14. Britnell, *The Marketing of Grain in England.*

15. Muhlberger, "Medieval England."

16. Ibid.

17. See the full account of Bury St. Edmonds at this time in Arnold, ed., "Memorials of St. Edmund's Abbey."

18. See Britnell, *The Marketing of Grain in England.*

19. L. W., "God's Great and Vvonderful Vvork in Somerset-Shire."

20. *The Country-Miser.*

21. Díaz del Castillo, *The True History of the Conquest of New Spain.*

22. Bromley and Symanski, "Marketplace Trade in Latin America."

23. Rafert, *The Miami Indians of Indiana,* 25–55.

24. Hall, *Historic Treasures,* 23.

25. Pyle, "Farmers' Markets in the United States," 172.

26. Wann et al., "Farmers' Produce Markets," 5–6.

27. Ibid., 5.

28. Compare to Bromley and Symanski, "Marketplace Trade in Latin America." During the same period in South America, the number of small markets also declined while activity at larger market centers has increased. In an exception, markets in Bolivia were established after the revolution of 1952 because land reform broke up large estates. They

then went as smaller holdings to growers who took their produce to new markets frequented by wholesale buyers. The result was a higher income for the small growers.

29. Pyle, "Farmers' Markets in the United States," 179.

30. These statistics are according to ibid., which cites the 1880 U.S. Census. This survey was not an exhaustive census of major urban areas.

31. Ibid., 176.

32. Ibid., 172.

33. From the *Judicium Pillorie,* quoted in Britnell, *The Marketing of Grain in England.*

34. Quoted from the *Composicio* (1274–75) in Britnell.

35. Lyson, Gillespie, and Hilchey, "Farmers' Markets and the Local Community."

36. Paul, "The New Face of Old McDonald."

37. Integrity Systems Cooperative Co., *Adding Values to Our Food System,* 3.

38. Wann et al., "Farmers' Produce Markets," 15.

39. Ibid., 2.

40. By 1993, only 1% of the food people ate was produced at home, according to Integrity Systems Cooperative Co., *Adding Values to Our Food System,* 64.

41. Wann et al., "Farmers' Produce Markets." This study counted four types of farmers' markets: wholesale markets, wholesale shipping point markets, retail markets, and "farm women's markets."

42. Ibid., 2. Pyle, "Farmers' Markets in the United States," 180–83, 92.

43. De Weese, *The Detroit Eastern Farmers' Market,* 14.

44. Brown, "Counting Farmers Markets," 665.

45. Pyle, "Farmers' Markets in the United States," 185.

46. Halweil, *Eat Here;* Halweil, "Home Grown," 7–8.

47. Lyson, Gillespie, and Hilchey, "Farmers' Markets and the Local Community," 108.

48. Brown, "Farmers' Market Research 1940–2000," 173.

49. Callahan, "America Growing a Taste for Organic Food."

50. Fox, "Paul K. Keene, 94, Organic Farming Pioneer." In 2000, the Hain Celestial Group added Walnut Acres to its growing portfolio of natural foods labels. Walnut Acres Farms had been among the first commercial producers of organic foods. It was founded by Paul K. Keene in Pennsylvania in the mid-1940s after he met Gandhi while he was teaching in India a decade earlier. Keene brought home lessons from the Indian independence movement, which had itself been influenced by Albert Howard's observations about traditional regenerative farming practices in India. Bucking mid-century agricultural conventions for more natural and traditional methods that used such things as manuring and ladybugs, Walnut Acres' organic operation was able to produce more than 350 products, with annual sales of nearly $8 million at its height.

51. Pretty, Lang, Morison, and Ball, "Food Miles and Farm Costs."

52. Halweil, *Eat Here,* 7.

53. Halweil, "Home Grown."

54. Ikerd, "The High Cost of Cheap Food," 3.

55. U.S. Census Bureau, "Geographic Comparison Table."

56. Planck, *Real Food: What to Eat and Why.*

2. New Markets

1. Howard, *An Agricultural Testament.*

2. Brucato, *The Farmer Goes to Town,* 17. A special sale of potatoes later sold "more than 20,000 sacks of surplus Sonoma County potatoes at 2½ cents per pound," half the retail price (32). Subsequent references to the early years of the San Francisco farmers' market refer to this book.

3. See Davis, Epp, and Riordan, "Changes in USDA Food Composition Data for 43 Garden Crops, 1950 to 1999." The breeding and planting based on yield rather than nutrition has led to a decline in some vitamins and minerals in certain vegetables since 1950.

4. See *Farmers Market.* Even today, that same Los Angeles market, featured in "Farmers' Market at Gilmore Island," advertises car racing, multiplex movie theaters, and a replicated "Village Square." See www .farmersmarketla.com.

5. The terms "producer-vendor" and "grower-vendor" have different connotations, in that some "producers" may not actually grow what they sell. Such products would include wild mushrooms and jam made from purchased fruit. Some markets have some small-scale producers who are not also growers. Many markets, however, try to control the number of non-growing producers (though most would not count wildcrafters as non-growers).

6. Schlosser, *Fast Food Nation.*

7. Howard, *An Agricultural Testament.*

8. Nearing and Nearing, *Living the Good Life.*

9. Ibid., vii.

10. Lappé, *Diet for a Small Planet.*

11. Thomas, *The Vegetarian Epicure;* Katzen, *Moosewood Cookbook.*

12. Madison, *About Deborah Madison.*

13. United States, "Farmer-to-Consumer Direct Marketing Act of 1976, Public Law 94-463." See also Brown, "Counting Farmers Markets." Brown debates the precise number of farmers' markets in operation in 1970, concluding that by 1976 it probably approximated another scholar's "educated guess" of 600 (665). In her review of literature, Brown notes that the quantitative descriptions of farmers' markets, including their prevalence, farmer income, and consumer spending are ballpark figures at best, pointing out discrepancies in the USDA Agricultural Census's method (168). For example, a study of direct marketing

conducted by the USDA and the University of Georgia in 1996 did not include sales of non-food items such as flowers, nursery products, wool, and value-added products (168).

14. Pyle, "Farmers' Markets in the United States," 188.

15. Callahan, "America Growing a Taste for Organic Food." Indiana did not opt into the organic movement as quickly as some other states. In 2005, the state-government certifier had approved only 54 organic farms. Meanwhile, across the nation, certified organic cropland was growing quickly, amounting to 2.3 million acres in 2001.

16. The term "market" can refer to many kinds of institutions. In general, they can be defined as "an organized public gathering of buyers and sellers of commodities meeting at an appointed place at regular intervals" (ibid., 3). The term "farmers' market" in contemporary North America is applied loosely to wholesale markets, at which the majority of the buyers are retailers rather than consumers and many of the vendors sell produce they have bought elsewhere rather than growing it themselves. Some so-called farmers' markets are really closer to flea markets or festivals, with a high proportion of stands featuring food and non-foodstuffs brought in from miles away or other states or countries. Sometimes the term is used to refer to private markets that are owned by one person who stocks the market with various kinds of vendors in order to make a profit. Some of these private markets have little if anything to do with farmers while others, in contrast, feature only local producer-vendors. Occasionally, people use "farmers' markets" for what would be better termed "farm markets" or "farm stands." These private operations are usually associated with a single farm or a few neighboring ones. Sometimes proprietors of these farm markets, particularly year-round ones, supplement what they can grow with produce purchased from wholesale distributors. The most defining characteristic in this discussion about farmers' markets as a site for building community in the prevailing North American corporate culture is that they bring producers and consumers into direct exchange.

17. For the 1974 statistics, see Brown, "Farmers' Market Research 1940–2000," 167; all other statistics are from USDA, "U.S. Farmers Markets—2000," iv.

18. Arnosky and Arnosky, "Reinventing the Farm," 16–17.

19. Paul, "The New Face of Old McDonald."

20. Integrity Systems Cooperative Co., *Adding Values to Our Food System,* 4.

21. Ikerd, "The New American Food Culture."

22. Indeed, in the 1940s farmers were beginning to realize that they would need to diversify crops and secure local sales outlets if they were to compete against big agribusiness. See Brucato, *The Farmer Goes to Town,* 121.

23. Integrity Systems Cooperative Co., *Adding Values to Our Food System,* 4. See also Flora, "Social Capital and Sustainability" for a dis-

cussion of a study that showed sustainable agriculture improves community wellbeing.

24. Kloppenburg et al. (1996) quoted in Integrity Systems Cooperative Co., *Adding Values to Our Food System,* 4.

25. Brown, "Counting Farmers Markets," 669.

26. Jonas Winklepleck, interview with Jennifer Meta Robinson, Bloomington, September 3, 2005.

27. Theresa Ochoa, interview with Jennifer Meta Robinson, Bloomington, May 13, 2005.

28. David Morgan, interview with Jennifer Meta Robinson, Bloomington, August 13, 2005.

29. Berry, *Another Turn of the Crank,* 13, 16.

30. Alexander, *The Timeless Way of Building,* 29.

3. The Bloomington Farmers' Market

1. Dan Cooper, interview with Jennifer Meta Robinson, Bloomington, June 4, 2005.

2. Veldman, "Lunch Wagon Discussion."

3. Wann et al., "Farmers' Produce Markets in the United States," 81–83.

4. Pyle, "Farmers' Markets in the United States," 185.

5. See Indianapolis City Market, *Indianapolis City Market.* In the early twenty-first century, the City of Indianapolis is capitalizing on the success of the revived Original City Market by building more housing units and retail storefronts on or near that downtown location.

6. Rafert, *The Miami Indians of Indiana,* 1–13.

7. Hall, *Historic Treasures,* 75. The description of early Bloomington and the market house are drawn from this source.

8. Pyle, "Farmers' Markets in the United States," 193. The Spencer fur market fielded half a dozen buyers and 25 or so sellers, and the prices averaged 25¢ for a pelt in 1971.

9. Adams, "What Kind of Farmer?"

10. "History and Heritage."

11. David LoCascio, interview with J. A. Hartenfeld, May 4, 2006.

12. The Belmont Farmers' Market Committee, "Beginnings."

13. Marcia Veldman, focus group with Jennifer Meta Robinson and J. A. Hartenfeld, Hart Farm, Solsberry, Ind., May 7, 2006.

14. City of Bloomington, *2006 Farm Vendor Handbook,* 3.

15. DeVault, "Persistence Pays Off for Farmers' Market."

16. *Santa Fe Farmers Market.*

17. See Koryta, "Showers Sale 50 Years Ago Marked the End of an Era."

18. Marcia Veldman, e-mail communication, April 3, 2006.

19. USDA, "U.S. Farmers Markets—2000," 4–5.

20. Veldman, e-mail communication.

21. The Holiday Market invites all of the regular season farmers to participate and is also open to artists upon application. All the artwork has to be original and made by the artist. Dried flower arrangements must be grown by the applicant, and work cannot include items made from kits or from molds that were not made by him or her. Work is selected with the intention of creating a diversity of items available, and also on the basis of quality, price, variety, and previous participation. People who participate during Affair of the Arts during the regular season are given special consideration.

22. Simone Robbins, interview with Jennifer Meta Robinson, September 5, 2006.

23. In 1946, fees for selling at a market ranged from 25¢ to $1 or more, and most markets rented space on daily or load basis, though others rented on a weekly, monthly, or annual basis (Wann et al., "Farmers' Produce Markets," iv). In 1990, the Boulder, Colorado, market followed a different fee structure. To have access to the 15,000 to 18,000 customers per week, vendors there paid fees according to a percentage of their income from the market—5% for farmers and 15% for food stalls—plus a membership fee of $50 per year for growers and $100 for food stalls (Festing, *Farmers' Markets,* 14).

24. Veldman, "Lunch Wagon Discussion."

25. Maria Cooper and Scott Cooper, interview with Jennifer Meta Robinson, Bloomington, August 20, 2005.

26. USDA, "U.S. Farmers Markets—2000." According to the U.S. Department of Agriculture, markets most commonly receive support from local governments through, for instance, grants or a rent-free space. The most significant support they can receive from that source is a manager. Thirty percent of all markets had paid managers (half of those had full-time managers), as of 2000. Markets with full-time workers average 2.2 full-time workers, while markets with part-time workers reported 1.9 part-time workers.

27. All statistics in this paragraph from USDA, "U.S. Farmers Markets—2000."

28. Ibid.

29. Burns and Johnson, *Farmers' Market Survey Report.*

30. National Association of Farmers Markets.

31. Ibid.

32. City of Bloomington, *2005 Farm Vendor Handbook.* The Bloomington market makes no conditions regarding quality. In contrast, the Athens, Ohio, market, for example, tries to ensure the quality of produce and the sustainability of the farmers by prohibiting "radical price cutting of top quality produce" or the selling of "poor quality or overripe produce" without appropriate labeling and discounting (see the website www.athensfarmersmarket.org). It also provides detailed rules for expelling producers from the market for "violations of any market regulations."

33. Veldman, "Lunch Wagon Discussion."

34. Occasionally people with city street–vending permits pull alongside the market area to sell prepared food that they have not grown. The market management responded by trying to get the city to exclude non-market food vendors from areas adjacent to the Common, arguing, "The Market cannot be all things to all people. Markets that try to do that become flea markets. . . . Somewhere a line has to be drawn on what type of commerce is and isn't permissible and no matter where you draw the line, some people will be unhappy. That is why it is so important to have sound reasons for drawing the line and not base it on the interest of a few individuals" (ibid.). While one might see these renegades as entrepreneurs, taking advantage of a sales opportunity by providing new options for customers, the market management believes that such infringements will eventually degrade the market and its local orientation. Allowing independent entrepreneurs to take advantage of the market scene, the market staff say, affords them, for free, the benefits of the market for which others pay. Those benefits cost Bloomington vendors $104 to $317 each to use a space for the 2006 season. After debate, however, the City Council decided against the market staff's recommendation and continues to allow licensed food vendors access to the blocks surrounding the market.

35. See especially Brown, "Farmers' Market Research 1940–2000"; and Hilchey, Lyson, and Gillespie, "Farmers' Markets and Rural Economic Development"; Paul, "The New Face of Old McDonald," 5.

36. Brown, "Farmers' Market Research 1940–2000," 173; Hilchey, Lyson, and Gillespie, "Farmers' Markets and Rural Economic Development."

37. Festing, *Farmers' Markets*.

38. For a cogent argument for professional market managers, see Planck, "Farmers' Markets & Beyond."

39. Such suspicions are not frequent but do occur occasionally at many markets. For a report of similar tensions, see De Weese, *The Detroit Eastern Farmers' Market*, 6.

40. Anonymous (C102), interview with Jennifer Meta Robinson, Bloomington, 2005; and Anonymous (C106), interview with Jennifer Meta Robinson, Hart Farm, Solsberry, Indiana, 2005.

41. Ibid.

42. See for example Kremen, Greene, and Hanson, "Organic Produce, Price Premiums, and Eco-Labeling in U.S. Farmers' Markets," 10; Integrity Systems Cooperative Co., *Adding Values to Our Food System*.

43. Putnam and Allhouse (1994), quoted in Integrity Systems Cooperative Co., *Adding Values to Our Food System,* 3; Plunkett Research, "Food, Beverage and Tobacco Trends."

44. Jewett and Braaten, *Local Foods: Where to Find It, How to Buy It*.

45. USDA, "U.S. Farmers Markets—2000." National market figures are from 2000, the most current available.

46. Brown, "Farmers' Market Research 1940–2000," 169; Festing, *Farmers' Markets,* 29; USDA, "U.S. Farmers Markets—2000," 6. A market survey in Alberta, Canada, showed that the majority of consumers at farmers' markets there were female (80%) and half of them lived alone or in two-person households (Paul, "The New Face of Old McDonald," 6).

47. Indiana Business Research Center, *Bloomington, IN Metro Area.* All Bloomington and Indiana statistics in the paragraph are from here.

48. Festing, *Farmers' Markets,* 13.

49. Economics Institute, *Crescent City Farmers Market.*

50. Fisher, *Hot Peppers and Parking Lot Peaches,* 9.

51. USDA, "U.S. Farmers Markets—2000."

52. Fisher, *Hot Peppers and Parking Lot Peaches.*

53. Warren and Tyagi, *The Two-Income Trap.* This research indicates that today's middle-class families earn about 75% more (adjusted for inflation) compared to those a generation ago in large part due to mothers entering the work force. However, after accounting for four fixed expenses—mortgage, health insurance, childcare or education, and car payments—today's median-income family has less money left over than the single-income family of the 1970s.

54. Theresa Ochoa, interview with Jennifer Meta Robinson, Bloomington, May 13, 2005; Josh Tenenberg, e-mail communication, March 11, 2005; Katie Levin, interview with Jennifer Meta Robinson, Bloomington, May 28, 2005; Anonymous (C209), interview with Jennifer Meta Robinson, Washington, D.C., June 19, 2005; Jane Goodman, interview with Jennifer Meta Robinson, Hart Farm, Solsberry, Indiana, June 19, 2005; Dan Cooper, interview with Jennifer Meta Robinson, Bloomington, June 4, 2005; Elisabeth McMahon and Christopher Harter, interview with Jennifer Meta Robinson, Bloomington, May 28, 2005; Peacock, "Farmers' Markets"; Brown, "Farmers' Market Research 1940–2000," 168–71; Madison, *Local Flavors,* xviii.

55. Ibid.; customer interviews 106, 102, 101, and 108.

56. USDA, *AMS Farmers Markets.* All national statistics in this paragraph are from this source.

57. Fisher, *Hot Peppers and Parking Lot Peaches.*

58. Veldman, e-mail communication.

59. As at other markets, customers at farmers' markets in low-income neighborhoods look for quality and freshness first and then price. While Americans as a whole eat more fruits and vegetables as their income increases, the lower income groups in California, especially Hispanics, tend to eat more fruits and vegetables on a daily basis than other ethnic groups with higher incomes (Fisher, *Hot Peppers and Parking Lot Peaches*).

60. USDA, "U.S. Farmers Markets—2000," iv. In comparison, the Dane County Farmers' Market (Madison, Wisc.) in 2003 did a survey that found on average people spent $15.80 at market (not including crafts). See Lemire, "Dane County Farmers' Market Survey."

61. Ibid. A survey of customers at the Dane County market found that about half the market customers shop and eat downtown on market days, spending about $22 additional dollars at downtown businesses.

62. Festing, *Farmers' Markets,* 7; Veldman, e-mail communication.

63. National figures in this paragraph from USDA, "U.S. Farmers Markets—2000," the most recent statistics available from the government.

64. Festing, *Farmers' Markets,* 35.

65. USDA, *AMS Farmers Markets.*

Vendor Notes, Part 2

1. Cheal, "Showing Them You Love Them," 158.

4. Market Customers

1. Cottingham, "Profile of Farmers and Consumers at Wisconsin Farmers' Markets," quoted in Festing, *Farmers' Markets;* De Weese, *The Detroit Eastern Farmers' Market,* 15; Hilchey, Lyson, and Gillespie, "Farmers' Markets and Rural Economic Development," 3. These studies and others show that 40% to 65% of people shopping at farmers' markets do so for the "atmosphere."

2. In Christopher Alexander's view, each place has the potential to generate a unique feeling that he describes as its "aliveness." That feeling, he says, comes in part from how well its architectural design matches human needs and uses and also from the "patterns" of experience we find there, created by "the people around us, and the most common ways we have of meeting them, of being with them" (*The Timeless Way of Building,* 26, 62). Such structures and patterns define, or key, the market as a special place and a kind of collective, cultural performance.

A market may not be practiced and staged in the same way as a theatrical performance or a religious service, but each of the participants has his or her part to prepare for and plays that role when the "cast" assembles for the special event (Bauman and Ritch, "Informing Performance").

Perhaps chief among the signals of the market as a performance is time. Many market participants point to its rhythms—its periodic regularity by season, by day, and by hour; its opening with the breaking day and closing with a blast from the market master's whistle—as part of what makes it special. Physical structures also help to evoke the mood of the market and transform it into a performance space. Canopies, umbrellas, and tables transform a parking lot into a marketplace. An umbrella of sensory inputs also united the market into a cohesive space: the colorfulness of the displays; the smells of popcorn, cooked meat, or aromatic flowers; the sounds of a steam engine, musical groups, and that distinctive noise of being equidistant between musical groups or numerous boisterous conversations; the place-evoking feel of osage oranges, honey sticks, edamame pods, or watermelons. The dress of the participants, for all their diversity, may create a sense of a distinctive event. (The Bloomington market shows an abundance of straw hats, suspenders, baskets, oversized bags, and wagons of produce that are not typically found elsewhere around town.) (See Stoeltje and Bauman, "The Semiotics of Folkloric Performance," for a discussion of the features of cultural performances.)

Within the larger context of the market are performances that take place on a smaller scale, in how individuals conduct themselves and relate to others in groups. A vendor who juggles and another who wears "old-timey" clothes or sings out a particular greeting to potential customers are helping to create the market atmosphere. The ways that people interact in a space like a farmers' market are both fresh and individual and also in many ways draw on behaviors and scripts familiar to others around them. These ways of being also create patterns. The patterns as enacted by individuals in conjunction with the market and collectively through the market are what this book explores, and those patterns, as Alexander says, "make it possible for us to be alive" (*The Timeless Way*, 65).

3. Jane Goodman, interview with Jennifer Meta Robinson, Hart Farm, Solsberry, Indiana, June 19, 2005.

4. Theresa Ochoa, interview with Jennifer Meta Robinson, Bloomington, May 13, 2005.

5. Brown, "Farmers' Market Research 1940–2000," 168, 70–71; Paul, "The New Face of Old McDonald," 6; Festing, *Farmers' Markets,* 30; Integrity Systems Cooperative Co., *Adding Values to Our Food System;* Hilchey, Lyson, and Gillespie, "Farmers' Markets"; Cottingham, "Profile of Farmers and Consumers," quoted in Festing, *Farmers' Markets.* See also Planck, "Farmers' Markets & Beyond"; Madison, *Local Flavors,* xxiii.

6. Kremen, Greene, and Hanson, "Organic Produce, Price Premiums, and Eco-Labeling," 4.

7. Some customers believe, often incorrectly, that they can tell who grows organically and who does not. One customer assumed that she could tell categorically that "older" vendors or those with more produce are not organic and that Amish, younger, or long-haired vendors are. But anyone who has had in-depth experience with farmers knows such assumptions are unfounded. Other customers may have the misconception that organic food is sold at a substantial markup, although studies indicate that the premiums on organic foods at most markets are very small. See also ibid., 10.

8. Madison, *Local Flavors,* xxiii; Anonymous (C213), interview with Jennifer Meta Robinson, Bloomington, 2005.

9. Anonymous (C213), interview.

10. Kremen, Greene, and Hanson, "Organic Produce, Price Premiums, and Eco-Labeling," 6.

11. Hilchey, Lyson, and Gillespie, "Farmers' Markets and Rural Eco-

nomic Development," 3; Kremen, Greene, and Hanson, "Organic Produce, Price Premiums, and Eco-Labeling," 6.

12. Cottingham, "Profile of Farmers and Consumers," quoted in Festing, *Farmers' Markets;* Fisher, "Hot Peppers and Parking Lot Peaches," 40; Kremen, Greene, and Hanson, "Organic Produce, Price Premiums, and Eco-Labeling," 1.

13. Economic Research Service, *Household Food Security in the United States,* 2.

14. Hilchey, Lyson, and Gillespie, "Farmers' Markets and Rural Economic Development," 3.

15. Elisabeth McMahon and Christopher Harter, interview with Jennifer Meta Robinson, Bloomington, May 28, 2005.

16. See Integrity Systems Cooperative Co., *Adding Values to Our Food System,* 65. This report, prepared for the USDA, cites a trend during the 1990s that suggests that organic produce moved beyond specialty markets of socially and environmentally aware consumers and into the mainstream where customers look first for quality and freshness. The report also notes that studies in the 1990s showed that the top three reasons consumers did not buy organic produce were lack of availability, price, and lack of knowledge. This suggests, the report says, that "as consumer knowledge improves; as organic produce becomes more readily available; and as organic growing matures (resulting in lower farm costs), locally produced organic foods should capture a great share of the total food market" (65). With the recent entry of Wal-Mart and other mega-retailers into the arena, organic food is sure to have a higher profile as well as greater production, which may provide collateral benefit to farmers' markets.

17. Paul, "The New Face of Old McDonald," 6; Festing, *Farmers' Markets,* 30; Hilchey, Lyson, and Gillespie, "Farmers' Markets and Rural Economic Development," 3; Brown, "Farmers' Market Research 1940–2000," 169. A market survey in Alberta, Canada, and one in Wisconsin found that, for as many as 72% of customers, supporting local farmers was one of the most important reasons people attended farmers' markets. A California study indicated that a majority of respondents were willing to pay a higher price for food that contributed to a living wage and safe working conditions (Howard, "Central Coast Consumers Want More Food-Related Information").

18. Anonymous (C106), interview with Jennifer Meta Robinson, Hart Farm, Solsberry, Indiana, 2005.

19. Katie Levin, interview with Jennifer Meta Robinson, Bloomington, May 28, 2005. Subsequent quotes from Levin are from this interview.

20. Anonymous (C101), interview with Jennifer Meta Robinson, Bloomington, 2005.

21. David Morgan, interview with Jennifer Meta Robinson, Bloomington, August 13, 2005.

22. Alexander, *Timeless Way*, 25.

23. Taylor and Harper, "Age-Old Practices in the 'New World'." In small towns, the networks of obligation can even become a burden, keeping people from attending the market because they want to avoid a particular person or because they anticipate exhaustion at having to meet and greet so many. Introverts, those who deal with the public in their jobs, and others may not find it relaxing to circulate in crowds of people they recognize.

24. Ochoa, interview with Jennifer Meta Robinson, Bloomington, May 13, 2005.

25. Cecilia Wade Hartfield, interview with Jennifer Meta Robinson, Bloomington, October 8, 2005.

26. Waters, "Keynote."

27. Madison, *Local Flavors*, xvii.

28. Sommer et al., "The Behavioral Ecology of Supermarkets and Farmers Markets," 13–19. Customers frequently mention the number of conversations they have at market, including Dan Cooper, interview with Jennifer Meta Robinson, Bloomington, June 4, 2005; Morgan, interview; and Anonymous (C212), interview with Jennifer Meta Robinson, Bloomington, August 9, 2005.

29. See Lauren Langman as quoted in Aldred, "Plastic Shamans and Astroturf Sun Dances"; Bauman, "Survival as a Social Construct." Lauren Langman suggests that identity becomes problematic in a society in which stable social networks of kinship and community have broken down. People relieve their sense of loneliness by purchasing items that identify them with a group (a "proto-community") defined by commercial society. However, this activity provides only short-lived and unsatisfactory gratification. Bauman (in "Survival"), too, recognizes the effort to mitigate feelings of isolation by buying products that associate them with a "neo-tribe."

30. De Weese, *The Detroit Eastern Farmers' Market*, 18.

31. Ochoa, interview.

32. Customers corroborated what De Weese found in her survey of the Detroit market in the 1970s that only a minority (13%) of the shoppers at the market cited nostalgia or tradition as reasons for attending (15–16).

5. Market Growers

1. Lyson, Gillespie, and Hilchey, "Farmers' Markets and the Local Community." Reasons such as "we want extra income," "our other income sources are limited," "we don't have the capital to open [another kind of outlet like a roadside stand or store]" top the list for why vendors attend farmers' markets. The fifth most common reason is "we have always sold at the farmers' market," which was not statistically different for full-time or part-time growers. The seventh most cited reason, "we

have no other options," also showed no statistical difference for full-time or part-time growers. Also in the top ten: "we want a learning experience for children."

2. Ibid.; Brown, "Farmers' Market Research 1940–2000," 168.

3. USDA, "U.S. Farmers Markets—2000."

4. Henderson and Linstrom, "Farmer-to-Consumer Direct Marketing in Six States."

5. Anonymous (V222), interview with Jennifer Meta Robinson, Bloomington, May 20, 2006.

6. Brown, "Farmers' Market Research 1940–2000," 168; Paul, "The New Face of Old McDonald," 5. This source reports on a study of farmers' markets in Alberta, Canada, which showed that most vendors "received only a modest return" for their time at market. Figures are fairly studiously left out of discussions among vendors of any cash business about whether the day was "a good one" or "slow."

7. USDA, "U.S. Farmers Markets—2000."

8. Lyson, Gillespie, and Hilchey, "Farmers' Markets and the Local Community."

9. Ibid.; Paul, "The New Face of Old McDonald," 5; Art Sherwood, interview with Jennifer Meta Robinson, Bloomington, June 8, 2005.

10. Lyson, Gillespie, and Hilchey, "Farmers' Markets and the Local Community."

11. Brenda Simmons, interview with Jennifer Meta Robinson, Bloomington, August 21, 2005.

12. Brown, "Farmers' Market Research 1940–2000," 168.

13. "Farm to Market: Fresh and Ripe for the Shopping," *New York Times*, June 1, 2005, sec. D5.

14. Brenda Simmons, interview with Jennifer Meta Robinson, Bloomington, August 21, 2005.

15. Marcia Veldman, e-mail communication, April 3, 2006.

16. Chris Hunter, interview with Jennifer Meta Robinson, Bloomington, September 17, 2005.

17. John Byers, interview with Jennifer Meta Robinson, Bloomington, August 21, 2005.

18. Gregory Ash and Kenny Hughes, interview with Jennifer Meta Robinson, Bloomington, October 1, 2005.

19. Lyson, Gillespie, and Hilchey, "Farmers' Markets and the Local Community," 111. All quotes and figures in this paragraph are from this source. On the other hand, full-time growers sell more (30%) at roadside stands or U-pick operations than do part-time growers (16%). Full-time growers sell wholesale 19% of their crop whereas part-time growers sell 4% of their crop wholesale. All quotes and figures in this paragraph are from the same source.

20. Jonas Winklepleck, interview with Jennifer Meta Robinson, Bloomington, September 3, 2005.

21. Bob Wise, interview with Jennifer Meta Robinson, Bloomington, October 1, 2005.

22. Tracy Branam, interview with Jennifer Meta Robinson, Bloomington, May 13, 2005.

23. Lyson, Gillespie, and Hilchey, "Farmers' Markets and the Local Community."

24. Anonymous (V121), interview with Jennifer Meta Robinson, Bloomington, 2005.

25. Brucato, *The Farmer Goes to Town,* 117. In the 1940s, Brucato described the San Francisco farmers' market as a kind of "agricultural clinic [where] the backyard gardeners of the city seek advice from farmers who have experience with the real thing." See also Theresa Ochoa, interview with Jennifer Meta Robinson, Bloomington, May 13, 2005, in chapter 4.

26. Brucato, *The Farmer Goes to Town,* 118.

6. Market Generations

1. J. D. Grove, focus group with Jennifer Meta Robinson and J. A. Hartenfeld, Hart Farm, Solsberry, Indiana, May 7, 2006.

2. Glassie, *Material Culture,* 16.

3. Cecilia Wade Hartfield, interview with Jennifer Meta Robinson, Bloomington, October 8, 2005.

4. Dan Cooper, interview with Jennifer Meta Robinson, Bloomington, June 4, 2005. This and subsequent quotes from Cooper in this chapter are from this interview.

5. Berry, *Another Turn of the Crank,* 17.

6. Anonymous (C111), interview with Jennifer Meta Robinson, Bloomington, 2005.

7. See McGrath, Sherry, and Heisley, "An Ethnographic Study of an Urban Marketplace"; and Aldred, "Plastic Shamans and Astroturf Sun Dances."

8. Langman quoted in Aldred.

9. Stephen Krecik and Amalia Krecik, interview with Jennifer Meta Robinson, Bloomington, May 27, 2006.

10. Glassie, *Material Culture,* 7.

7. New Farms, New Farmers

1. Logsdon, *The Contrary Farmer.*

2. John Byers, interview with Jennifer Meta Robinson, Bloomington, August 21, 2005.

3. Pamela Kinnaman and Timothy Kinnaman, interview with Jennifer Meta Robinson, Bloomington, October 1, 2005.

4. Byczynski, "Farming."

5. See Jonsson, "A Comeback for Small Farms."

6. Art Sherwood, interview with Jennifer Meta Robinson, Bloomington, June 8, 2005.

7. McFadden, "The History of Community Supported Agriculture."

8. Bobbi Boos, interview with Jennifer Meta Robinson, Hart Farm, Solsberry, Indiana, May 17, 2005.

9. Hilchey, Lyson, and Gillespie, "Farmers' Markets and Rural Economic Development."

10. Large-scale farmer processing cooperatives have had success in the Midwest, including one in Minnesota formed by 383 corn producers at the cost of $22 million and a cooperative plant for making pasta that was formed by North Dakota wheat farmers at a cost of $43 million (Integrity Systems Cooperative Co., *Adding Values to Our Food System*, 29). In Bloomington, a much smaller-scale kitchen incubator is envisioned by some people in the Local Growers Guild. The kitchen would be certified by the health department and would provide a place for growers to add value to small quantities of homegrown or purchased products. One challenge to a community food-processing kitchen at this scale would be whether the volumes that small-scale entrepreneurs can produce will contribute meaningfully to the support of a family. On the other hand, as farmers' markets have shown, even small businesses can provide a worthwhile supplement to income and put otherwise surplus or second-quality produce to use. In any case, this concept of "income patching"—having multiple streams of income that together support an individual or family—is now standard for the majority of farm families.

11. Economic Research Service, *State Fact Sheets;* Ibid.; Economic Research Service, *Structural and Financial Characteristics of U.S. Farms.*

12. Maria Cooper and Scott Cooper, interview with Jennifer Meta Robinson, Bloomington, August 20, 2005.

13. Anthony Blondin, interview with Jennifer Meta Robinson, Sun Circle Farm, Paoli, Indiana, September 5, 2005.

14. Integrity Systems Cooperative Co., *Adding Values to Our Food System.* While it is commonly thought that sustainable and organic food production results in lower yields, in fact the research findings are far from clear. Many variables impact yield, including soil fertility, climate, fertilizer application, length of growing season, seeing densities, management capabilities, and irrigations systems. While some studies found lower or higher yield with organic growing, a number of studies have found that there was in fact no significant yield difference among growers in a given year.

15. Jeff Evard and Melissa Evard, interview with Jennifer Meta Robinson, Martinsville, Indiana, September 7, 2005.

16. Integrity Systems Cooperative Co., *Adding Values to Our Food System.*

8. Market Futures

1. The transcriptions included in this chapter are excerpted from a longer, two-and-a-half-hour conversation that emerged with little prompting and followed the logic of the developing thoughts of the participants. The questions inserted were implicit rather than actually asked

during the discussion. They have been added here to help orient the reader. In some places, spoken grammar, redundancy, and other stumbling blocks to meaning have been eliminated.

2. Byczynski, "What's Ahead for Farmers' Markets?"

3. Brenda Simmons, interview with Jennifer Meta Robinson, Bloomington, August 21, 2005; Anonymous (V222), interview with Jennifer Meta Robinson, Bloomington, May 20, 2006.

4. The USDA-funded National Center for Appropriate Technology (NCAT) maintains a database of internship and employment opportunities at http://attrainternships.ncat.org, accessed September 11, 2006.

Conclusion

1. See Aldred, "Plastic Shamans and Astroturf Sun Dances." In mass-produced shopping experiences, styles are purchased as a way into membership in what Langman calls "proto-communities" of strangers who seek to buy more gratifying, but finally empty markers of self.

2. Flora, "Social Capital and Sustainability." Flora's study shows that farmers using more sustainable methods were viewed as success stories in their communities because of the perception of their problem-solving skills, judgment, and independence. Their communities also showed greater benefits than those without sustainable growers in the areas of mutual trust and reciprocity.

3. Berry, *Another Turn of the Crank.*

4. Gulliver and Silverman, *Merchants and Shopkeepers,* 7.

5. Stoeltje and Bauman, "The Semiotics of Folkloric Performance," 589.

6. See Clark, "Price Control of Local Foodstuffs in Kumasi, Ghana, 1979." This anthropological study describes how the Kumasi market in Ghana was bulldozed by a revolutionary government in 1979. Clark also describes how, within a week of the neat rows of kiosks and simple metal roofs being scraped away, the women traders came back out to sell their wares. Each in her same spot with her same commodities spread on the ground around her, waiting for customers. And the customers came. Little changed, Clark reports, other than that the sun beat down on sensitive babies and perishable produce.

7. Nash, "Introduction"; Brondizio, "Brazilian Acai Crops."

8. Alexander et al., *A Pattern Language,* and Alexander, *The Timeless Way of Building.* Alexander argues that, for architecture, "in our time the languages have broken down" (*Timeless Way,* xii). These landmark volumes discuss archetypical patterns of human action and interaction as made manifest in architecture. His comments about architecture, community, and marketplaces discuss the social and cultural meanings of the places of human interaction. They argue that patterns of behavior and interaction can be inductively derived and transferred from one context to the next.

9. Berry, *Another Turn of the Crank,* 5–7.

10. Halweil, "Home Grown," 6–7, 16; Halweil, *Eat Here,* 15. An analysis by food giant Unilever showed that power in the food industry has moved since 1900 from the hands of the farmers to those of the manufacturers to the wholesalers to, now, the retailers. Farmers' markets allow farmers access to a measure of that power and simultaneously re-empower consumers to jump the line in a preternaturally extended food system (Schirach-Szmigiel, *Power in the Food Industry*).

Bibliography

Adams, Ryan Thomas. "What Kind of Farmer? Local Vs. Market Farming and Organic Vs. Conventional Farming in Bloomington, Indiana." Unpublished manuscript, 2003.

Aldred, Lisa. "Plastic Shamans and Astroturf Sun Dances: New Age Commercialization of Native American Spirituality." *The American Indian Quarterly* 24, no. 3 (2000): 329–52.

Alexander, Christopher. *The Timeless Way of Building.* New York: Oxford University Press, 1979.

Alexander, Christopher, et al. *A Pattern Language: Towns, Buildings, Construction.* New York: Oxford University Press, 1977.

Arnold, Thomas, ed. "Memorials of St. Edmund's Abbey, Vol. 1 ("Cronica, by Jocelin De Brakelonde")." In *British Library, Harleian Ms.1005, ff.141–143, 147, 149–151* (Bury St. Edmunds: 1180s–1190s). http://www.the-orb.net/encyclop/culture/towns/florilegium/government/gvcons14.html (accessed September 12, 2006).

Arnosky, Pamela, and Frank Arnosky. "Reinventing the Farm: From Wholesaling to Agritourism." *Growing for Market* 14, no. 12 (2005): 16–18.

"Athens Farmers Market." http://www.athensfarmersmarket.org (accessed September 12, 2006).

Bakhtin, Mikhail M. *The Dialogic Imagination.* Trans. Caryl Emerson and Michael Holquist. Ed. Michael Holquist. Austin: University of Texas, 1981.

Bauman, Richard. *Verbal Art as Performance.* Prospect Heights, Ill.: Waveland, 1977.

Bauman, Richard, and Pamela Ritch. "Informing Performance: Producing the *Coloquio* in Tierra Blanca." *Oral Tradition* 9, no. 2 (1994): 255–80.

Bauman, Z. "Survival as a Social Construct." *Theory, Culture, and Society* 9 (1992): 1–36.

The Belmont Farmers' Market Committee. "Beginnings: How the Belmont Farmers' Market Came to Be." Pp. 1, 4 in *Roots & Sprouts: News and Ideas from the Belmont Farmers' Market.* Belmont, Mass., 2006.

Berry, Wendell. *Another Turn of the Crank*. Washington, D.C.: Counterpoint, 1995.

———. "How to Be a Poet (to Remind Myself)." In *Given: New Poems*. Washington, D.C.: Shoemaker, Hoard, 2005.

Botsford, George Willis, and Charles Alexander Robinson, Jr. *Hellenic History*. 4th ed. New York: Macmillan, 1956.

Briggs, Charles L. *Competence in Performance: The Creativity of Tradition in Mexicano Verbal Art*. Philadelphia: University of Pennsylvania Press, 1988.

Britnell, Richard H. *The Marketing of Grain in England, 1250–1350*. http://www.dur.ac.uk/r.h.britnell/articles/Grainframe.htm (accessed June 30, 2006).

Bromley, R. J., and Richard Symanski. "Marketplace Trade in Latin America." *Latin American Research Review* 9, no. 3 (1974): 3–38.

Brondizio, Eduardo. "Brazilian Acai Crops." Presentation at Indiana University, 2005.

Brown, Allison. "Counting Farmers Markets." *The Geographical Review* 91, no. 4 (2001): 655–74.

———. "Farmers' Market Research 1940–2000: An Inventory and Review." *American Journal of Alternative Agriculture* 17, no. 4 (2002): 167–76.

Brucato, John G. *The Farmer Goes to Town: The Story of San Francisco's Farmers' Market*. San Francisco: Burke, 1948.

Burns, Arthur, and Denny Johnson. *Farmers' Market Survey Report*. USDA, 1996. www.ams.usda.gov/farmersmarkets (accessed January 29, 2006).

Byczynski, Lynn. "Farming: The Perfect Retirement Job?" *Growing for Market* 14 (August 2005): 1, 4–6.

———. "What's Ahead for Farmers' Markets? Keep Your Eye on These Trends." *Growing for Market* (January 2001): 14.

Callahan, Rick. "America Growing a Taste for Organic Food: Trend Creates Opportunity for Hoosier Farmers." *Hoosier Times,* April 24, 2005, sec. A12.

Carson, Rachel. *Silent Spring*. Boston: Houghton Mifflin, 1962.

Cheal, D. "Showing Them You Love Them: Gift Giving and the Dialectic of Intimacy." *The Sociological Review* 35, no. 1 (1987): 150–69.

City of Bloomington Parks and Recreation Department. *2005 Farm Vendor Handbook*. City of Bloomington, Indiana, 2005.

———. *2006 Farm Vendor Handbook*. City of Bloomington, 2006.

Clark, Gracia. *Onions Are My Husband: Survival and Accumulation by West African Market Women*. Chicago: University of Chicago Press, 1994.

———. "Price Control of Local Foodstuffs in Kumasi, Ghana, 1979." In *Traders Versus the State: Anthropological Approaches to Unofficial Economies,* 57–79. Boulder, Colo.: Westview, 1988.

"The Country-Miser, or, the Unhappy Farmers Dear Market." *Early*

English Books Online, 1693. http://wwwlib.umi.com/eebo/image/ 104024 (accessed May 1, 2006).

Davis, Donald R., Melvin D. Epp, and Hugh D. Riordan. "Changes in USDA Food Composition Data for 43 Garden Crops, 1950 to 1999." *Journal of the American College of Nutrition* 23, no. 6 (2004): 669–82.

De Weese, Pamela Marshall. *The Detroit Eastern Farmers' Market: Its Social Structure and Functions.* Detroit: Ethnic Studies Division, Center for Urban Studies, Wayne State University, 1975.

DeVault, George. "Persistence Pays Off for Farmers' Market." *Growing for Market* 14, no. 9 (2005): 8–10.

Díaz del Castillo, Bernal. *The True History of the Conquest of New Spain.* Trans. Alfred Percival Maudslay. London: Hakluyt Society, 1908–16.

The Domesday Book Online. 1999–2004. http://www.domesdaybook .co.uk/ (accessed September 22, 2006).

Economic Research Service. *See* U.S. Department of Agriculture.

Economics Institute. *Crescent City Farmers Market.* 2006. http://www .crescentcityfarmersmarket.org/ (accessed February 24, 2006).

Farmers Market. 2005. www.farmersmarketla.com/ (accessed June 12, 2005).

Festing, Harriet. *Farmers' Markets: An American Success Story.* Bath, U.K.: Eco-logic, 1998.

Fisher, Andy. *Hot Peppers and Parking Lot Peaches: Evaluating Farmers' Markets in Low Income Communities.* Community Food Security Coalition, 1999.

Flora, Cornelia Butler. "Social Capital and Sustainability: Agriculture and Communities in the Great Plains and Corn Belt." *Sustainable Agriculture Research and Education Program Newsletter* 7, no. 4 (1995).

Fox, Margalit. "Paul K. Keene, 94, Organic Farming Pioneer." Obituary, *New York Times,* May 18, 2005, sec. C21.

Glassie, Henry. *Material Culture.* Bloomington: Indiana University Press, 1999.

Goffman, Erving. *The Presentation of Self in Everyday Life.* Garden City, N.Y.: Doubleday/Anchor, 1959.

Gulliver, P. H., and Marilyn Silverman. *Merchants and Shopkeepers: A Historical Anthropology of an Irish Market Town, 1200–1991.* Toronto: University of Toronto Press, 1995.

Hall, Forest M. *Historic Treasures: True Tales of Deeds with Interesting Data in the Life of Bloomington.* 1922. Reprint, Bloomington: Indiana University Press, 1979.

Hallam, H. E. *Rural England, 1066–1348.* Atlantic Highlands, N.J.: Humanities Press, 1981.

Halweil, Brian. *Eat Here: Reclaiming Homegrown Pleasures in a Global Supermarket.* New York: W.W. Norton, 2004.

———. "Home Grown: The Case for Local Food in a Global Market." In *World Watch Paper 163,* ed. Thomas Prugh. Washington, D.C.: Worldwatch, 2002.

Heiser, Charles B., Jr. *Seed to Civilization: The Story of Food.* New ed. Cambridge, Mass.: Harvard University Press, 1990.

Henderson, P. L., and H. R. Linstrom. "Farmer-to-Consumer Direct Marketing in Six States." Agriculture Information Bulletin. USDA. Number 436. Washington, D.C., 1980.

Hilchey, Duncan, Thomas Lyson, and Gilbert W. Gillespie, Jr. "Farmers' Markets and Rural Economic Development: Entrepreneurship, Business Incubation, and Job Creation in the Northeast." In *Farming Alternatives Program Community Agriculture Development Series.* Ithaca: Cornell University, 1995.

"History and Heritage." In *Break Away Bloomington, Indiana.* Bloomington Indiana Tourism Center. http://www.visitbloomington.com/static/index.cfm?contentID=206 (accessed January 5, 2006).

Howard, Albert. *An Agricultural Testament.* New York: Oxford University Press, 1943. http://www.gutenberg.net.au/ebooks02/0200301.txt (accessed September 12, 2006).

Howard, Philip H. "Central Coast Consumers Want More Food-Related Information, from Safety to Ethics." *California Agriculture* 60, no. 1 (2006): 14–19.

Ikerd, John. "The High Cost of Cheap Food." *Small Farm Today,* July/August (2001).

———. "The New American Food Culture." *Field Notes* 31 (2005): 6–8.

Indiana Business Research Center. 2006 "Bloomington, IN Metro Area: In Depth Profile." In *STATS Indiana* ed. Indiana University's Kelley School of Business. State of Indiana and the Indiana Department of Workforce Development. http://www.stats.indiana.edu/profiles/prmsa1020.html (accessed April 19, 2006).

Indianapolis City Market. *Indianapolis City Market.* 2004. http://www.indianapoliscitymarket.com (accessed May 4, 2006).

Integrity Systems Cooperative Co. *Adding Values to Our Food System: An Economic Analysis of Sustainable Community Food Systems.* Ed. USDA, *Sustainable Agriculture Research and Education Program.* Logan, Utah: USDA, 1997.

Jewett, Jane Grimsbo, and Derrick Braaten. *Local Foods: Where to Find It, How to Buy It.* St. Paul: Minnesota Institute for Sustainable Agriculture, 2005.

Jonsson, Patrik. "A Comeback for Small Farms." *Christian Science Monitor.* February 9, 2006. http://www.csmonitor.com/2006/0209/po3s03-ussc.html (accessed September 12, 2006).

Katzen, Mollie. *Moosewood Cookbook.* Berkeley: Ten Speed, 1977.

Knox, Ellis L. 1999. "Medieval Society: Introduction." In *On-line Reference Book for Medieval Studies,* ed. Laura V. Blanchard and Caro-

lyn Schriber. http://www.the-orb.net/textbooks/westciv/medievalsoc
.html (accessed May 28, 2005).

Koryta, Michael. "Showers Sale 50 Years Ago Marked the End of an Era." *Herald-Times,* May 16, 2005, sec. A1, A9.

Kremen, Amy, Catherine Greene, and Jim Hanson. *See* U.S. Department of Agriculture.

L. W. "God's Great and Vvonderful Vvork in Somerset-Shire." *Early English Books Online,* 1676. http://wwwlib.umi.com/eebo/image/ 33724 (accessed September 12, 2006).

Lappé, Frances Moore. *Diet for a Small Planet.* New York: Ballantine, 1971.

Lemire, Steven. "Dane County Farmers' Market Survey." *Summary Report,* 2003.

Logsdon, Gene. *The Contrary Farmer.* White River Junction, Vt.: Chelsea Green, 1994.

Lyson, T. A., G. W. Gillespie, Jr., and D. Hilchey. "Farmers' Markets and the Local Community: Bridging the Formal and Informal Economy." *American Journal of Alternative Agriculture* 10, no. 3 (1995): 108–13.

Madison, Deborah. *About Deborah Madison.* http://www.randomhouse .com/features/deborahmadison/about.html (accessed June 12, 2005).

———. *Local Flavors: Cooking and Eating from America's Farmers' Markets.* New York: Broadway, 2002.

McFadden, Steven. "The History of Community Supported Agriculture: Part II, CSA's World of Possibilities." *The New Farm* (2003).

McGrath, M. A., Jr., J. F. Sherry, and D. D. Heisley. "An Ethnographic Study of an Urban Marketplace: Lessons from the Midville Farmers' Market." *Journal of Retailing* 69, no. 3 (1993): 280–319.

Muhlberger, Steven. 1999. "Medieval England: Economy and Society up to the Thirteenth Century." In *On-line Reference Book for Medieval Studies,* ed. Laura V. Blanchard and Carolyn Schriber. http://www.the-orb.net/textbooks/muhlberger/econ_to_1300.html (accessed May 28, 2005).

Nash, June. "Introduction: Traditional Arts and Changing Markets in Middle America." In *Crafts in the World Market: The Impact of Global Exchange on Middle American Artisans,* ed. June Nash, 1– 22. Albany: State University of New York Press, 1993.

National Association of Farmers Markets (UK). http://www.farmers markets.net (accessed June 12, 2005).

Nearing, Helen, and Scott Nearing. *Living the Good Life: How to Live Sanely and Simply in a Troubled World.* New York: Schocken, 1970. Originally published 1954.

Paul, Christine. "The New Face of Old McDonald—Part 1 Farmers' Markets." *Practical Hydroponics and Greenhouses.* November/December (2002).

Peacock, Alison. 1999. "Farmers' Markets." In *Aisling Magazine,* http://

aislingmagazine.com/aislingmagazine/articles/TAM27/Farmers .html (accessed June 12, 2005).

Planck, Nina. "Farmers' Markets & Beyond: Expanding the Market for Local Foods." In *The New Farm*, Rodale Institute, www.newfarm .org/features/1004/npmarket/index.shtml (accessed April 17, 2006).

———. *Real Food: What to Eat and Why.* New York: Bloomsbury, 2006.

Plunkett Research. "Food, Beverage and Tobacco Trends." In *Industry Statistics, Trends and In-depth Analysis of Top Companies*, 2006. www.plunkettresearch.com (accessed June 3, 2006).

Pretty, J. N., T. Lang, J. Morison, A. S. Ball. "Food Miles and Farm Costs: The Full Cost of the British Food Basket." *Food Policy* 30, no. 1 (2005): 1–20.

Project for Public Spaces. 2006. *Great Public Spaces.* http://www.pps .org/great_public_spaces/one?public_place_id=392&type_id=8 (accessed May 31, 2006).

Pyle, Jane. "Farmers' Markets in the United States: Functional Anachronisms?" *The Geographical Review* 61, no. 2 (1971): 167–97.

Rafert, Stewart. *The Miami Indians of Indiana: A Persistent People, 1654–1994.* Indianapolis: Indiana Historical Society, 1996.

Santa Fe Farmers Market. 2005. http://www.santafefarmersmarket.com (accessed June 12, 2005).

Schirach-Szmigiel, Christopher von. *Power in the Food Industry.* 2005. The Farm Foundation, http://www.farmfoundation.org/documents/ Chris-VSS.pdf (accessed June 2, 2006).

Schlosser, Eric. *Fast Food Nation.* New York: Houghton Mifflin, 2001.

Sherry, John F., Jr. "Market Pitching and the Ethnography of Speaking." *Advances in Consumer Research* 15 (1988): 543–47.

Sommer, Robert, et al. "The Behavioral Ecology of Supermarkets and Farmers Markets." *Journal of Environmental Psychology* 1, no. 1 (1981): 13–19.

Stoeltje, Beverly, and Richard Bauman. "The Semiotics of Folkloric Performance." In *The Semiotic Web 1987*, 585–99. New York: Mouton de Gruyter, 1987.

Taylor, Alex S., and Richard Harper. "Age-Old Practices in the 'New World': A Study of Gift-Giving between Teenage Mobile Phone Users." *CHI* 4, no. 1 (2002): 439–46.

Thomas, Anna. *The Vegetarian Epicure.* New York: Vintage. 1972.

Turner, Victor. *From Ritual to Theatre: The Human Seriousness of Play.* New York: PAJ, 1982.

U.S. Bureau of the Census. *Geographic Comparison Table, Occupation, Industry, and Class of Worker of Employed Civilians 16 Years and Over: 2000.* Census 2000 Summary File 3, Matrices P49, P50, and P51. Washington, D.C., 2000.

U.S. Code. *Farmer-to-Consumer Direct Marketing Act of 1976*, Public Law 94-463. As Amended Through Public Law 107-293, Nov. 13, 2002, 1976.

U.S. Department of Agriculture. Agricultural Marketing Service. *Farmers' Market Facts*. 2005. USDA. http://www.ams.usda.gov/farmers markets (accessed January 30, 2006).

———. Agricultural Marketing Service. *U.S. Farmers Markets—2000: A Study of Emerging Trends.* Ed. Tim Payne, 2002.

———. Economic Research Service. "Female Farm Operators and Their Farms." In *Structural and Financial Characteristics of U.S. Farms: 2001 Family Farm Report.* Ed. Robert A. Hoppe. Agriculture Information Bulletin No. 768. 2001. 38–50.

———. Economic Research Service. *Household Food Security in the United States.* FANRR-42. 2003.

———. Economic Research Service. *Organic Produce, Price Premiums, and Eco-Labeling in U.S. Farmers' Markets.* Amy Kremen, Catherine Greene, and Jim Hanson. Report VGS-301-01. 2004.

———. Economic Research Service. *State Fact Sheets: United States.* 2006. www.ers.usda.gov/StateFacts/US.htm (accessed May 17, 2006).

———. *Farmers' Produce Markets in the United States, Part 1: History and Description.* John L. Wann et al. 1948.

Veldman, Marcia. "Lunch Wagon Discussion." Bloomington, Ind.: Parks and Recreation Department, 2005.

Wann, John L., et al. *See* U.S. Department of Agriculture.

Warren, Elizabeth, and Amelia Warren Tyagi. *The Two-Income Trap: Why Middle-Class Mothers and Fathers Are Going Broke.* New York: Basic Books, 2003.

Waters, Alice. "Keynote." Paper presented at the Terra Madre World Meeting of Food Communities, Turin, Italy, October 20–23, 2004.

Index

of farms and businesses, 49, 87, 206, 229, 247n32; and food systems, 202, 206–208, 215, 217; growing choices for, 6, 108; lifestyle choices for, 67, 143, 130; yields and, 226, 256n14

sustainable growing methods, social status, 234, 257n2 (Conclusion)

Tassajara, 62
Tewksbury, Lloyd and Tamo, 59
Texas, *37, 39, 41,* 64
Thailand, markets, 26, 74
Thomas, Anna, 60
Traders Point Farmers' Market, 207
tradition, 3, 6, 17, 127, 155–156, 235; family, 139–141, 145–146, 155, 172. *See also* ritual
transportation, 6, 67; changes in, 30, 32, 36–38, 47, 235; costs of, 43–45, 236

United Kingdom. *See* Great Britain
urban gardening, 129, 193, 204, 228
urbanization, 4, 36–37, 40–42, 45
utopianism, 52, 58

Veldman, Marcia, 77, 80–83, 214, *217,* 221, 223, 225–227, *229*
vendor, definition, 244n5
Victory Gardens, 40, 48
Vietnam, markets, 26
Vigo County, Indiana, 156, 158

Waltham, Massachusetts, market, 5
Washington, D.C., markets, 7, 160
Washington County, Indiana, 216
Waters, Alice, 62, 121
Wayland, Massachusetts, market, 109
Weatherford, Texas, *37, 41*
Weber, Dan, 156–162, 164
Weber, Tom, 156
Weekend Women's Market, 26
West Berkeley Farmers' Markets, 89
Whole Earth Catalog, 56
Whole Earth Review, 56
Whole Foods Market, 43, 106
wholesale buyers, 32, 38, 40, 49, 84, 243n28
wholesale markets, 42, 71, 245n16, 258n10
WIC, 92, 93
wild-gathering, 86, 146–152, 172; place in markets, 83, 215, 244n5
William the Conqueror, 29
Williams, Jessica, 215, 225
Windsor Locks, Connecticut, *44*
Winklepleck: Betty, 145; Jonas, 143–145
Wise, Bob, 145–146
women in farming, 133–139, 190–193

Zanzibar, Old Town Market, 26–27

Jennifer Meta Robinson directs Campus Instructional Consulting and the award-winning Scholarship of Teaching and Learning Program at Indiana University. She has been closely involved with the Bloomington Farmers' Market since 1991. Robinson holds a doctorate in English with an emphasis on folklore and performance.

J. A. Hartenfeld, Jennifer's husband, has been a grower since 1977. He has sold at the Bloomington Farmers' Market consistently since then. In a past life, Jeff was a photography and graphic design instructor in the Indiana University School of Journalism.

Dan Schlapbach is Associate Professor of Fine Arts and Director of the Photography Program at Loyola College in Baltimore.

Jennifer Roebuck is an independent illustrator whose mixed media work has been exhibited nationally.